P9-DVJ-215
3 1404 00815 6868

Reading Aloud Across the Curriculum

DEC 2 0 2006

WITHDRAWN

MAY 0 7 2024

DAVID O. McKAY LIBRARY
BYU-IDAHO

MAY 0 7 2024

Reading Aloud Across the Curriculum

How to Build Bridges in Language Arts, Math, Science, and Social Studies

Lester L. Laminack

Reba M. Wadsworth

HEINEMANN

Portsmouth, NH

Heinemann
A division of Reed Elsevier Inc.
361 Hanover Street
Portsmouth, NH 03801–3912
www.heinemann.com

Offices and agents throughout the world

© 2006 by Lester L. Laminack and Reba M. Wadsworth

All rights reserved. No part of this book may be reproduced in any form or by any electronic or mechanical means, including information storage and retrieval systems, without permission in writing from the publisher, except by a reviewer, who may quote brief passages in a review.

Library of Congress Cataloging-in-Publication Data
Laminack, Lester L., 1956–
    Reading aloud across the curriculum : how to build bridges in language arts, math, science, and social studies / Lester L. Laminack, Reba M. Wadsworth.
       p.   cm.
    Includes bibliographical references and index.
    ISBN-13: 978-0-325-00982-7
    ISBN-10: 0-325-00982-1
    1. Oral reading.   2. Language arts (Elementary).
3. Content area reading.   4. Picture books for children.
I. Wadsworth, Reba M.   II. Title.
LB1573.5.L347 2006
372.45′2—dc22   2006012287

Editor: Lois Bridges
Production: Elizabeth Valway
Cover and interior design: Joyce Weston
Cover image: © William James/Images.com
Composition: Technologies 'N Typography, Inc.
Manufacturing: Louise Richardson

Printed in the United States of America on acid-free paper
10 09 08 07 06 RRD 1 2 3 4 5

Contents

Acknowledgments

W E GRATEFULLY ACKNOWLEDGE our editor and friend, Lois Bridges, whose keen insight and vision led us to make this book a reality. In addition, we wish to acknowledge the wisdom and guidance of Elizabeth Valway whose day-to-day communications kept us on track. And finally we wish to acknowledge Joyce Weston's talents as she created for us yet another stunning cover that embraced our work with dignity and grace.

Introduction

MOST OF US would be shocked by the wealth of resources being overlooked if we had the time to carefully and thoroughly examine the picture book collections in school and classroom libraries. Many well-written and tightly focused books are available to help layer children's understanding of most any topic in the curriculum. Yet, picture books continue to be greatly underutilized in our teaching, so we have revisited our personal libraries with a lens focused on weaving picture books into lessons throughout the day and across the curriculum.

In *Learning Under the Influence of Language and Literature* (2006), we delineated six opportunities for reading aloud across the day. The fifth of those opportunities, described in Chapter 6 of that book, is to use reading aloud as a curriculum bridge. That chapter suggested using read-alouds as an instructional act designed to help students build background for a unit of study through a conceptual framework of thought, language, and image. The specific example provided there was for a study of the civil rights movement in the United States. We developed a rationale for using read-alouds as a means of exploring the topic with a thorough collection of picture books that are listed in the chapter's annotated bibliography.

This book extends the focus to other areas of the curriculum and strengthens the connections between well-chosen picture books and learning in the content areas. You will find listings of books and descriptions here to support many units of study; lines of inquiry; and individual research in language arts, mathematics, science, and social studies. The collections included are not intended to be exhaustive lists; no single book has space to do that. Instead, we have examined the national standards as described by the leading professional organizations in each area of the curriculum and used those as the lens for choosing which books to include. Every collection contains a set of "bookshelves" that we think of as "starter sets." Each set is intended as a springboard of sorts—an introduction to authors and topics in picture-book format that will help you launch or extend your teaching.

Our hope is that these starter sets can be the beginning of a growing collection of titles you can rely on again and again. The size of our personal collections certainly has increased as a result of the search for titles to include on each of the shelves in this book. While there are current titles, you will also note that several of our favorites are books that have been around a while, so it is likely they are already in local school, community, and/or classroom libraries.

As you locate the books on our shelves and begin to weave them into your curriculum and teaching, the emphasis can clearly remain on the power of reading aloud as a deliberate and thoughtful act of instruction. However, we hope the information here on the collection of books is adequate and broad enough—that is, represents a variety of genres, topics, formats, and illustration styles—to help you find titles to extend your instruction and support students in their personal inquiries as well.

We suggest that you create a small text set from each collection of books to support a study you have planned. Consider the following as a thoughtful way to use such a set to layer in concepts and vocabulary related to a topic.

- Preview the titles included in each set.
- Identify concepts that could be developed and/or extended by using a particular set of books.
- Identify essential vocabulary related to the unit of study to be undertaken.
- Identify the core understandings needed to connect to the new information.
- Notice how the writer develops the concepts—that is, through the use of language, illustrations, captions, labels, and so on.

Next, for each set of books, place the titles in order from simple to complex. Then, select one for an opening read-aloud.

- Begin with a launching title from the set. This should be a book you feel has the potential to introduce the necessary concepts and vocabulary.
- Read the title and the names of the author and illustrator.
- Speak to the connection you hope the book you are using will establish. For example:

    "Readers, we have been learning about slavery in American history. Today as I read this book, I hope you will notice that many people in that time believed that slavery was wrong. Pay attention to how courageous individual slaves risked everything to gain freedom. Notice too how others who were free risked everything to help slaves gain freedom. When we reach the end of the book, I will ask you to turn and talk with your partners about it."

- As you read, occasionally speak to your insights—the ones you are leading students toward—by commenting on what you've noticed and wonder about and the connections you have made.

Be *very* cautious; don't overdo this. Too much commentary may take away the need for readers and listeners to think independently and may even reduce the extent to which they are able to engage with the story. For some books, this will not be necessary. In any case, it should not overpower the language of the text and the interplay between the mind of the writer and the mind of the reader or listener. Remember your goal is to slowly move students toward *independence* and that this work *is instructional*. Your role is to serve as the one who is *demonstrating* the thinking, not *thinking for* them.

Let this first story serve as a foundation—a common ground of sorts. As you reach the end, ask students to turn and talk with their partners; this could also be done in a group of three or four. Remind them of your opening statement and invite students to reflect on that before they begin: "I hope you noticed how courageous individuals risked everything to gain freedom or to help others gain freedom." As they begin their conversations, move around the room and listen in.

Now, speak to the group's work:

"So readers, as I was walking about, I heard comments like these [give a few examples and continue]. Now I'm wondering what we have learned from this book? This author shows us that freedom was not easy to attain and came at great risk. Think about the risks involved and how one person made a difference. Think now about how [name individual being profiled in one of the books—Harriet Tubman, John Parker, Sojourner Truth, Levi and Katy Coffin] did that. What difference did her [his] actions make? Think about something we might take from this book to put into practice in our lives. OK, turn and talk with your partners [group] about that."

Let this buzz a bit. Don't wait too long or the conversation will naturally drift away from the focus. In fact, we find it builds energy to cut it a bit shorter. When there is energy and focus about the topic, there is an eagerness to share and continue the dialogue: "Readers, your attention please. Thank you. Let's talk for a moment about what you and your classmates have been thinking here."

As students begin to talk and share, continue to guide the direction of the discussion:

"Let's think about what we've learned from this. What did you realize . . . ? When did you realize that . . . ? What were you wondering . . . ? What did you notice . . . ? Can you identify a place in the book that led you to that thinking? Can you talk about how the author or illustrator led you to that thinking?"

Each of the preceding questions has the potential to open further dialogue. You will have to decide which of them to pursue and which to redirect as you consider time constraints and goals and, most important, students' growing understandings.

Begin charting the main points when the students begin to talk. Be sure to include the language you identified when organizing the set of books you're using. Take this opportunity to do the following.

- Feature the vocabulary
- Introduce or extend the concepts you hope to scaffold with the set of books
- Have students use the book's language to express their ideas, insights, and connections
- Have students articulate confusions, wonderings, and longings for more insight

This chart should become a touchstone for subsequent books in a set and for designing your instruction to meet the growing understandings of your students. Now as you read each book in the collection in sequence, make consistent references to the chart and add to it to show the connections between individual books and among those within the text set.

As the concepts and/or language become more and more complex in successive books, you may choose to pause within a book to have children turn to each other and discuss it. However, use the charting at the conclusion of the book to bring closure for students. Review the chart before reading the next book as you and your students continue through the set's remaining titles.

When you finish a set of books, have students refer to the chart, turn to their partners or group, and talk through the threads of thinking they can see. With the first set, you may need to lead that process and scaffold the thinking required to arrive at specific generalizations. For later sets, this should become a more and more independent exercise.

Now let's take a look at one collection of books and see what it looks like with a focus on The Underground Railroad. Assume that the following is your collection.

Almost to Freedom

Written by Vaunda Micheaux Nelson
Illustrated by Colin Bootman
Scholastic 2003, ISBN 0–439–63156–4

Aunt Harriet's Underground Railroad in the Sky

Written and Illustrated by Faith Ringgold
Dragonfly/Crown 1992 (Scholastic), 1995, ISBN 0–517–88543–3

Enemies of Slavery

Written by David A. Adler
Illustrated by Donald A. Smith
Holiday House 2004, ISBN 0–8234–1596–1

Freedom River

Written by Doreen Rappaport
Illustrated by Bryan Collier
Jump at the Sun/Hyperion 2000, ISBN 0–7868–0350–9

A Good Night for Freedom

Written by Barbara Olenyik Morrow
Illustrated by Leonard Jenkins
Holiday House 2004, ISBN 0–8234–1709–3

. . . If You Traveled on The Underground Railroad

Written by Ellen Levine
Illustrated by Larry Johnson
Scholastic 1992, ISBN 0–590–45156–1

Liberty Street

Written by Candice Ransom
Illustrated by Eric Velasquez
Walker Books 2003, ISBN 0–8027–8869–6

Sweet Clara and the Freedom Quilt

Written by Deborah Hopkinson
Illustrated by James Ransome
Dragonfly Books/Knopf 1993, 1995, ISBN 0–697–87472–0

Under the Quilt of Night

Written by Deborah Hopkinson
Illustrated by James Ransome
Aladdin 2002 (Atheneum), 2005, ISBN 0–689–87700–5

After reading each of the preceding titles, we considered the following to decide on a sequence for presenting the books.

- Background knowledge of the learners
- Previous exposure to the vocabulary and concepts presented in the set
- Complexity of each text in the set
- Potential for each book to serve as a scaffold, or springboard, to growing insights and understandings within the unit of study

Consider those that follow and reflect on our rationale for using the books in this order. You may, of course, find that a different sequence better suits the needs of your learners.

Under the Quilt of Night

The story remains tightly focused on the escape of a group of slaves led by one young girl. The young girl is our narrator. The telling of the story is presented in the "phases" of an escape (running, waiting, watching, hiding, traveling, singing). The story layers in the major concepts and introduces and embeds key vocabulary for the set.

Liberty Street

The setting for the story is in contrast to the typical plantation setting. The narrator, Kezia, is a young girl born to slaves who work in and around the home of a widow named Missus Grace. The escape here is to protect Kezia from the prospects of being bonded out to the sister of Missus Grace. Kezia's father has been sold to help pay the widow's debts. Kezia's mom is a conductor. Here again the focus remains tight. The story reveals all the planning that leads up to an escape, reveals signals for safety, and layers in some of the dangers faced.

Almost to Freedom

The story is told through the perspective of a doll who accompanies a young girl as she and her family make the escape to freedom. The story reveals some aspects of life as a slave and helps to develop concepts of conductors, safe houses, and other vocabulary for the set. The text is more complex and detailed and of greater length than the previous book.

Sweet Clara and the Freedom Quilt

The book reveals how slaves could be separated from family to serve the needs of the master. It shows various jobs slaves performed (field hands, seamstresses, cooks, drivers). The story reveals how word of freedom, escape to Canada or North, and the making of maps could spread among the slaves. The author describes the ingenuity of the slaves in search of freedom and the careful planning necessary to avoid capture.

A Good Night for Freedom

This story layers in a new dimension with a white child who meets two runaway slaves in the home of a Quaker woman known to help runaways. When the slave catchers confront her, she has the dilemma of deciding what to do. The book extends concepts introduced in earlier books and layers in vocabulary.

Freedom River

In this true story, we meet a former slave (John Parker) who bought his freedom and moved to a free state (Ohio). He has a successful business and employs both black and white men. Kentucky, a slave state, lies across the river and John Parker routinely helps slaves make the escape into Ohio and further north where they will be safe. This book layers in new concepts and vocabulary.

Aunt Harriet's Underground Railroad in the Sky

This story provides a brief history of The Underground Railroad. The narrator is a young girl who is *flying among the stars* . . . with her baby brother. This "fantasy" setting provides a backdrop for the children to witness (experience) an escape.

The story commemorates the one hundredth anniversary of Harriet Tubman's first flight to freedom.

Enemies of Slavery

This book extends concepts by departing from a story format and moving to one-page profiles of fourteen individuals—black, white, male, and female—who stood against slavery at risk to their own safety. The previous books, told as stories, will have built a foundation for understanding the significance of the actions of each of these individuals.

. . . If You Traveled on The Underground Railroad

This book is presented last because it has the greatest depth of detail and the most text. The content is organized around a series of questions about life in the time of slavery with a tight focus on escaping via The Underground Railroad. The scaffolding provided through previous books in this set will lessen the impact of the concept density and vocabulary in this title. This book should serve well as a way to pull concepts from the set together into a cohesive whole.

The next move is to identify a set of concepts that could be developed and/or extended through use of this set of books, including:

- Slavery
- The Underground Railroad
- Emancipation

Then it's time to review the set to identify essential vocabulary related to the unit of study. For this set, you could include the following.

- Abolition
- Abolitionists
- Bonding out
- Bounty hunters
- Conductors
- Free state
- Jump the broom
- Liberty
- Master (sometimes printed as *massa*)
- Overseer

- Paterollers
- Runaways
- Safe house
- Skiff
- Slave catcher
- Slave state
- Stations and agents of The Underground Railroad

Next, identify the core understandings needed, such as the following, to connect to the new information.

- Slaves were captured, brought to America, and sold as property.
- Slaves could be bought and sold.
- Slaves could be sold and separated from family members.
- Slaves were not free to move about as they wished.
- Slaves could be whipped and/or otherwise severely punished by the master for anything that didn't please him.
- There were no laws to protect slaves.
- Slaves were not allowed to learn to read and write.
- Slaves who tried to escape and were captured could be subjected to severe forms of punishment (e.g. , having toes or a foot cut off to prevent them from running again, being sold away from their families).
- There were many people, both black and white, who risked much to help slaves gain freedom.
- Those who helped slaves escape could be severely punished if caught.
- The nation was divided between slave states and free states.
- There were supporters of slavery in both slave states and free states.
- There were antislavery movements in both slave states and free states.

It is also important to make notes about how the writer develops the concepts—for example, by using language, illustrations, captions, labels, and so on.

This line of thinking can be extended using a variation of a literature circle. In this situation, the circle could be a vehicle for building vocabulary; developing or extending (breadth and depth) concepts; and building a repertoire of images that will serve as a connector (like the loop side of Velcro) for the language, concepts, charts, and diagrams so frequently found in content-area textbooks and in teacher talk (the hook side of Velcro). The books can be organized in the following two or three ways.

1. By time, especially in social studies because the books can be sorted by events on a timeline for the unit of study.
2. By complexity within a time period—that is, the same as for the stories featuring events of The Underground Railroad—or within a topic of study, especially for mathematics or science.
3. By standards or strands in the curriculum or in the guidelines set forth by professional organizations (e.g., NSTA, NCTM, NCSS, NCTE).

1

Picture Books and Read-Alouds to Support the Language Arts Curriculum

*T*HE LANGUAGE ARTS curriculum is most likely the first area one thinks of when talking about using picture books in teaching. The natural connections between reading and writing and listening and oral language are very visible in picture books. So, for that reason, we want to look more deeply into the use of them in the language arts curriculum. As a starting point, we encourage you to visit the twelve standards for literacy education developed jointly by the National Council of Teachers of English (www.ncte.org) and the International Reading Association (www.reading.org)—two of the most respected organizations dedicated to literacy.

> **The Standards**
>
> 1. Students read a wide range of print and nonprint texts to build an understanding of texts, of themselves, and of the cultures of the United States and the world; to acquire new information; to respond to the needs and demands of society and the workplace; and for personal fulfillment. Among these texts are fiction and nonfiction, classic and contemporary works.
> 2. Students read a wide range of literature from many periods in many genres to build an understanding of the many dimensions (e.g., philosophical, ethical, aesthetic) of human experience.

3. Students apply a wide range of strategies to comprehend, interpret, evaluate, and appreciate texts. They draw on their prior experience, their interactions with other readers and writers, their knowledge of word meaning and of other texts, their word identification strategies, and their understanding of textual features (e.g., sound-letter correspondence, sentence structure, context, graphics).

4. Students adjust their use of spoken, written, and visual language (e.g., conventions, style, vocabulary) to communicate effectively with a variety of audiences and for different purposes.

5. Students employ a wide range of strategies as they write and use different writing process elements appropriately to communicate with different audiences for a variety of purposes.

6. Students apply knowledge of language structure, language conventions (e.g., spelling and punctuation), media techniques, figurative language, and genre to create, critique, and discuss print and nonprint texts.

7. Students conduct research on issues and interests by generating ideas and questions, and by posing problems. They gather, evaluate, and synthesize data from a variety of sources (e.g., print and nonprint texts, artifacts, people) to communicate their discoveries in ways that suit their purpose and audience.

8. Students use a variety of technological and information resources (e.g., libraries, databases, computer networks, video) to gather and synthesize information and to create and communicate knowledge.

9. Students develop an understanding of and respect for diversity in language use, patterns, and dialects across cultures, ethnic groups, geographic regions, and social roles.

10. Students whose first language is not English make use of their first language to develop competency in the English language arts and to develop understanding of content across the curriculum.

11. Students participate as knowledgeable, reflective, creative, and critical members of a variety of literacy communities.

12. Students use spoken, written, and visual language to accomplish their own purposes (e.g., for learning, enjoyment, persuasion, and the exchange of information).

These standards can be used as a lens for choosing and using books to expand and enrich the development of language skills and strategies to help children make connections in ways that maintain their dignity as learners and their integrity as human beings. The selection of books for this chapter was filtered through the twelve standards for literacy growth.

As we began selecting books and looking for connections, we used the thinking found in *Standards for the English Language Arts* published by NCTE (1996). The first two standards deal with the range of reading materials that should be made available. Children need to be encouraged to read all genres and to be able to communicate why they are drawn to one genre over another. As children grow toward more fluent and competent readers, the texts themselves need to be high-quality works that offer much diversity. In addition, as teachers we should consider both print and nonprint materials while we help children understand themselves and others within their culture. In planning for these two standards, you could move beyond the books listed in this chapter and look in our companion book, *Learning Under the Influence of Language and Literature* (2006). You may find the Building Community bookshelf in Chapter 2 particularly helpful.

Standard three moves away from the types of texts to focus on the strategies successful readers need to apply while reading. Although this standard is very concise, and there are many strategies that can help meet it, it is sometimes very difficult to match the strategies with the task. But choosing the appropriate strategy is critical if we are to develop fluent readers. Recently we had the privilege to hear Stephanie Harvey talk about the research she and her colleague, Anne Goudvis, did for their book *The Comprehension Toolkit* (2005). The package of research is presented in a clear and easy-to-follow structure. The toolkit format offers many useful and powerful strategies to use with readers and matches those strategies to a type of text.

Standard four can be easily met using a carefully chosen read-aloud if we invite students to communicate their personal reflections about the story in a "turn and talk" period at critical points during the story or at the end. We know that comprehension has to be an active process with the reader totally engaged throughout the text. To ensure that young readers are engaged, we need to structure activities to allow them to communicate about how the text is written, how the author used various conventions, and how those conventions facilitate understanding of the meaning of the story. As you read the annotations provided for the books, you will find many comments concerning the visual impact some books had on us. As always, we encourage you to share the illustrations with students while reading. Another way to address this standard occurs when you give children an opportunity to respond in writing about the impact a book has had on them.

Standards five and six are devoted to the written language that communicates with others for a variety of purposes. These standards offer an excellent opportunity to bring in books featuring the ways an author uses language to evoke a mood or emotion or response. It could include featuring the deliberate use of certain structural devices to signal pauses or tone or intensity when the text is read. It can also be an opportunity to demonstrate how writers use a variety of formats to communicate their ideas depending on topic and audience. For example, this would be a good time to pull out Debra Frazee's *Roller Coaster* to look at how she chose to use conventions and font changes to signal the reader how the text might sound and to make the meaning more robust. Or you might consider using Ralph Fletcher's *Hello Harvest Moon* for figurative language to examine how his word choices make the reader feel the tone and evoke emotional responses. Cynthia Rylant's *Scarecrow* or *In November* could also serve you well in meeting these two standards. Remember the standards invite children to use their own written language to communicate in the same ways Frazee, Fletcher, and Rylant do.

In meeting standards seven and eight, you may want to move to nonfiction text and demonstrate for students how to research and analyze data. A rich resource for these standards can be found on the shelves for social studies and science. Gail Gibbons favors a text structure that can be made visible with attention to the similarities among each of her books regardless of the subject. Simon Seymour is another who offers richly descriptive work vastly different in text structure from Gibbons' books. Jerry Pallotta, another nonfiction writer, favors the structure of an alphabet book to share his research. All three serve a valuable purpose in the elementary classroom while you teach students to conduct research and analyze information as they create their own work.

Standards nine and ten take on greater importance as we move further into the twenty-first century because of the richness of cultural diversity our children are now experiencing in classrooms and neighborhoods across America. Once again, picture books abound to assist in broadening the world of students well beyond the walls of classrooms, to help all children see themselves as fully worthy humans, to see themselves and others as having the right to be on this planet. We encourage you to consider our suggestions, but to also search your shelves and those of the school library for books that will enable students to value the lives of others as fully worthy. To broaden your list of possibilities, see our companion book, *Learning Under the Influence of Language and Literature;* look in Chapter 2—the first opportunity for reading aloud—Building Community Bookshelf One: Celebrating Ourselves and Others.

The last two standards explore the collaboration found in well-developed communities of learners. The learners in these communities value each other, but realize that it is equally important to be aware of their own uniqueness. Once again our companion book (2006) offers a rich, annotated list of books focused on Building Community.

After we begin to work with these national standards to develop young literacy learners in all areas of language arts—reading, writing, listening, speaking, viewing, and visually representing—picture books can serve as the heart of lessons as we pull children into rich literacy learning. Instead of using an overwhelming textbook with young children, let's examine a few well-chosen picture books to attain our goals.

Now, let's consider how we can use picture books to enrich the language arts classroom in addition to, or in place of, the standard textbook. For the following sample lesson on the use of adjectives, we feature three picture books that provide rich usage and descriptions of adjectives: *Puppies! Puppies! Puppies!* by Susan Meyers (see summary on page 10); *Many Luscious Lollipops: A Book About Adjectives* by Ruth Heller; and *Hairy, Scary, Ordinary: What Is an Adjective?* by Brian P. Cleary.

"Today I want to share with you one of my favorite new books for read-alouds. For our first reading, I just want you to listen to Susan Meyers' words as she talks about all the playful little puppies in her story." Following the reading: "Now can you share with your neighbor some of the descriptions you remember about the puppies in the story?"

After a minute, have children share with you some of their noticings. List the adjectives on an anchor chart, which is to be left up in the classroom for everyone to add to as they discover adjectives in their readings. Discuss what adjectives do for a story. Refer to *Puppies! Puppies! Puppies!* On the rereading, leave out many of the adjectives. Have the partners discuss the differences.

"Now I'd like to share another text that features adjectives in a different way. Let's read a few pages and you tell me what you notice. The author of this book wrote a series of books to make children fall in love with language, and she put them in a structure that makes it easy for you to understand all the parts of speech. Listen as I read you a section from Ruth Heller's book, *Many Luscious Lollipops.*"

After reading this book about adjectives, let children discuss and identify adjectives. If they don't notice the difference between the books, lead them. Once again, add to the anchor chart as the children list off the descriptive words Heller chose to use to describe.

Review the chart and tell them you are going to leave it available for them to add other adjectives they notice as they read. For the children who are ready to move on, provide a collection of books on their independent reading level.

"Now readers, I would like you to return to your reading area and select one or two books you'd like to read while I work with a small group. As you are reading, I want you to read with glasses that zoom in on the use of adjectives. Inside each book you will find small sticky notes to use as your detective notebook for recording all the adjectives you spy. If you finish one book before I finish with my group work, please feel free to read another. Does everyone understand what I need you to do? OK readers off you go!"

For a small group of children that need additional support, use Brian Cleary's book *Hairy, Scary, Ordinary*. Get the group engaged by discussing the work as you read to ensure that they understand specifically how to identify and use adjectives. If time permits, at the end of the discussion, use a set of books and have them spy adjectives as a group. Have them share the pen with you and list them on the anchor chart.

Invite both groups back to the carpet and remind them of the power of adjectives throughout their own writing as they move out into their next work.

We have assembled the collection of books in this chapter to support and enrich the language arts curriculum. Many of these listed in the starter sets at the beginning can be read aloud to introduce, explore, or extend various aspects of your study of content within the language arts curriculum. You will find titles that feature most parts of speech to move you beyond a textbook when trying to interest children in gaining a greater command of language.

The latter part of the chapter contains lovely read-aloud books that feature various elements of the language arts curriculum. Once you read through this chapter, begin to read books from your own shelves with a new lens and you will find a wealth of additional support from your favorite authors to bring into the classroom to enrich the study of language arts.

Once again, this collection is just a starter set and the titles are organized on different bookshelves with the hope that this beginning point will only whet your appetite. Now we invite you into our libraries with your paper and pencil in hand to begin making your own connections with books to use to stretch children's understanding of the joys of language.

■ *When Dialogue Matters*

The Conversation Club

Written and Illustrated by Douglas Stanley
Aladdin 1990, ISBN 0–689–71401–7

This adorable book can help children understand the importance of talking, but also reminds readers that being a good listener is essential to conversation. Peter Fieldmouse is very happy living a simple life in his new house. He enjoys listening to the sounds around him in peaceful reflection. He hears the leaves blowing in the wind, the gurgle of running water, the birds singing, and even the crunch of footsteps. The first visitors to welcome him to the neighborhood invite Peter to their Conversation Club. Once there Peter finds that everybody talks at once so no one can listen to anything. So, Peter forms his own club—the Listening Club. Soon, everyone wants to join the new club. Once there, Peter teaches them the importance of listening when others are talking so that you can learn from them. *The Conversation Club* is a short story with a powerful lesson for children.

Quiet, Wyatt!

Written by Bill Maynard
Illustrated by Frank Remkiewicz
Putnam 1999, ISBN 0–399–23217–6

It seemed to Wyatt that no matter who he asked a question of he was always told the same answer: *Quiet, Wyatt!* He wanted to help the big boys fly an airplane, to help his big sister wash the car, he even wanted to help his dad fry an egg, but no one wanted his help. In fact, they didn't even want him to talk. Finally Wyatt decides he's had enough of being told to be quiet so he decides to be quiet. When the big kids lost their airplane and Wyatt knows where it is, he keeps quiet. You can imagine how Maynard solved Wyatt's problem and your children will as well but will adore having this one read to them. Remkiewicz's art just perfectly reflects Wyatt's story.

The Scarecrow's Hat

Written and Illustrated by Ken Brown
Peachtree 2001, ISBN 1–56145–240–8

> *The Scarecrow's Hat* can be read aloud to show children how to be problem solvers and communicators. Chicken needs a new nest and she knows the Scarecrow's hat would make a perfect one. When she approaches him, he tells her he'll trade his hat any day for a walking stick because he gets so tired holding his arms up. Chicken doesn't have a walking stick but she knows someone who does so she sets to work to exchange one item after another. By the end of this charmer, every single animal had their needs met: the scarecrow has his walking stick, badger has his ribbon, crow has his wool, sheep has his glasses, owl has his blanket, donkey has his feathers, and best of all chicken has her nest! Use this one to explore how negotiating, working together, and talking things out can often solve problems.

The Very Busy Spider

Written and Illustrated by Eric Carle
Philomel 1984, ISBN 0–399–21166–7

> Very young children will adore this multisensory book about *The Very Busy Spider* who doesn't have time to talk to all the barnyard animals because she is too busy spinning her web. With a repetitive and rhythmic tale, Carle invites children to join in making the sounds of each of the barnyard animals as they greet the humble but busy spider to invite her to join them in having fun. This one belongs in the patterned text as well because it would be ideal for young writers to use as a mentor text.

■ *The Study of Language and Words*

The irresistible Ruth Heller will assist you in teaching the parts of speech in a delightful and often playful pattern paired with strikingly colorful artwork. Children will never moan when you begin a lesson on grammar using Heller's work to introduce it to them. Instead, many will be inspired to use language more richly and with greater command. Once read, this little collection of books will become a valuable resource for children throughout the year.

Behind the Mask: A Book About Prepositions

Written and Illustrated by Ruth Heller
Putnam 1995, 1998, ISBN 0–698–11698–4

A Cache of Jewels and Other Collective Nouns
Written and Illustrated by Ruth Heller
Putnam 1987, 1998, ISBN 0–698–11354–3

Fantastic! Wow! And Unreal!: A Book About Interjections and Conjunctions
Written and Illustrated by Ruth Heller
Putnam 1998, 2000, ISBN 0–698–11875–8

Kites Sail High: A Book About Verbs
Written and Illustrated by Ruth Heller
Grosset & Dunlap 1968, 1995, ISBN 0–448–41267–5

Many Luscious Lollipops: A Book About Adjectives
Written and Illustrated by Ruth Heller
Putnam 1989, 1998, ISBN 0–698–11641–0

Merry-Go-Round: A Book About Nouns
Written and Illustrated by Ruth Heller
Putnam 1990, 1998, ISBN 0–698–11642–9

Mine, All Mine: A Book About Pronouns
Written and Illustrated by Ruth Heller
Putnam 1997, 1999, ISBN 0–698–11797–2

Up, Up and Away: A Book About Adverbs
Written and Illustrated by Ruth Heller
Putnam 1991, 1998, ISBN 0–698–11663–1

Another author who introduces the parts of speech with kid-friendly artwork is Brian P. Cleary. These playful books engage children in a study of language that is painless and often leaves them begging for more.

Hairy, Scary, Ordinary: What Is an Adjective?
Written by Brian P. Cleary
Illustrated by Jenya Prosmitsky
Carolrhoda 2000, ISBN 1–57505–401–9

A Mink, a Fink, a Skating Rink: What Is a Noun?

Written by Brian P. Cleary
Illustrated by Jenya Prosmitsky
Carolrhoda 1999, ISBN 1–57505–402–7

To Root, to Toot, to Parachute: What Is a Verb?

Written by Brian P. Cleary
Illustrated by Jenya Prosmitsky
Carolrhoda 2001, ISBN 1–57505–403–5

 *Adjectives*

In My New Yellow Shirt

Written by Eileen Spinelli
Illustrated by Hideko Takahashi
Henry Holt 2001, ISBN 0–8050–6242–4

> Aunt Betty gives our young narrator a yellow shirt at his birthday party, but his best friend Sam makes fun of him. He likes his new yellow shirt despite Sam's words. On every page that follows, our delightful young friend finds all the wonderful yellow things he can be in his new yellow shirt: *a duck quacking, splashing in a puddle, a lion scaring crows, a taxi zooming down the street, a lazy caterpillar taking a nap, a dancing daffodil, a swimming fish, a bouncing tennis ball, a tooting brass trumpet, a fluttering butterfly, a singing canary, a golden treasure, a silly banana, a yellow submarine, and at last a blinking fireflies that gets to fly through the night right by Sam's window.* Little ones will adore this story.

Puppies! Puppies! Puppies!

Written by Susan Meyers
Illustrated by David Walker
Harry N. Abrams 2005, ISBN 0–8109–5856–2

> *Puppies big and puppies small, Puppies short and puppies tall. Spotty, wrinkly, shaggy puppies, bouncey, wriggly, waggy puppies. Here and there and everywhere, Puppies! Puppies! Puppies!* If you are the lucky person to have a little one at home to read to or if you are the teacher of many little ones at school, you simply must have this oversized adorable read-aloud filled with

enriching vocabulary, playful art, and discussion-inviting story. Each page is equally delicious and sure to get little minds engaged. Don't miss it.

Compound Words

Once There Was a Bull . . . (frog)

Written by Rick Walton
Illustrated by Greg Hally
Putnam 1995, 1998, ISBN 0–698–11607–0

What a fun book to read. There is only one sentence per page and the compound word is always split between pages, adding a little tension and drama and suspense. *When the bull . . . frog lost his hop, he went looking for it everywhere. He looked under a toad . . . stool but it wasn't there.* His search takes him on quite an adventure to find his hop. This is a very brief book, but it is one that will give children a laugh-out-loud demonstration of how compound words work.

Idioms

Even More Parts

Written and Illustrated by Tedd Arnold
Dial 2004, ISBN 0–8037–2938–3

If you are familiar with the work of Tedd Arnold, you won't be disappointed with this book. He has taken idioms to a new level with his crafty words and his delightful art. He reminds us how idioms can confuse children. To set up the story, Arnold begins: *Sometimes I wish my stupid ears weren't always open wide. They hear such strange and crazy talk—I'm scared to go outside! I jotted down a list of all the scary things I've heard. Believe me, all of these are real. I wrote them word for word. To leave my bedroom unprepared, I'd have to be a fool! Excuse me now. There's work to do before I go to school.* Then Arnold launches into the idioms. This book is simply wonderful.

A Little Pigeon Toad

Written and Illustrated by Fred Gwynne
Alladin 1988, 1990, ISBN 0–671–69444–8

Gwynne illustrates one idiom on every spread. The illustration depicts the most literal meaning. For example, when the text reads, *Mommy says her coat is a little thread bear,* the illustration shows a little girl looking with a sad face at a little bear completely covered in thread. And when the text reads, *Daddy says he wants a pool table,* the illustration shows daddy about to dive into a pool atop a very large table while the little girl looks on. Children will laugh out loud and delight in coming up with more to add on their own. Gwynne's two earlier books—*A Chocolate Moose for Dinner* (Aladdin 1976, 1988; ISBN 0–671–66741–6) and *The King Who Rained* (Aladdin 1970, 1988; ISBN 0–671–66744–0)—follow the same pattern.

My Teacher Likes to Say

Written by Denise Brennan-Nelson
Illustrated by Jane Monroe Donovan
Sleeping Bear Press 2004, ISBN 1–58536–212–3

If we want children to fall in love with language, then we need books on our shelves to help them explore and play with it. This book, filled with idioms, maxims, proverbs, and clichés commonly heard in classrooms, is delightful. After reading and discussing it, you and your children will think of many more. The author gives the background for many of the items she has chosen to use.

There's a Frog in My Throat: 440 Animal Sayings a Little Bird Told Me

Written by Loreen Leedy and Pat Street
Illustrated by Loreen Leedy
Holiday House 2003, ISBN 0–8234–1774–3

Leedy (known for her math books) and Street give us this treasure to explore 440 idioms featuring animals. The idioms are grouped by the type of animal in the saying. For example, *It's raining cats and dogs* would be found in the domestic animals section. The book includes a table of contents and an index to help readers locate favorite idioms. The authors pair every idiom with an illustration and also give the meaning of the idiom in a smaller font. This one will be well worn if left available for children.

Nouns

Your Foot's on My Feet! And Other Tricky Nouns

Written by Marvin Terban
Illustrated by Giulio Maestro
Clarion 1986, ISBN 0–89919–413–3

Terban provides us with another book to help children discover how "irregular" the English language can be. In this one, he takes ninety irregular nouns and uses them in humorous rhymes that will tickle the ear, clear up some tricky words, and leave a ripple of word play in the wake. The following are other titles by Terban.

> *The Dove Dove* (Homograph riddles)
> *Eight Ate* (Homonym riddles)
> *Guppies in Tuxedos* (Eponyms)
> *Hey, Hay!* (Homonyms)
> *In a Pickle* (Idioms)
> *I Think I Thought* (Tricky verbs)
> *Mad as a Wet Hen* (Idioms)
> *Punching the Clock* (Funny action idioms)
> *Too Hot to Hoot* (Palindrome riddles)
> *Superdupers!* (Funny real words)

Opposites

Fortunately

Written and Illustrated by Remy Charlip
Aladdin 1964, 1993, 0–689–71660–5

This one is sure to get children inspired to write their own version of *Fortunately* once they go on the adventure with Ned. The text is very short and each page gives the opposite of the page before. *Fortunately once, Ned got a letter that said, "Please come to a surprise party." But unfortunately the party was in Florida and he was in New York. Fortunately a friend loaned him an airplane. Unfortunately the motor exploded.* Follow along with Ned as this series of events unfolds with every new page. The last page holds the surprise ending.

That's Good! That's Bad!

Written by Margery Cuyler
Illustrated by David Catrow
Henry Holt 1991, ISBN 0–8050–2954–0

Another word-play book is written on the same pattern as *Fortunately,* but it has highly recognizable full-color illustrations by David Catrow. This story is told as an adventure with a little boy who is visiting the zoo with his parents. They buy him a balloon and *it lifted him high up into the sky, WOW! Oh, that's good. NO, that's bad!* Then the adventure begins with him floating off mile after mile before a tree pops the balloon. *Oh, that's bad. No, that's good.* (Notice the reversal of phrases.) Of course, he falls into a muddy river full of hippopotamuses. And then, off he goes once more. Finally, he does arrive— by stork—back safely into his mother's arms.

Oxymorons

Who Ordered the Jumbo Shrimp? And Other Oxymorons

Written and Illustrated by Jon Agee
Farrar, Straus and Giroux 1998, 2002, ISBN 0–374–48372–8

The *New York Times* called this little book "laugh-out-loud-brilliant," and we all know that is high praise. Adults will have fun using this one with children. As you thumb through, you will see how children can easily get such mixed messages from the oxymorons we use every day.

Playing with Words

Autumn: An Alphabet Acrostic

Written by Steven Schnur
Illustrated by Leslie Evans
Clarion 1997, ISBN 0–395–77043–2

This book looks so simple at first glance. You flip through the pages and notice that every one begins with a word related to the autumn season. Each page features a word beginning with the next letter of the alphabet. OK, pretty simple, we could do that. Now, each word is presented as an acrostic poem—yeah, we could do that. So what's the catch you might be thinking?

Well, on a closer read, we realize that every acrostic is not *just* a stand-alone poem, but that each one leads into the next so that all twenty-six can be read one after the other as one long poem. And if you find this one intriguing then you will also love the others in this set. Yep, there are four; one for every season and they all follow the same very clever format. Schnur wrote, Evans illustrated, and Clarion published them: *Winter: An Alphabet Acrostic,* 2002 (ISBN 0–618–02374–7), *Spring: An Alphabet Acrostic,* 1997 (ISBN 0–395–82269–6), *Summer: An Alphabet Acrostic,* 2001 (ISBN 0–618–02372–0).

CDB!

Written and Illustrated by William Steig
Simon & Schuster 1987, 2000, ISBN 0–689–83160–9

> *If U R reading this, solving the puzzles N this book should B E-Z 4 U.* And if this intrigues you, then this is a book for you, and it's full of playful twists on every page. But for those of you who aren't sure you can keep up with the kids in solving the puzzle, you will find all the answers at the back of the book. Steig has written several books like this and kids love the idea of playing with language this way. Of course, this is one you have to see while you are listening. Go ahead and open this one for a few moments of fabulous fun with language.

The Circus of Words

Written by Richard Lederer
Illustrated by Dave Morice
Chicago Review 2001, ISBN 1–55652–380–7

> This one is just full of all types of word play: anagrams, palindromes, spoonerisms, puns, acrostics, riddles, and other activities. Open it up and have a blast.

Doodler Doodling

Written by Rita Golden Gelman
Illustrated by Paul O. Zelinsky
Greenwillow 2004, ISBN 0–688–16645–8

> What does a doodler's doodlings mean? Gelman's play with words and imagination with Zelinsky's reflective art will fuel chuckles at times and puzzlement at others, but on every page, children will be filled with wonder about

what comes next. The front flap of the dust jacket tells the reader: *Here is a book starring twenty-one words, a blank piece of paper, and a train of thought. And you will be amazed. WOW!* And we think you and your students will agree.

Fibblestax

Written by Devin Scillian
Illustrated by Kathryn Darnell
Sleeping Bear Press 2000, ISBN 1–886947–90–2

All of us want children to fall in love with words. What better way to get them interested in learning where words come from and how things got the names they have than to read a delightful fable one morning. The text is filled with beautiful language and illustrated with soft intricate details in colored pencil. In this fable *Fibblestax,* a sweet boy with a heart of gold, thinks of only lovely wonderful names for things. But Carr, a grouchy old man, was just the opposite. He gives terrible names even to lovely things. He uses awful words in a careless, haughty way. Finally, the Lord Mayor has had enough and declares a contest between the two wordsmiths. They are each given five objects that needs names, including the drops of water that fall from the sky, a name for the crispy little squares we eat with soup, and more. But the final one is the feeling we get as we gather together with others: . . . *a dreamy kind of cheer.* Carr, a person who has never experienced that feeling, is speechless and runs away but *Fibblestax* with tears in his eyes names that feeling "love." Following this book you and your students could have great fun exploring the origins of the names for common things in the classroom. One thing for sure, you will all be more aware of the words you use.

The Hungry Thing

Written by Jan Slepian and Ann Seidler
Illustrated by Richard E. Martin
Scholastic 1967, ISBN 0–439–27598–9

When you read this one aloud, you can have a great time with the children while you give them a delightful opportunity to listen oh so carefully. When *The Hungry Thing* comes to town and wants to be fed, none of the people in town can understand what he is asking for when he says such things as *tickles* when he really means *pickles* and *feetloaf* when he really wants *meatloaf.* Once children understand the pattern used by these clever authors, they will clamor to tell you what *The Hungry Thing* really wants to eat.

Word Wizard

Written and Illustrated by Cathryn Falwell
Clarion 1998, 2006, ISBN 0–395–85580–2

Children will adore this magical book as Anna discovers she can make new words in her cereal bowl by dipping her spoon into the mix and watching the letters float around. When she dips the spoon, readers will notice *dawn* becomes *wand*, *pat* becomes *tap*, and *flea* becomes *leaf*. This book will inspire young word magicians to fall in love with playing with words. Have fun!

 Puns

Pun and Games: Jokes, Riddles, Rhymes, Daffynitions, Tairy Fales, and More Word Play for Kids

Written by Richard Lederer
Illustrated by Dave Morice
Chicago Review 1996, ISBN 1–55652–264–9

Children will have fun with this one because they've been hearing puns all their lives without knowing they are puns. This book is more of a resource tool than a read-aloud. You and your students will find fun word play opportunities to try out during those times of transition and lining up. The puns in this book are sure to make children fall in love with language.

 *Superlatives*

Pig, Pigger, Piggest

Written by Rick Walton
Illustrated by Jimmy Holder
Gibbs Smith 1997, 2003, ISBN 1–58685–318–X

Walton took humorous liberties with a remake of *The Three Pigs* to give us a book filled with superlatives. From the pig's names to the Witch, the Witcher, and the Witchest who are rich and want to buy the castle built by the Pigs. If you chose this one to help explain the use of superlatives, you'd better practice before trying to read it aloud. It can be tricky in places, and you are likely to get your tongue twisted around your eye teeth and not be able to see what you are saying.

Things That Are MOST in the World

Written by Judi Barrett
Illustrated by John Nickle
Aladdin 1998 (Atheneum), 2001, ISBN 0–689–84449–2

Barrett is at her best in this book of superlatives. Every superlative is printed in an enlarged font and appears in color. There is only one sentence per page supported by an illustration that extends across the opposite page.

For additional read-aloud books that use superlatives, look on the math bookshelf in Chapter 2 for the two books by Steve Jenkins: *Hottest, Coldest, Highest, Deepest* and *Biggest, Strongest, Fastest.*

Verbs

Frog Legs: A Picture Book of Action Verse

Written by George Shannon
Illustrated by Amit Trynan
Greenwillow 2000, ISBN 0–688–17047–1

There's nothing serious about this rip-romping, stomping, tipping, slipping poetry book about frogs. Each one will have children giggling and wanting to read it again and again. All the poems are very short, but the vocabulary you will be exposing children to is amazing. We can see your physical education teachers loving this one!

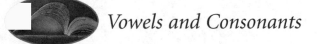

Vowels and Consonants

The War Between the Vowels and the Consonants

Written by Priscilla Turner
Illustrated by Whitney Turner
Sunburst/Farrar, Straus and Giroux 1996, 1999, ISBN 0–374–48217–9

Many children have problems remembering which letters are called vowels and which ones are the consonants. While that is important, their significance emerges when those letters are joined together to make words, phrases, sentences, paragraphs, stories, books, and so on. This clever little book goes a long way in getting that message across as the Vowels wage a battle with the Consonants. Until they are confronted with a common enemy, they never realize that together they are much more powerful. This one entertains and informs.

Words Within Words

ANTics!

Written and Illustrated by Cathi Hepworth
PaperStar/Putnam & Grosset 1992, 1996, ISBN 0–399–11350–0

The PIG in the sPIGot

Written by Richard Wilbur
Illustrated by J. Otto Seibold
Harcourt 2000, ISBN 0–15–202019–5

There's an ANT in ANThony

Written and Illustrated by Bernard Most
HarperTrophy 1980 (Mulberry), 1992, ISBN 0–688–11513–6

Anthony learns to spell his name once he notices that there is an ANT in its spelling. Once he notices the ANT in his name, he begins to search for other words where ANT was chunked into a larger word. He looks all over his room before he finds a plANT and then an ANTenna on his radio. On a walk around town, he finds a fire hydrANT and an elephANT. This simple little book will get kids fascinated with word play and have them noticing chunks and smaller words hidden in larger words.

■ Books That Illustrate the Features of Writing

Alliteration

Some Smug Slug

Written by Pamela Duncan Edwards
Illustrated by Henry Cole
HarperCollins 1996, ISBN 0–06–024792–4

Some Smug Slug will be a task to test your talent to read troublesome alliteration without tripping over your tongue. The surprise ending will be . . . well, it will be a surprise. The moral of the story is that smugness will get you into trouble and this sad lesson is one the Smug Slug learns just a bit too late. Read as he is warned by a sparrow, a spider, a swallowtail, a skink, and a squirrel while he only smirks and slithers up the slippery slope to finally become a succulent slug. What vocabulary this one will provide your students. The very short text is presented in an enlarged font nestled on Henry Cole's cheerful art.

The Worrywarts

Written by Pamela Duncan Edwards
Illustrated by Henry Cole
HarperTrophy 1999, 2003, ISBN 0–06–443516–4

The team that brought us *Some Smug Slug* now gives us *The Worrywarts,* which is just as much fun to read, and it is just as clever in the use of alliteration. Wombat asks Weasel and Woodchuck to go on a walk with her on Wednesday. Wombat is a worrier and that habit rubs off on her friends as they walk. Every time a new worry creeps up, the font is enlarged to help the reader know how to use his or her voice with the text. This could be a fun follow-up for *Some Smug Slug.*

Relevant Details

Weaving the Rainbow

Written by George Ella Lyon
Illustrated by Stephanie Anderson
Atheneum 2004, ISBN 0–689–85169–3

A story is woven in the poetic prose we have come to expect in Lyon's writing. On the surface, it is a simple telling of the process of raising sheep, gathering and preparing wool—combing and washing and carding, pulling and twisting and spinning. It is a story of the weaver drawing a plan, making dyes from what nature has provided, dying the yarn and weaving a picture. But its more than that. It is a story of envisioning, planning, working toward something beautiful that lives within you—a story of believing your vision into reality. Anderson's watercolor art (the perfect companion to Lyon's luscious language) is soft as lambs' wool, inviting the reader to lean in, tempting the reader to reach in and dare to touch. To sum it up in a single word—gorgeous!

Interesting Use of Italics

The Ghost-Eye Tree

Written by Bill Martin Jr. and John Archambault
Illustrated by Ted Rand
Henry Holt 1985, 1988, ISBN 0–8050–0947–7

One dark and windy autumn night when the sun had long gone down, Mama asked my sister and me to take the road to the end of town to get a bucket of milk. Oooo . . . I dreaded to go . . . I dreaded the tree . . . And so begins the exciting tale of two young children whose imaginations take them across town right by the ghost-eye tree. As the winds howl, their fears grow, but despite all the fright, they make it safely back home boasting to each other about how they really weren't afraid. Yet, from that time on, neither could be found when it was time to go get milk.

Language That Extends Vocabulary

Giddy Goat

Written by Jamie Rix
Illustrated by Lynne Chapman
Gingham Dog/McGraw-Hill 2003, ISBN 0–7696–3161–4

Giddy Goat teaches us how to dig deep within ourselves to find courage to deal with challenges in life. Giddy was deathly afraid of heights. No matter how hard he tried or how often his parents soothed him, he just couldn't cope with this fear. Enjoy the charm of Rix's words as you discover how *Giddy Goat* learned to overcome his fear. As you read aloud, children will be introduced to rich vocabulary such as *ravine, perched, cliffs, acrobatic, quivering, grazed, molehills, bleating,* and *measly* for starters.

Imagine a Night

Written by Sarah L. Thomson
Illustrated by Rob Gonsalves
Atheneum 2003, ISBN 0–689–85218–5

Before you open this one, before you even peek inside, you must spend time with the stunning art that envelops the cover. Linger there and examine the images to get ready for the remarkably descriptive language on every page. *Imagine a night . . . when snow white sheets grow crisp and cold, and someone whispers, "Follow me." Imagine a night . . . when a snowfall tucks you in and the evening star kisses you asleep. Imagine . . . tonight.* Created by the same team that brought us *Imagine a Day,* this one is equally delightful.

The Listening Walk

Written by Paul Showers
Illustrated by Aliki
HarperTrophy 1961, 1991, 1993, ISBN 0–06–443322–6

The Listening Walk is a simple text told in first person as a young girl and her father go on a walk where there is no talking, just listening. The book could be used so well by teachers to feature the power of the sense of hearing and the art of listening. Onomatopoeia is used throughout the text—*the twick of the dog's nails; the dop, dup, dop, dup of the father's shoes*—to reveal the sounds of each of the things they see on their listening walk. Many children will love hearing this story and then going for their very own listening walk.

The Long and Short of It

Written by Cheryl Nathan and Lisa McCourt
Illustrated by Cheryl Nathan
BridgeWater/Troll 1998, ISBN 0–8167–4545–5

You will absolutely adore this book after one read-aloud, but even better, children will beg for it over and over again. The language is delightful. The vocabulary is outstanding. What more could you ask for? Well, if it is a book full of unusual facts about animals, then this is the one for you. The font often follows the shape of the animal it is describing. Nathan's art might remind you of Eric Carle's work, which is always a winner with children.

Snow Music

Written and Illustrated by Lynne Rae Perkins
Greenwillow 2003, ISBN 0–06–623956–7

Before reading this book, take time to meander through the pages to examine the text structure and the amazing art. Only after the visual senses have been satisfied should you begin to put the language into the air. What does *Snow Music* sound like? Let's let Perkins describe how that music is made and who helps to make it. The thread she chooses to hold the story together is a little boy who goes out on a snowy day to find his runaway dog. During his search, the little boy meets and listens to the sounds made by various creatures and things.

Memoir Like Story

The Raft

Written and Illustrated by Jim LaMarche
HarperTrophy 2000, 2002, ISBN 0–06–443856–2

Having a raft turns a typical summer into an adventure for Nicky who isn't happy at all about having to spend his summer with his grandmother in the middle of the Wisconsin woods. Like many young people, he is concerned about how he will spend all the time in the middle of the woods without a TV. What Nicky doesn't count on is his discovery of a raft that seems to be waiting just for him at the edge of the river. Drifting down the river made fishing better for a city boy as he slowly begins to notice all the life around him—life he has never seen before. Like most grandmas, Nicky's can be talked into letting him camp out on the raft and even helps him set up his tent. But the greatest gift Grandma gives him that summer is a big sketchpad and crayons. By the end of the summer, Nicky becomes an artist and a river rat just like his Grandma. The Author's Note at the beginning tells the reader that the book is somewhat like a memoir of LaMarche's summer as a boy when he spent time with his grandparents in the north woods.

Metaphors and Similes

Grandfather's Lovesong

Written by Reeve Lindbergh
Illustrated by Rachel Isadora
Viking 1993, ISBN 0–670–84842–5

Grandfather's Lovesong is full of similes used by the grandfather to describe his vast love for his grandson—*I love you high like the top of the sky where the sun and moon go floating by. I love you low like the world below where parents watch their children grow.* The structure of it uses some of the months of the year and the seasons to carry the story from beginning to end. This one is gentle and poetic and is likely to influence both oral and written language in the community.

Looking for Diamonds

Written by Brenda Seabrooke
Illustrated by Nancy Mantha
Cobblehill/Dutton 1995, ISBN 0–525–65173–X

> *Looking for Diamonds* highlights the special relationship between young Amy and her grandparents. Amy cuddles with grandmother under the quilt in a bed like no other. And shortly after breakfast, Amy and Granddaddy go looking for diamonds. In the summer, they look for dew diamonds and in winter it is frost diamonds. And after a rain, there are even rain diamonds. Diamonds are formed in *that special moment when the sun catches the fire in a drop of water and glitters with color.* They even find *dishwasher diamonds as they shimmered and glowed* after Amy's grandmother threw out the dishwater. Mantha's soft pastel illustrations are soothing and reflect the tender relationship described by the words of the text.

When I Go Camping with Grandma

Written by Marion Dane Bauer
Illustrated by Allen Garns
Troll 1996, ISBN 0–8167–3449–6

> With lush language, Bauer tells us a very short but significant story about a young girl's special camping trip with her Grandma. Phrases—for example, *sunlight spread on black water; tree bones stand in the lake; gone in the wiggle of light; the moon floats low in the bluing sky like a balloon left from a night party*—move the story along and elicit such wonderful images that readers and listeners will "Ooooo" and "Aaaah" over the use of descriptive language. Garns' chalk art is just the right balance for the tone of the story.

Onomatopoeia

Achoo! Bang! Crash! The Noisy Alphabet

Written and Illustrated by Ross MacDonald
Roaring Brook Press 2003, ISBN 0–7613–1796–1

> Get your head wrapped around onomatopoeia for this fun-with-language alphabet book. Once you get halfway though it, stop and let children work in

small groups to think of onomatopoeia words with the rest of the alphabet. Then go back and compare their work with MacDonald's. We've tried this one even with adults and had fun. And don't forget to read the Illustrator Notes at the end. Then, return to the art for a fresh look.

Click, Clack, Moo: Cows That Type

Written by Doreen Cronin
Illustrated by Betsy Lewin
Simon & Schuster 2000, ISBN 0–689–83213–3

What happens when the cows find an old typewriter in Farmer Brown's barn? What happens when he hears more typing than mooing? If you guessed that he begins finding notes around the barn, you guessed right! It seems the cows aren't satisfied with the way Farmer Brown runs his farm. Duck enters the story as an intermediary between the cows and Farmer Brown as they try to work out their differences. With enlarged font and playful onomatopoeia, this will become one of children's favorites . . . regardless of age. Just read it once and you'll hear them chant, "Read it again."

Night in the Barn

Written by Faye Gibbons
Illustrated by Erick Ingraham
Morrow Junior Books 1995, ISBN 0–688–13326–6

It was darker than dark that cold fall night. And so begins the story of a group of boys who dare each other to sleep out in the barn all night. The mood of the dark windy night is enhanced with appropriately placed onomatopoeia. The art extends the feeling with each full-page spread. Relive your own childhood as you battle the fears of the night and its strange sounds. This story will filter into your writing workshop as some students are likely to springboard off the topic and others will play around with sound effects in their pieces.

Patterned Text

Brown Bear, Brown Bear, What Do You See?

Written by Bill Martin Jr.
Illustrated by Eric Carle
Henry Holt 1967, 1970, 1992, 1995, ISBN 0–8050–4790–5

Brown Bear, Brown Bear, a beloved classic for very young children, shouldn't be missed during those precious early childhood years. Widely known for its very predictable structure, this one will have even the very young chanting the text along with you after only one reading. Eric Carle's art, which is so distinctive, leads the children with the expected line of text.

Chicka Chicka Boom Boom
Written by Bill Martin Jr. and John Archambault
Illustrated by Lois Ehlert
Alladin/Simon & Schuster 1989, 2000, ISBN 0–617–83568–X

All young children deserve to hear an enthusiastic teacher read this captivating book. And to make the experience even more special, let them listen to a recording of John Archambault and David Plumer singing the book. After listening just once, it will play around in your head for many days to come. You'll walk around hearing: *A told B, and B told C, I'll meet you at the top of the coconut tree. Whee! Said D to E, F, G, I'll beat you to the top of the coconut tree . . . . Chicka Chicka Chicka Boom Boom! Will there be enough room? Look who's coming L M N O P! And Q R S! And T U V. Still more—W! And X Y Z!* You and your students will adore the rhyme and rhythm of this text. And Ehlert's bright and colorful and simple art is a treat for the eyes.

Click, Clack, Quackity-Quack: An Alphabet Adventure
Written by Doreen Cronin
Illustrated by Betsy Lewin
Atheneum 2005, ISBN 13–978–0–689–87715–5

For all of you who first fell in love with *Click, Clack, Moo: Cows That Type,* here's a new one for you. Using the alphabet as the structure, Cronin gives us a perfect example of careful word choice, strong nouns and verbs, onomatopoeia, and alliteration. With all this going for it, this latest work of Cronin and Lewin will be equally at home in a preschool classroom that features the alphabet and in a fifth-grade one that looks at language structure.

The Hidden Alphabet
Written and Illustrated by Laura Vaccaro Seeger
Roaring Brook Press 2003, ISBN 0–7613–1941–7

If you don't know this book but think you know a lot about books, get ready because Seeger has one for you that is so unbelievably clever you'll be sharing it with everyone you know. [It's true. We have even pulled it from our shelves to share it with adult friends who drop by.] Just the cover will spark your interest *but* wait until you see the unique way she presents each letter of the alphabet. On every glossy black page you will see a picture of an object framed within a cutout. All the illustrations feature an object that begins with the page's letter. The name of each object is printed in white letters. Now, lift the cut-out page to reveal that the object is really embedded within a larger illustration of the specific letter. Once children understand the structure, they will eagerly begin guessing what is hidden underneath each flap.

The Napping House

Written by Audrey Wood
Illustrated by Don Wood
Harcourt 1984, 1991, ISBN 0–15–256711–9

The pattern in this story is layered in as a cumulative tale. You may use it as a read-aloud to illustrate a pattern, but this one is such fun to read you will find yourself reading it for the pure enjoyment of putting the language in the air. The art is just as delightful as Audrey and Don Wood team up to show the reader Granny sleeping in a cozy bed on a rainy day in a napping house where everyone is sleeping. Each page adds a detail to the growing tale, creating a cumulative pattern. Look closely and notice how the art changes in tone and point of view. This one is a favorite of ours, so we think it must be read in every classroom.

Naughty Little Monkeys

Written by Jim Aylesworth
Illustrated by Henry Cole
Dutton 2003, ISBN 0–525–46940–0

This alphabet book is written in rhyme about the antics of twenty-six *Naughty Little Monkeys* whose mom thinks are perfect. Once tucked in for the night, those naughty monkeys get into all kinds of trouble. The first little monkey folds an airplane (A) to send flying around the room. The second one begins jumping on the bed (B) until she bonks her head. However, by the time we get to the naughty little monkey splashing soapy water (W), the parents come home to discover their precious little monkeys aren't so precious after all. The very next morning after discovering all the mess they had made, all twenty-six are sent to the zoo (Z) where all little monkeys go!

Don't worry, the last page reassures children that the monkeys aren't left at the zoo. That Jim Ayelsworth is so clever.

The Racecar Alphabet

Written and Illustrated by Brian Floca
Atheneum 2003, ISBN 0–689–85091–3

Beginning with the endpapers, this book will inspire and intrigue any students who are interested in race cars. The illustrations in this oversized book portray different periods of history in racing with each turn of a page. The text takes you through one race zipping through the alphabet. Each page features one letter and uses alliteration as it pulls the reader through the race. A sharp reader will notice that as the alphabet progresses so does the history of race cars. The book's size with its enlarged font makes it splendid for a read-aloud with a classroom full of children.

Read Anything Good Lately?

Written by Susan Allen and Jane Lindaman
Illustrated by Vicky Enright
Millbrook Press 2003, ISBN 0–7613–1889–5

Read Anything Good Lately? is a clever alphabet book about all the things around us that we can read. Beginning with the atlas in the airport and a biography in bed, Susan and Jane provide playful alliteration throughout the alphabet that can be a springboard to get children engrossed in searching for special places and things with other letters of the alphabet to read. *Warning:* Read at your own risk. You may begin speaking in alliteration and find yourself searching for new places and things to read.

This Is the House That Was Tidy and Neat

Written by Teri Sloat
Illustrated by R. W. Alley
Henry Holt 2005, ISBN 0–8050–6921–6

When mom left her house neat and tidy, she never stopped to think about the nanny going to sleep and leaving her son, daughter, a dog, a cat, and a mouse to wreck havoc in her neat and tidy house. Each page tells the cumulative tale of the destruction that ends when dad came home to begin the clean up. The text is fun to read and shows children another perfect example of how a story builds across the pages. Other stories to show cumulative text examples include *The House That Jack Built* and *The Napping House.*

Tomorrow's Alphabet

Written by George Shannon
Illustrated by Donald Crews
Greenwillow 1996, 1999, ISBN 0–688–13504–8

If you and your students are fans of alphabet books, this is one for you. It is a most unusual book that is such fun to use with kids. The clever before-and-after pattern will jump-start the creative juices in your community; for example: *A is for seed—tomorrow's APPLE. B is for eggs—tomorrow's BIRDS. C is for milk—tomorrow's CHEESE.* The book is so clever and Crew's large and colorful art is the finishing touch that makes the package a delicious one.

Personification

Book! Book! Book!

Written by Deborah Bruss
Illustrated by Tiphanie Beeke
Arthur A. Levine 2001, ISBN 0–439–13525–7

What happens when all the children go back to school and the barnyard animals get bored? Well, of course, like all smart animals, they go to visit the library to get a book. The problem is that the librarian can't understand any of them as they *moo, neigh, oink,* and *baaah.* But when the hen takes over, the librarian understands perfectly. This is one you'll need to practice to get your reading of *Book! Book! Book!* to sound just right. Once read, you'll want to read it over and over. It is so much fun to hear children's chuckles as the words "cluck" out. The book is just so clever it is bound to become a favorite.

Cock-a-Moo-Moo

Written by Juliet Dallas-Conté
Illustrated by Alison Bartlett
Little, Brown 2001, ISBN 0–316–60505–0

This is a great companion book to read with *Bob*—see Building Community Bookshelf Six: Overcoming Obstacles and Facing Life's Challenges in Chapter 2 of *Learning Under the Influence of Language and Literature* (2006). This poor rooster had forgotten how to crow as well. When the sun comes up, instead of cock-a-doodle-doo, out comes *Cock-a-Moo-Moo!* Of course, the cows don't like a rooster imitating them, so rooster tries again and again.

Each time his cock-a-doodle-doo comes out sounding like all the other animals on the farm. Dallas-Conté gives readers and/or listeners a predictable ending that is satisfying and has everyone living happily ever after.

Crackers

Written by Becky Bloom
Illustrated by Pascal Biet
Orchard 2001, ISBN 0–531–30326–8

Crackers is a very strong cat with many wonderful abilities and talents—but he doesn't have a job. Since he is big and strong, he applies for a job as a security guard. But when a tiny mouse asks for some scrap lumber, Crackers gives it to him. He gets fired. Next, he applies to be an assistant at the marina and because he is such a good swimmer, he is hired immediately. But he lets a family of mice fish from the pier. He gets fired. Then, he applies to be a waiter in a fancy restaurant and since he also speaks French, they hire him immediately. But when he ushers a family of mice to a table, that scares all the other customers. You know what happened and children will be giggling by the time they get the pattern of this wonderful story. And you will all be pleased when you reach the end and discover how Bloom solves the problem.

Goodnight, My Duckling

Written and Illustrated by Nancy Tafuri
Scholastic 2005, ISBN 0–439–39881–9

This simple little text is a gentle, soothing naptime story for little ones. When read aloud, the reassuring words will lull listeners into a sense of calm or ease them off into sleep. Like Tafuri's other work, *Goodnight, My Duckling* is appealing to young children because of the uncluttered, full-spread illustrations, the sparse language, and the enlarged font. And as a note from a couple of folks who know, this one makes a lovely gift for any new parents. It is destined to be read as a rocking-chair lullaby.

Mole Music

Written and Illustrated by David McPhail
Owlet/Henry Holt 1999, 2001, ISBN 0–8050–6766–3

Mole Music is a modern fantasy about a mole who lives all alone and becomes intrigued when he hears someone play a violin on TV. Mole wants to play one himself. So he orders one and dedicates himself to practice until he plays beautiful music . . . one piece after another. All along he wonders what would happen if only he could play for others. What he doesn't know is that his music floats out from the tunnels and charms everyone who hears it . . . even his enemies.

Spring's Sprung

Written by Lynne Plourde
Illustrated by Greg Couch
Simon & Schuster 2002, ISBN 0–689–84229–5

Plourde introduces spring through personification of Mother Earth and the months of the spring season as her daughters . . . *Mother Earth rouses her daughters— / March, April, and May. / "You must wake the world / to start a new day."* The sisters argue back and forth about who is the favorite until finally, to settle the argument (like all good mothers), she tells her girls: *A mother's heart is big enough to grow and grow, and stretch and stretch. The truth—I love you ALL the best.*

Wolf!

Written by Becky Bloom
Illustrated by Pascal Biet
Orchard 1999, ISBN 0–531–30155–9

When the Wolf comes to town broke and hungry, he immediately begins thinking of ways to feed himself. A farm with lots of animals would provide him with everything he needs. When he arrives at the farm, there sits a pig, a duck, and a cow *reading*. He's never seen anything like that before. When they don't react to his howl, he becomes irate. How dare they ignore a big bad wolf. Well no matter how he growls, they are just too involved in their reading. So being the smart wolf that he is, he goes into town and uses the little money he has left to buy a book. The problem is that he has not yet learned to read. His first attempts are a bit stilted: *Run, wolf, run! See wolf run* and that certainly doesn't appeal to the other animals. His next attempt is almost as bad when he tries to impress the others by reading as fast as he can and all the words run together. Those educated animals know no self-respecting reader reads that way. So they turn him away again! Finally, the Wolf goes to the library and checks out lots of books because he is determined to become as good a reader as the other animals. Will he succeed? You'll only know if you read this adorable book.

Questions as a Story Structure

Dad, Aren't You Glad?

Written by Lynn Plourde
Illustrated by Amy Wummer
Dutton 2005, ISBN 0–525–47362–9

> With only two sentences and the rest of the text in questions, Plourde's work is one of pure pleasure as you chuckle throughout at the antics of the little boy who longs to do all his dad's chores to make his father's day special. Wummer's art complements the mischievous text to make this one a winner. Even though most of the text is told in the form of questions, the editors (or Plourde) chose not to use question marks. Regardless, it is a perfect example of telling a story using questions.

Slows Time and Shows a Small Moment

Salt Hands

Written by Jane Chelsea Aragon
Illustrated by Ted Rand
Puffin 1989, 1994, ISBN 0–14–050321–8

> This spectacular little book so clearly models what Lucy Calkins called "expanding a small moment." The entire story is only a moment in time as a young girl wakes in the middle of the night to discover a deer on the lawn. The back cover of this dynamic book so clearly describes this treasure: *Readers will hold their breath and watch in awe as a majestic wild deer comes close enough to lick salt from a little girl's hands in this magical, whisper-soft picture book luminously illustrated by Ted Rand.* Cross your fingers before you check the library shelves because this one is out of print.

Unusual Punctuation

The Stars Will Still Shine

Written by Cynthia Rylant
Illustrated by Tiphanie Beeke
HarperCollins 2005, ISBN 0–06–054640–9

Get ready to fall absolutely in love with this lyrical book by Rylant. If it had been published before *Learning Under the Influence of Language and Literature* (2006), we would have placed it on the Building Community Bookshelf One: Celebrating Ourselves and Others. Because it wasn't available then and we could not bear for you not to know about it, we are placing it here with other books that illustrate unusual punctuation. On its glorious pages, you will find only one phrase and often no punctuation. However, by the placement on the pages, Rylant has given you the pacing to read it slowly and melodiously. Beeke's art envelops the story in child-friendly watercolors that will sing to children.

Train Song

Written by Diane Siebert
Illustrated by Mike Wimmer
HarperTrophy 1981, 1993, ISBN 0–064–43340–4

Siebert does an incredible job of describing the journey of various trains. The rhythmic language is nestled in a box surrounded by Wimmer's rich and crisp illustrations that fill every spread. Siebert uses no capital letters or punctuation marks, but the phrasing helps the reader know how this lovely piece should sound when read aloud.

The Wonderful Happens

Written by Cynthia Rylant
Illustrated by Coco Dowley
Simon & Schuster 2000, ISBN 0–689–83177–3

This lovely book could easily fit into the Building Community read-alouds because of the focus it places on how wonderful and special each child is. However, we chose to include it here because of the interesting use of punctuation and because it is a delight to read. Rylant uses cycles to explain how the egg becomes a bird and the seed becomes a wonderful rose and a grain of wheat becomes a loaf of bread. Then, she turns this to focus on little special "you" whose ears are being filled with this wonderful, lyrical language. And she explains how very wonderful every one of us truly is.

Varied Sentence Length

Rosie and the Nightmares

Written and Illustrated by Philip Waechter
Handprint 2005, ISBN 1–59354–115–5

Here is a new one for your language arts classroom that illustrates how authors use the varied length of sentences to build a powerful story. Rosie, a little bunny, has a recurring nightmare that haunts her every night. When she has had enough of her sleepless nights, she visits a dream specialist who prescribes a good book to read about monsters. The book prepares her to face her fear and the tension begins to build as she visits an amusement park to confront the monsters. Inside the tunnel as her eyes *adjust quickly to the darkness. Everything was just as creepy as she had imagined. Huge eyes stared at her. Pointy teeth flashed. Sharp claws scratched. Great mouths hissed. . . . There's no turning back now. She was ready.* The children will delight in how Rosie confronts and wins over her fears before being banned from the park. Waechter's whimsical illustrations will empower children as they garner strength to face and overcome their own nightmares.

■ Building a Reader and a Writer

Books That Feature an Author's Visit

My Special Day at Third Street School

Written by Eve Bunting
Illustrated by Suzanne Bloom
Boyds Mills 2004, ISBN 1–59078–075–2

All children should have the opportunity to have authors visit their school every year. In this playful story, Eve Bunting lets us join the children at Third Street School as they prepare for and then welcome author Miss Amanda Drake. The day is a delight as Miss Drake tells them all about her work as a writer. Because of this visit, the children write even more as they eagerly await the book Miss Drake is writing about her visit to their school. Suzanne Bloom's lively art complements the rhyme and rhythm of the language.

Books That Illustrate a Fractured Tale (Parody)

Bubba, the Cowboy Prince: A Fractured Texas Tale

Written by Helen Ketteman
Illustrated by James Warhola
Scholastic 1997, ISBN 0–590–25506–1

> Based on the Cinderella fairy tale, *Bubba, the Cowboy Prince* will get even the most hardened adult laughing. Read about Bubba, the stepson, and his wicked stepdad with two lazy stepbrothers and the beautiful Miz Lurleen. Bubba (not unlike Cinderella) wants to go to Miz Lurleen's ball. But there is a little problem since he doesn't have any fancy duds, he knows he can't even think about going. True to the Cinderella tales, his fairy godcow works her magic and he ends up in Miz Lurleen's arms. Practice a few times before reading this one aloud. Then just mosey on into the part—accent and all—to truly hook children. It's never failed us yet!

Cook-a-Doodle-Doo!

Written by Janet Stevens and Susan Stevens Crummel
Illustrated by Janet Stevens
Harcourt Brace 1999, 2005, ISBN 0–15–201924–3

> Those silly sisters bring us another tickle-your-funny-bone retelling of a classic tale. This time we meet Big Brown Rooster, who just happens to be the great-grandson of *Little Red Hen*. Among the things Big Brown Rooster inherited from his great-grandmother was her recipe book—*The Joys of Cooking Alone* (chuckle-chuckle). As the Rooster begins the process of baking the very same strawberry shortcake his famous great-grandmother made, he encounters the same problems she faced all those years ago. (Do we never learn from these stories?) Not one of his friends, neither Dog nor Cat nor Goose wants to help him with the work of cooking. But in this retelling, three new friends—Iguana and Turtle and Pig—come to the rescue and become the "I can do that!" team. All but the pig stay busy. Each time he wants to help, the others want him to wait. When the finished cake is accidentally dumped on the floor, the pig goes to work cleaning up the mess. When Iguana and Turtle become angry, it is the Big Brown Rooster who reminds them that the second cake will be even easier to make. Sure enough, the second one is a masterpiece! Even though the text doesn't mention the Dog, the

Cat, or the Goose being invited to join Rooster and his new friends for the strawberry shortcake, the art on the last page shows them with the completed masterpiece. When you read it aloud, see whether children notice the similarity to the original.

And the Dish Ran Away with the Spoon

Written by Janet Stevens and Susan Stevens Crummel
Illustrated by Janet Stevens
Harcourt 2001, ISBN 0–15–202298–8

Sisters Janet and Susan collaborated on another very clever spin on one of our favorite nursery rhymes. The book begins with the standard: *Hey diddle diddle, the cat and the fiddle, The cow jumped over the moon; The little dog laughed to see such sport, And the dish ran away with the spoon.* All is well until the Cat realizes that Dish and Spoon did not come back as they always did. And so begins the quest of the Cat and the Dog and the Cow as they travel from place to place searching for Dish and Spoon. Remind children to keep their eyes open and focused as you join the search. You will all be amused by the other favorite nursery rhyme characters they encounter in this frantic search. Janet's art is indispensable to this story; reading the book aloud may take more than one class period because of its length. So, find a good stopping place that will whet the appetite of children for the ending . . . which according to all nursery rhymes is a good one.

The Horned Toad Prince

Written by Jackie Mims Hopkins
Illustrated by Michael Austin
Peachtree 2000, ISBN 1–56145–195–9

Here's another version of the *Frog Prince* with a western twist and a sprinkling of Spanish throughout the story. Reba Jo is an independent cowgirl who knows her way around and won't take much from anyone. In short, she has a bit of an attitude. However, circumstances don't always work her way and when she finds herself in a spot of trouble she must make a deal with a horned toad. There is a twist to this version of the *Frog Prince* because Reba Jo doesn't ride off into the sunset with a prince. You'll just have to read to find out how this tale ends.

The Three Little Wolves and the Big Bad Pig

Written by Eugene Trivizas
Illustrated by Helen Oxenbury
Aladdin 1993 (Heinemann), 1997, ISBN 0–689–81528–X

If you are expecting a clever twist and a surprise ending in this rendition of a traditional tale, you won't be disappointed. When the three little wolves are told it is time for them to go out into the world, the first thing they do is build a strong house of brick, but it proves to be no trouble to the Big Bad Pig when he wants to blow it down. The same thing happens to their house of concrete, then to their house of iron and steel. But when they build their next house of flowers, it charms the Big Bad Pig and suddenly he wants to become a good pig. The happy ever after is when the wolves invite him to live with them and he does!

 *Books About the Importance of Reading*

Amber on the Mountain

Written by Tony Johnston
Illustrated by Robert Duncan
Puffin 1994 (Dial), 1998, ISBN 0–14–056408–X

Amber lives on a beautiful mountain but is lonely until Anna moves nearby. Anna's family came from the city because her father is helping to build a road down the mountain to the city. Not only do the girls become close friends, but when Anna discovers that Amber can't read, Anna becomes committed to teaching her. When the road is finished and Anna's family moves back to the city, she leaves Amber with lots of friends—friends she discovers in the books Anna left behind. This is a wonderful book about the power of setting your mind to a task and accomplishing a goal, and about the life-changing effect of learning to read.

The Library Dragon

Written by Carmen Agra Deedy
Illustrated by Michael P. White
Peachtree 1994, ISBN 1–56145–091–X

All of us who work in schools know that the librarian (well, that would be media specialist now) has an important job—keeping everything in its place so we can find just what we need. Miss Lotta Scales, the librarian, has a motto: *A place for everything and that's where it stays.* No one can make her see things differently until she falls under the charm of the language of a young girl named Molly. The music of Molly's read-aloud so charms Miss Scales that the dragon is transformed (well almost) into Miss Lotta Scales—librarian extraordinaire. Children will chuckle in all the right places and will share the delight as Molly saves the day. And they just might search for evidence of a dragon in the library.

Once Upon a Time

Written and Illustrated by Niki Daly
Farrar, Straus and Giroux 2003, ISBN 0–374–35635–5

You and your children will fall in love with Sarie, a young African girl, as you follow her struggles to make sense of letters and words. The other children read so easily and make fun of her struggles. Their teasing follows her everywhere she goes even after warnings from kind Mr. Adonis who shows great patience with Sarie's efforts in trying to make sense of the reading. Sarie's one joy is spending Sunday afternoons with her Auntie Anna. Every Sunday they "drive" in a rusted, tire-less old car pretending to travel far, far away. On these wonderful afternoon adventures, Auntie Anna tells stories . . . stories that make Sarie want to read so badly. As you might expect, she does do just that with the help of Auntie Anna. This one will warm your heart and inspire children to do their best in the face of struggle. In addition, you'll have a perfect opportunity to open a conversation about supporting friends in times of struggle.

Thank You, Mr. Falker

Written and Illustrated by Patricia Polacco
Philomel 1998, ISBN 0–399–23166–8

Thank You, Mr. Falker, a story from Polacco's own childhood, is a wonderful picture book to read aloud to children. The young girl in the story reaches fifth grade unable to read. Because of her struggle with reading, the young girl becomes the object of taunts from her classmates. One boy is particularly cruel as he zeros in on her greatest weakness. Share this one and discover how one teacher, Mr. Falker, recognizes the problems in this child's life and becomes the one person who refuses to give up. You and your students will be touched by the power of kindness, belief, tenacity, and knowledge.

The Wednesday Surprise

Written by Eve Bunting
Illustrated by Donald Carrick
Clarion 1989, ISBN 0–395–54776–8

Savor the relationship between a grandmother and her granddaughter as you read this heartwarming story. Page by page Bunting reveals the trusting bond they share as the young girl teaches her grandmother to read. Every Wednesday night, the grandmother travels across town to sit with her granddaughter while her parents work. The secret goal of these Wednesday nights is to have the grandmother reading as a gift for her son's birthday. That gift is the Wednesday surprise.

2

Picture Books and Read-Alouds to Support the Mathematics Curriculum

*U*SING LITERATURE is one of the most inviting ways to get children involved in mathematical thinking. Stories offer readers and listeners an array of possibilities when seeking solutions to open-ended problems. When mathematical concepts are contextualized in stories, the meaning of those concepts is naturally carried by the medium of story (xi). The mathematics standards of the National Council of Teachers of Mathematics (NCTM) seek to build a solid foundation for each strand of math. In contrast to past practices, which focused on covering as much as possible in a curriculum of extreme breadth with little depth, the more recent standards were designed to delve more deeply.

We like to think of this as taking the time to *hover* with ideas and concepts as opposed to rushing to *cover* the curriculum. The goal, then, is for children to develop a depth of knowledge—a thorough understanding—because they must be users of math in the world beyond school. Indeed, math education is changing rapidly because these more recent standards have become the "yardstick" with which the mathematics curriculum is being measured.

The five content standards, or strands, of mathematics apply to all grade levels—kindergarten through twelfth—and include the following.

- Number and Operations
- Algebra

- Geometry
- Measurement
- Data Analysis and Probability

In addition to these five content standards, NCTM has developed five process standards.

- Problem Solving
- Reasoning and Proof
- Communication
- Connections
- Representation

Each process standard is used in all areas of mathematical thinking and, in our opinion, in all literacy education. Therefore, as concepts are introduced to young students who must understand what they are learning and actively build new knowledge from the interplay of new experiences and prior knowledge, we feel that literature can be an essential resource. With this in mind, here is a collection of carefully selected picture books for those who want to establish a classroom learning environment to address the more recent standards for mathematics education. This bookshelf provides books that offer wonderful read-alouds to introduce children to concepts that may be new and sometimes difficult for them.

Now let's take Marc Harshman's picture book, *Only One* (1993), and consider how you might use it to extend the math thinking of primary children. First, read the book aloud to explore the concept of the number of individuals, items, or pieces it takes to make one new something. For example, it takes 50,000 bees to make one hive, 500 seeds to make one pumpkin, 100 patches to make one quilt, 12 eggs to make one dozen, 11 cows to make one herd, and so on.

After inviting children to get together with their partners, provide them with chart paper and markers. Then, show them the page with eleven cows. Begin to think aloud about the possible number of legs shown in the picture, and invite students into the thinking with something like this:

Investigators, today I want you to use your markers and chart paper to show how you and your partner can help me determine the total number of legs these eleven cows have. To explain your answer, you can show your thinking in any way you would like.

If children can manage this, you can extend their thinking by inviting them to show how they would determine the total number of eyes or ears or tails in the same illustration.

By having them work with this strategy, you are exposing children to each of the process standards while working within the Number and Operations content standard. To briefly show how each process principle is used, consider doing the following.

> After the problem is posed to them, have partners reason out how they will solve the problem. Through such reasoning, they must communicate to partners a reasonable method to represent their thinking. For the partners to be able to complete each of the other processes, they must be able to connect a reasonable method of solving the problem as posed by you.

The absolute beauty of inviting young mathematicians to participate in this kind of thinking is that it allows them to become actively engaged in each of the critical process standards while at the same time displaying the depth of their understanding of the Number and Operations content standard and how they choose to solve the problem.

If you are working with older children, you may want to address this same content standard using Annegert Fuchshuber's *Two Peas in a Pod* (1996). Following the read-aloud, and with the assistance of the children, make an anchor chart for all of the book's characters and animals—Paul and Peter, Mama Bear and her two cubs, Papa Lion and his three cubs, Mother Mole and her four baby moles, Mother Owl and her five baby owls, Mother Cat and her six kittens, and so on. The chart will serve to ensure that every character will be available for the children to refer to as they work together to solve the problem you pose. The invitation should follow the pattern of the one used with the younger children, but the content needs to be more diverse. With older children, invite partners to figure out the total number of legs shown in the illustration.

> Investigators, today I want you and your partners to use markers and chart paper to show your thinking about how many legs are shown in the illustrations of *Only One*—the total number. Refer back to the anchor chart we've just created to help you as you solve the problem on each of the spreads of the book. For instance, think of the picture of Paul and Peter. We know very quickly that the illustrator shows us four legs on that spread. But what about on the page with the Mama Bear and her two

cubs? Turn to your partner and discuss how many legs are shown on this page.

After a short time, let one of the children explain his or her thinking. If they seem to clearly understand the process, move on. If not, discuss the next page in the book to clarify your expectations.

Now, work with your partners to solve the puzzle of the total number of legs we would find if you look at each of the pages of *Two Peas in a Pod*. Your chart paper should show your thinking as you solve the problem.

Once again, by using a lovely read-aloud, you've shown children a connection between literature and math. In addition, you've provided them a challenging problem in an environment that is appealing and also safe for them to explore. By keeping the standards in mind as you choose books for read-alouds, you can move far beyond the initial concept, as we just illustrated with both *Two Peas in a Pod* and *Only One*. This is what is often referred to as "working smarter rather than harder"!

Now it's time for you to explore this bookshelf on your own. So, let your imagination run free and consider all the ways literature can be used to build bridges across the mathematics curriculum. One quick note before you get started with this collection: The books are grouped by specific content area under each of the five national standards.

Again, we realize this is not a comprehensive list for any of the standards; however, we so hope that the shelves here will be the starting point for your collection of excellent picture books. This collection includes many great read-alouds, we think, to help you introduce concepts that will help children learn about unfamiliar topics. It is our hope that the read-aloud experiences children have when you use the books will create a supportive environment that can lead students toward a deeper understanding of mathematical thinking.

■ *Standard One: Number and Operations*

Addition

Dominoes Around the World

Written by Mary D. Lankford
Illustrated by Karen Dugan
HarperCollins 1998, ISBN 0–688–14051–3

> The game of dominoes has been a favorite of people for many years. Lankford's book gives the history of the game and provides the various ways it is played by people in different countries. Since playing dominoes is an engaging way to use addition, this book offers a nice opportunity for a read-aloud that will get children into the game. It offers several alternative ways, other than the one we are most familiar with, to practice it. The procedures for game play in other lands (e.g., Cuba, France, Malta, The Netherlands, Spain, Ukraine, and Vietnam) are described. Dugan provides a picture of the countries to go along with the rules of play in each locale.

Fish Eyes (Number Sense)

Written and Illustrated by Lois Ehlert
Harcourt Brace 1990, ISBN 0–15–228051–0

> From the Booklist review: *Ehlert's sense of color and graphic design is amazing. . . . The dramatic effect of the brilliant tropical colors of the fish against a polished navy background makes the book a show stopper . . . a visual treat from start to finish.* And, equally, it will be a welcome addition to your math class as you attempt to develop number sense with children. Every time you see Lois Ehlert's name on a book, you can trust it to be a beautiful one for young children.

The Grapes of Math: Mind-Stretching Math Riddles

Written by Greg Tang
Illustrated by Harry Briggs
Scholastic 2001, 2004, ISBN 0–439–59840–0

> With very clever riddles, Tang will have children solving math problems long before the last page of this wonderful read-aloud. The question posed is

always printed in a contrasting color, while the riddle provides clues on how to quickly arrive at the answer. Once you read and solve several, children will be bouncing to do the rest by themselves. We find that children catch on much more quickly than most adults. Once again, Greg provides the answers at the back. As usual, Briggs' illustrations are vibrant and provide the perfect visual support for solving the riddles.

Let's Go Visiting

Written by Sue Williams
Illustrated by Julie Vivas
Voyager/Harcourt 1998 (Scholastic), 2000, ISBN 0–15–202410–7

Here's one young children will beg to hear again and again. The cumulative, repetitive pattern in the art is one that they will just delight in. The language follows a pattern of increasing the number by one every time you turn the page. *Let's go visiting. . . . What do you say? . . . One brown foal is ready to play . . . Let's go visiting . . . What do you say? . . . Two red calves are ready to play.* Following each *Let' s Go Visiting . . .* , readers meet a new animal and each time we meet a new animal, there is one more than on the previous page. So turn page after page and meet three black kittens, four pink piglets, five green ducklings, and six yellow puppies. Then, *No more visiting. No more play . . . Let's curl up and sleep in the hay!*

Math Appeal: Mind-Stretching Math Riddles

Written by Greg Tang
Illustrated by Harry Briggs
Scholastic 2003, ISBN 0–439–21046–1

Greg Tang has stepped up his invitation to children to engage in mathematical thinking with his third book. Once you read these books aloud, children will never leave them on the shelf. This book is written in the same style as his first two, but without a theme, so each page is a new surprise. Here's a typical one to give you an example:

> *Boston Pea Party*
> *A pea would find it rather odd,*
> *To be alone inside a pod.*
> *They like to hang out with their friends,*
> *For them the party never ends!*

Can you count up all the peas?
With 11's it's a breeze!

The art is carefully designed to provide a visual that will assist in solving the riddle. For this example, Briggs depicts eight pods of green peas. Four pods have six peas and four pods have five peas. The clue given in the poem was to group by 11. For each of these clever riddles, children will be so thrilled when they find the solution.

Math for All Seasons: Mind-Stretching Math Riddles

Written by Greg Tang
Illustrated by Henry Briggs
Scholastic 2002, ISBN 0–439–21042–9

What Tang did in his first book, *Grapes of Math* (2001) for older children, he has now provided for younger children with this second one. In this book of math riddles, children are treated to lessons in problem solving that show them how to group rather than count one by one. After solving the riddles, they will be subtracting in order to add. They will begin looking for patterns, but most of all, children will find math is interesting and fun. Oh, in case you get stumped, the answers are at the back.

MATH-terpieces: The Art of Problem Solving

Written by Greg Tang
Illustrated by Greg Paprocki
Scholastic 2003, ISBN 0–439–44388–1

Just when you think you've got his technique figured out, Greg Tang comes up with this stunning book. In this one, he builds poems around the artwork of twelve of the great masters. Now you are providing children an introduction to the work of the master artists while you are giving them additional time with addition. Here's a little sample:

A ballerina strikes a pose,
Another rests her weary toes.
Edgar Degas liked to portray
The varied scenes of a ballet.
Can you make 7 with these shoes?
THREE clever ways earn rave reviews.

The page opposite the poem provides five sets of ballet shoes: one set of five, one set of four, one set of three, one set of two, and one set of one. The children are to work to name three ways of grouping the shoes to make seven. Each set of problems is based on another painting by a famous artist paired with one of Greg's clever poems, setting up yet another math problem. Read this aloud and listen to the buzz humming through the room as students turn and talk as they try finding the solutions.

One Grain of Rice: A Mathematical Folktale

Written and Illustrated by Demi
Scholastic 1997, ISBN 0–590–93998–X

This folktale was written with the same number sense story found in *The King's Chessboard* (1993), which can be found on the Multiplication shelf later in this book. In this story, a raja from India, believed by his countrymen to be very wise and fair, asks his people to give him most of their rice. When they do as he asks, he stores it, but when a famine hits, he becomes too selfish to share the stored rice. In his selfishness, he declares that he and his staff will have a feast using the rice. As the elephants are bringing him the rice from storage, one basket breaks and rice spills out on the ground. A young girl runs alongside the elephant gathering the spilled rice in her skirt. Rather than keep the rice for herself, she presents it to the raja. He wants to reward her for her work. She asks for one grain of rice on the first day and that's to be doubled every day for thirty days. In the end, the raja is broke and the girl now has control over all his stored rice. She begins to give it out to the hungry and even shares it with the selfish raja.

One More Bunny: Adding from One to Ten

Written by Rick Walton
Illustrated by Paige Miglio
Lothrop, Lee & Shepard 2000, ISBN 0–688–16847–7

This one introduces young children to simple addition from one to ten. Every page shows a sketch of the addition problem, followed by the algorithm, and then a short simple verse that describes the problem. The page always ends with *Here comes one more bunny* to set up the new addition problem that's on the next page.

Six-Dinner Sid

Written and Illustrated by Inga Moore
Aladdin 1991, 1993, ISBN 0–671–79613–5

Children in the primary grades will fall in love with this one on the first read-aloud. Each night Sid, a black cat, goes to six different houses on Aristole Street and eats six different dinners. Of course, he answers to six different names, but he doesn' t mind because the alternative would be only one dinner. All is well until Sid gets sick and each of his owners takes him to the vet. After taking the medicine six different times, Sid isn't so sure of his duplicity. However, his secret is discovered by the vet and the six owners are not happy with Sid. Not to worry, Sid solves that problem by moving one street over and adopting six new owners. Can't you just hear the chuckles?

Splash!

Written and Illustrated by Ann Jonas
Greenwillow 1995, 1997, ISBN 0–688–15284–8

> *I have a pond in my backyard,*
> *I have one turtle, two catfish,*
> *Three frogs, and four goldfish.*
> *I feed them every day.*
> *How many are in my pond?*
> *My cat comes home.*
> *He wakes my dog.*
> *The turtle jumps into the pond. SPLASH!*
> *How many are in my pond?*

Every page continues to offer you math problems for which you either add or subtract to find the number of animals in the pond. The illustrations are enchanting and so child-friendly. You might want to take children on a picture walk before reading the text. If you don't, they are likely to be so enthralled with the art they might not listen closely to problems that are posed.

12 Ways to Get to 11

Written by Eve Merriam
Illustrated by Bernie Karlin
Aladdin 1993, 1996, ISBN 0–689–80892–5

For early childhood classrooms that are beginning to help children develop number sense, this book will fit like a glove. Every page is very colorful and inviting for young eyes and the same is true of the text, which will invite readers to explore the many ways to make eleven. In fact, Merriam and

Karlin show *12 Ways to Get to 11*. The book could also be used with older students who are beginning to work with number families.

 *Algorithms*

Alice in Pastaland: A Math Adventure

Written by Alexandra Wright
Illustrated by Reagan Word
Charlesbridge 1997, ISBN 1–57091–151–7

Wright provides a parody of Lewis Carroll's *Alice in Wonderland;* here Alice is very mathematically astute. As she goes from one adventure to another, each turn of events offers another math possibility. Many mathematical concepts are mentioned without elaboration; therefore, the book reads more as an adventure than as an introduction to math facts.

Counting

The Baseball Counting Book

Written by Barbara Barbieri McGrath
Illustrated by Brian Shaw
Charlesbridge 1999, ISBN 0–88106–333–9

If you have a few young baseball fans in your group, you will want to use this one when helping them develop number sense. As you read, you will find yourself wondering what McGrath will use to get beyond six, but she does it using baseball. Shaw's striking full-page illustrations clearly feature the number concept.

The Cheerios Counting Book

Written by Barbara Barbieri McGrath
Illustrated by Rob Bolster and Frank Mazzola Jr.
Scholastic 1998, ISBN 0–590–68357–8

For children nothing is better during math than getting to eat the manipulative. Just dump out a cup of Cheerios and mimic McGrath's text. The first part gives children practice with one to ten number sense. Then, she introduces grouping from ten to one hundred. Bolster and Mazzola use the

Cheerios to illustrate the math concept and include pieces of fruit as a border to further illustrate grouping.

Count and See

Written and Photographs by Tana Hoban
Simon & Schuster 1972, ISBN 0–02–744800–2

This one contains dramatic black-and-white photographs with large white numerals and dots on a black background. On the facing page is a full-page photograph of objects to represent the number. There are pages that represent one through twenty followed by pages illustrating how to count by tens. The book is very appealing because of its crisp presentation and simplistic way of explaining number sense to young children.

Count to a Million (Place Value)

Written by Jerry Pallotta
Illustrated by Rob Bolster
Scholastic 2003, ISBN 0–439–38915–1

Do you sometimes get confused by very large numbers? When you see a million written out do you have to stop and look at the place value to be sure? If so, can you imagine how large numbers appear when looking through the eyes of a child? In *Count to a Million,* Pallotta and Bolster have once again teamed up to produce a book using simple language and pictures familiar to children to explain a complex concept. Most children can understand that a large college football stadium can hold 100,000 people. But just picture an aerial view that shows ten stadiums each filled with 100,000 people. (Check out the dedication and you'll find another reason why we like this one.)

Counting Is for the Birds

Written and Illustrated by Frank Mazzola Jr.
Charlesbridge 1997, ISBN 0–88106–950–7

With rhyme and rhythm, Mazzola brings us this gorgeous book that is not only beautiful but also presents basic counting in three ways: numbers, number words embedded in the text, and illustrations. In addition, he gives readers interesting facts about the various species of birds in a smaller font at the bottom of every page.

Daisy 1 2 3

Written and Illustrated by Peter Catalanotto

Atheneum 2003, ISBN 0–689–85457–9

> *Mrs. Tuttle has twenty Dalmatians in her Saturday morning obedience class. They are all named Daisy. Her assistant, Doris, wonders how Mrs. Tuttle tells them apart.* Of course, Mrs. Tuttle knows her students well and explains on the next twenty pages how she tells each of her students apart. *Daisy 1 2 3* will be loved by young students as they begin to grasp the number sense concept in this very safe and memorable opportunity for working with numbers.

Five Little Ducks: An Old Rhyme

Illustrated by Pamela Paparone

North-South Books 1995, 1997, ISBN 1–55858–700–4

> *Five little ducks went out one day, over the hills and faraway. Mother duck said, Quack, quack, quack, quack. But only four little ducks came back.* This is a treasure that is just as wonderful today as it was when it was originally published. This one is very simple, very predictable, and very adorable.

Five Little Monkeys Jumping on the Bed

Retold and Illustrated by Eileen Christelow

Clarion 1998, ISBN 0–395–90023–9

> This charming counting book begins with five little monkeys getting ready for bed by bathing, brushing their teeth, and being tucked into bed. When the lights go off and mama leaves, they begin jumping on the bed. One monkey falls off the bed and bumps his head, leaving only four still jumping. One by one the monkeys fall off bumping head after head. When mama finally calls the doctor, he says, *No more monkeys jumping on the bed!*

Hide & Seek

Written by Janet S. Wong

Illustrated by Margaret Chodos-Irvine

Harcourt 2005, ISBN 0–15–204934–7

> Here is a "must-have" for a primary classroom because of its unusual side-by-side story structure. The first story about a little boy who is trying to find the best place to hide from his dad while they wait for their cookies to bake is told in rhyming text. The second story has the dad calling out his count

(with no peeking) from one to ten. As he counts, the numerals appear in colors in a block on the page. The colors of the numbers give the reader a hint to the objects that appear on that page.

How Many Feet in the Bed?

Written by Diane Johnston Hamm
Illustrated by Kate Salley Palmer
Aladdin 1991, 1994, ISBN 0–671–89903–1

This is a great read-aloud book that will invite young children to join in the math game by counting the feet in Dad's bed. With a precious little girl hanging onto the end of the bed early in the morning watching her father sleep, she asks, *How many feet are in the bed?* Father replies, *I thought there were two.* Then, as she playfully tumbles into the bed, *Not Now! With me here, I see four!* Keep counting as brother Tom climbs in and then Baby Jane, and Mom says, *Look again! With Baby Jane, you now have eight!* The art is just perfect for this wonderful read-aloud as the family counts the number of feet in the bed!

Jake's 100th Day of School

Written by Lester L. Laminack
Illustrated by Judith Love
Peachtree 2006, ISBN 1–56145–355–2

Judy Love's wonderful child-friendly art showcases this outstanding narrative about all the math-related things children do on the hundredth day of school. *Jake's 100th Day of School* is Lester's third picture book. In the story, which he based on an event that happened in Reba's school, Jake forgets his hundredth-day project on this all important school day. When Jake's tears begin, Mrs. Wadsworth suggests many things they can gather up right there at school, but none pleased Jake until the thought of a hundred books comes up. Read with delight about the events Mr. Thompson had his children do to make this day a truly memorable one. Recently, math guru and author Greg Tang shared with us a discovery he had made about fifth graders on the hundredth day of the school year. Did you know that if a fifth grader has attended school since kindergarten for 180 days every year, on the hundredth day of school he or she would be celebrating one thousand days of school? Even to literacy folks like us, that is fascinating to think about! [This annotation has been borrowed from *Learning Under the Influence* . . . because this book is so important to each of us.]

Just a Minute: A Trickster Tale and Counting Book

Written and Illustrated by Yuyi Morales
Chronicle 2003, ISBN 0–8118–3758–0

Morales tells readers on the front flap that this is an original trickster tale told within the Mexican culture. The text is delightful; however, we caution you to read it several times before reading to children to make sure that parts of the adventure in the tale won't disturb them. The story tells about a skeleton named Señor Galavera who visits Grandma Beetle to take her to her "next life." But Grandma Beetle outsmarts Señor Galavera by getting him to help her count (in both English and Spanish) all the birthday preparations she is making for her own birthday party with her grandchildren. Each of the counting words is in an enlarged font, making this a great read-aloud for getting students to join in the counting. By the end of the party, Señor Galavera decides he would rather come back for her next birthday and leaves her a note telling of his plans. The story is adorable if the beginning won't upset children. Morales' art is truly delightful.

Let's Count It Out, Jesse Bear

Written by Nancy White Carlstrom
Illustrated by Bruce Degen
Aladdin 1996, 2001, ISBN 0–689–84257–0

Carlstrom helps children understand and practice counting, adding, and subtracting through these lively and lovely poems. The predictable structure for the book will be appealing to young children. The first rhyming poem is followed with *None and one more is 1. One is fun!* The opposite page always shows the numeral plus the number word in a small box. The second poem is followed with *1 and one more are 2. Happy hopping two shoes!* Each new page and each new poem builds one greater. Poems stop after ten, but the numbers continue up to twenty following the same format: *10 and one more are 11. Eleven Clowns. 11 and one more are 12. Twelve Hats.* Degen's illustrations of Jesse Bear and his family will be adored by students.

One Cow Moo!

Written by David Bennett
Illustrated by Andy Cooke
Henry Holt 1990, ISBN 0–8050–1416–0

Young children will find joy in math when playing with this cow as she runs back and forth between the various barnyard animals. With each trip, the number of animals chasing her increases. And all along while you are reading aloud, children are gaining number sense.

One Hundred Is a Family

Written by Pam Muñoz Ryan
Illustrated by Benrei Huang
Hyperion 1994, 1996, ISBN 0–7868–1120–X

Through rhyme and rhythm, Ryan takes the reader on a counting adventure from one to ten and then from ten to one hundred as she explores which numbers make a family. In Huang's delicious illustrations, we see families doing all the things families like to do from counting stars to planting seedlings. Readers' understanding of counting will grow when you use this book.

One Is a Snail, Ten Is a Crab

Written by April Pulley Sayre and Jeff Sayre
Illustrated by Randy Cecil
Candlewick 2003, ISBN 0–7636–1406–8

If you want to get children involved in thinking about math, try this one. Here is a sample of how the book reads: *1 is a snail* (with an arrow pointing to the snail's foot); *2 is a person* (with an arrow pointing to the boy's feet); *3 is a person and a snail* (and in each one the arrows point out the feet); *4 is a dog; 5 is a dog and a snail; 6 is an insect; 7 is an insect and a snail; 8 is a spider; 9 is a spider and a snail; 10 is a crab and THAT means . . . 20 is two crabs.* And so the story goes all the way to a hundred, with an extraordinary ending that will delight kids. This one has many possibilities.

Only One

Written by Marc Harshman
Illustrated by Barbara Garrison
Dutton 1993 0–525–65116–0

There may be a million stars, But there is only one sky. There may be 50,000 bees, But there is only one hive. There may be 500 seeds, But there is only one pumpkin. Each page follows this descending pattern with illustrations to match. Once the beginning number gets to ten, every page decreases by one until finally we reach, *But the best thing of all is that there is only one me and there is only one you!*

Quack and Count

Written and Illustrated by Keith Baker

Voyager/Harcourt 1999 (Scholastic), 2004, ISBN 0–15–205025–6

> *7 ducklings in a row, count those ducklings as they go!*
> *Slipping, sliding, having fun 7 ducklings, 6 plus 1*
> *7 ducklings, 5 plus 2*
> *Playing games of peekaboo*
> *Chasing busy bumblebees*
> *7 ducklings, 4 plus 3 . . .*

The book continues with this predictable pattern, demonstrating all the ways to make seven until all seven ducklings fly away. And, of course, the artwork is done in the bright and colorful style we've come to expect from Keith Baker.

A Place for Zero: A Math Adventure

Written by Angeline Sparagna LoPresti
Illustrated by Phyllis Hornung

Charlesbridge 2003, ISBN 1–57091–196–7

> *Not long ago, Zero lay floating on the calm waters of Central Lake. He could hear the happy cries of the other numbers, 1 through 9, as they played in the meadow. Zero didn't play Addemup because he had nothing to add. He felt he had no place among the other digits. . . . Every number knew its place. A 7 was the number of days in a week, and a 5 was the number of points on a star. A 2 was handy for counting the wheels on a bicycle.* But no one in Digitaria knows what to do with the Zero because he cannot add anything of value to the other digits. That is, he can't add value until one day when he discovers that the number value changes when he stands next to the 1. On that day, King Multiplus declares a new number, which he names Ten. Thus, Zero finally finds a new value as he makes new numbers—number after number.

Reece's Pieces: Count by Fives

Written by Jerry Pallotta
Illustrated by Rob Bolster

Cartwheel 2000, ISBN 0–439–13520–6

Using construction equipment to move the *Reece's Pieces,* Pallotta once again invites children into the world of math through a clever theme (not to mention a popular candy). The book begins with the equipment moving candy one at a time (counting to ten by ones). When there are ten, the candies are moved in groups of five and fifteen are on the very next page. And off you go, counting by fives. Pallotta deftly slips in the name of each piece of equipment as it works to lift and move the candy into the proper groups. Students will love this one. Oh yeah, we should warn you, it might make you hungry.

Roar!: A Noisy Counting Book

Written by Pamela Duncan Edwards
Illustrated by Henry Cole
HarperCollins 2000, ISBN 0–06–028384–X

This one takes you on a playful romp with a young lion cub as he seeks a playmate. He first encounters *one red monkey who rushes up a tree.* And when *he roars by the lake, two pink flamingos flap and fly away.* Puzzled and more than a little upset, he roars even louder and, of course, three orange warthogs take off. The little cub continues his roaring until he comes upon nine other roaring little lion cubs and that makes *ten happy little lion cubs!* As with other books from the team of Edwards and Cole, this is sure to delight young listeners when you read it aloud.

Sitting Down to Eat

Written by Bill Harley
Illustrated by Kitty Harvill
August House 1996, ISBN 0–87483–603–4

A little boy is just *Sitting Down to Eat* when there is a knock on the door. The elephant at the door says, *Well if you have enough for one then you've got enough for two.* So, they both sit down to eat just as another knock comes. The tiger at the door says, *Well if you've got enough for two then you'll have enough for me.* So, three sit down to eat. The pattern is repeated throughout the book in a phrasing and tone reminiscent of *Brown Bear, Brown Bear.* Young listeners will enjoy the surprise ending when the ninth little animal crawls in to join the others as they eat.

Ten Flashing Fireflies

Written by Philemon Sturges
Illustrated by Anna Vojtech
North-South Books 1995, 1997, ISBN 1–55858–674–1

What do you see in the summer night?
Ten flashing fireflies burning bright!
Catch the one twinkling there
Like a star.
One flashing firefly in our jar.
What do we see in the summer night?
Nine flashing fireflies burning bright!
Capture another one.
Now there are . . .

And this pattern continues throughout the gorgeous book until ten flashing fireflies are all captured in the jar. As the children are preparing for bed, the fireflies begin to blink very slowly and they set them free. And as the fireflies leave the jar, the children count down . . . *ten, nine, eight, seven, six, five, four, three, two, one . . . Now there are none.*

Ten Little Fish

Written by Audrey Wood
Illustrated by Bruce Wood
Blue Sky Press 2004, ISBN 0–439–63569–1

Take a dive deep into the sea to begin a rhyming counting adventure filled with surprise. The colorful art adds to the playful text telling about those lit-tle fish *who swim in line until one dives down, and then there are . . . Nine lit-tle fish, swimming 'round a crate. One goes in, and now there are . . .* The story continues until there is only one little fish left. Now what will he do? *Along comes another fish, and that makes . . . Two little fish, in love with each other. Soon one is a father, and the other is a . . . Mother!* Then the rhyme begins again, but adding each time. This one is a keeper.

Ten in the Den

Written and Illustrated by John Butler
Peachtree 2005, ISBN 1–56145–344–7

Ten in the Den is such a joy to read that you will want to read it to young children more than once during the day. If you know Butler's work, you know before opening the cover that it will be visually pleasing. This one is a treat for the ears as well. Language flows through the playful font and readers find ten little animals snuggled in the den. When it's time to roll over, all ten must do it at the same time because space is so limited. But when they rolled, *rabbit fell out . . . floppetty, hoppetty, bump!* Now nine animals are left to roll over. This time *mole fell out, roly, poly, bump!* The sumptuous art on every spread shows yet another little animal rolling out of bed. When only one animal is left, he misses his friends, so he rolls over and scampers out to join them. Now the ten friends are together again. It is simply wonderful and, just think, you can teach math while you read it aloud.

Ten Seeds

Written and Illustrated by Ruth Brown
Alfred A. Knopf 2001, ISBN 0–375–80697–0

This book, written for young children, is absolutely stunning. The presentation is so clever and the art is divine. Readers begin planting ten seeds, but one ant pulls one of the seeds out before it can grow. Now we have nine seeds, but one pigeon picks another seed to eat. Next, we have eight seeds sprouting, but one mouse pulls one for food. And then, we are left with seven seedlings when one slug eats another. And the pattern continues until the next to the last page. There readers find a glorious flower and one bee . . . and then ten seeds again when they fall from the flower.

Two Ways to Count to Ten: A Liberian Folktale

Retold by Ruby Dee
Illustrated by Susan Meddaugh
Henry Holt 1988, ISBN 0–8050–1314–8

Who shall I name to rule after me when I die? King Leopard said one day to his beloved daughter. I must seek out the cleverest beast in our jungle. I must find one who is wise enough to rule well. I shall make him a prince. Someday, dear daughter, the two of you shall be queen and king. And so begins the plan to bring all the animals in the jungle together for a great feast so King Leopard can judge and select the possible future ruler. When the animals arrive, the King asks them to form a large circle. He demonstrates his strength by thrusting a spear high into the air and challenges each of the animals to match his skill. The elephant tries first, but before he can count to four, the spear returns to the ground. Then, the bush ox tries and he only gets to five. Animal after animal attempts and each fails. Finally, the young antelope steps up. As he dances so gracefully and thrusts the spear into the air, he counts *Two, Four, Six, Eight, Ten!* The king roars his approval and agrees he never said how the counting had to go, so the clever young antelope becomes the new prince.

Underwater Counting: Even Numbers

Written by Jerry Pallotta
Illustrated by David Biedrzychi
Charlesbridge 2001, ISBN 0–88106–800–4

> *There are zero fish swimming on this page. Maybe they were chased away by a shark. Or maybe you scared them off when you opened this book!* What child could resist a lead like this? On each gloriously, colorful underwater page, you will meet some of the most interesting fish. You won't be meeting shrimp or catfish. Instead, you'll find species such as one Green Moray Eel, two Coral Groupers, four Clown Triggerfish, and six Manta Rays. Not only are the even numbers distinctly written on every page in both algorithms and words, but each is also hidden once again in the art. Children can spend many moments hunting for those elusive numbers, and we assure you they will find them before your adult eyes do.

What Comes in 2's, 3's, & 4's?

Written by Suzanne Aker
Illustrated by Bernie Karlin
Aladdin 1990, 1992, ISBN 0–671–79247–4

> Using realistic pictures to support the introduction of the number concepts of 2's, 3's, and 4's, Aker and Karlin provide a book that is still very popular years after it was first published. It is so clearly presented that once you've read it aloud, children will understand the value of the numbers just by playing around with the ideas. To give you an example, the book opens with an adorable young boy who serves as a model for the concepts in the text: *What comes in 2's? Just look at you! You have 2 eyes, 2 ears, 2 arms, 2 hands, 2 legs and 2 feet.* Every page is just as cleverly illustrated. This one belongs on the shelf in every primary classroom.

Division

The Doorbell Rang

Written and Illustrated by Pat Hutchins
Mulberry/HarperTrophy 1986 (Greenwillow), 1989, ISBN 0–688–09234–9

> Ma makes very good cookies and she tells her two children to share them. They quickly divide the cookies into two piles of six cookies each. Before they can eat even one cookie, the doorbell rings and two friends come to

visit. So the cookies are divided into four piles of four cookies each. While they are bragging about how good the cookies smell, the doorbell rings again. Here comes two more to share the cookies with. The doorbell continues to ring until there are twelve friends with only one cookie each to eat. And, wouldn't you know it, just as they are about to eat, the doorbell rings again. This time it is Grandma with a fresh batch of cookies. This one has been a favorite of ours with many groups of children.

One Hundred Hungry Ants

Written by Elinor J. Pinczes
Illustrated by Bonnie MacKain
Houghton Mifflin 1993, 1999, ISBN 0–395–97123–3

What happens when one hundred ants are hungry and they smell food in the air? Well, of course, they begin to march toward the picnic to fill their hungry tummies. But soon the smallest of the ants has the idea that it's taking too much time to march one-by-one, so he suggests that they form two lines of fifty ants and they will get there twice as fast. Soon the idea occurs to him that four lines of twenty-five is an even better idea, but no sooner than they begin marching, he comes up with five rows of twenty then ten rows of ten. However, with each change, time is wasted and when they arrive at the picnic all the food is gone. The text tells the mathematical story in a rhyme students will be chanting.

One of Each

Written by Mary Ann Hoberman
Illustrated by Marjorie Priceman
Megan Tingley 1997, ISBN 0–316–36644–7

Oliver lived all alone in one perfect house with one little bed, one little pillow, one little chair, and one little blanket. But there was only one person to enjoy all the wonderful things and Oliver Tolliver wanted company. But when company comes there is no place to sit because the house was built for only one. So Oliver goes shopping and soon there is two of everything and his friend comes back to visit. Two soon grow to many more friends and Oliver learns how to divide one pear into many pears so that each person still has *One of Each*. The rhythm of this one makes such a joyful read-aloud that you will enjoy it as much as children.

A Remainder of One

Written by Elinor J. Pinczes
Illustrated by Bonnie MacKain
Houghton Mifflin 1995, 2002, ISBN 0–618–25077–8

Through a rhyming tale, Pinczes takes children along with a bug named Joe who is left out of the partnership as a group of twenty-five bugs forms lines of four to march past the queen. The queen is not pleased with the *Remainder of One.* She demands neatness. After many nights of trying to figure out how to become part of the squad with even lines, Joe finally figures out the division, form five lines of five rather than four lines of six. The queen is very pleased when there are no remainders to ruin her parade. Children will be clamoring to tell you how to solve Joe's problem long before he figures it out.

Greater Than and Less Than

One Less Fish

Written by Kim Michelle Toft and Allan Sheather
Illustrated by Kim Michelle Toft
Charlesbridge 1998, ISBN 0–88106–323–1

> *Twelve gracious angelfish*
> *Thinking they're in heaven.*
> *Along came the divers—*
> *Now there are . . . eleven.*

The number of fish decreases by one from twelve to zero with each page turned. Not only is the book cleverly written, but it also offers a treat for the eye. Every vibrant page is filled with sea life and embedded in the mathematical story are many facts about tropical fish. The authors provide readers with a glossary and additional facts.

Skittles Riddles: Math

Written by Barbara Barbieri McGrath
Illustrated by Roger Glass
Charlesbridge 2001, ISBN 1–57091–413–3

McGrath introduces the basic problem for each of the various mathematical concepts that Glass illustrates using Skittles. Most pages offer the problem in a visual pattern of Skittles on the left page with the answer given (upside down) on right page.

Fractions

Apple Fractions

Written by Jerry Pallotta
Illustrated by Rob Bolster
Cartwheel/Scholastic 2003, ISBN 0–439–38901–1

The task of explaining fractions has been made simple with this "delicious" book using the most tempting apples Bolster could produce. Every page clearly shows children both the fraction number and a model using the cut-up apple to demonstrate the fraction. This one belongs in the hands of a teacher on the very first day fractions are to be introduced. By using it to demonstrate, factions can be made simple. And you will have a healthy snack in the process.

Fraction Action

Written and Illustrated by Loreen Leedy
Holiday House 1994, 1996, ISBN 0–8234–1244–X

Have fractions ever proved to be difficult for some children? Well, then pull this book off the shelf and begin to teach the concept through the cartoons in this picture book. The text has a running commentary, but it is the cartoons that teach. At first, the pages appear to be busy, but take the time to examine them carefully. It is really a clever way to explain how fractions work. If children should have difficulty with any of the problems in the book, the answers are given at the back.

Fraction Fun

Written by David A. Adler
Illustrated by Nancy Tobin
Holiday House 1996, 1997, ISBN 0–8234–1314–1

A fraction is a part of something. We use fractions all the time. When someone says she is eight and a half years old, she is using a fraction. . . . When you have read one of many chapters in a book, you have read only a part, just a fraction, of the book. . . . Fractions are everywhere. Read this one aloud and you will present all sorts of problems children must use a fraction to solve. Although some problems are more complex than others, this book provides a basic introduction to the concept of fractions.

The Hersey's Fractions Book

Written by Jerry Pallotta
Illustrated by Rob Bolster
Cartwheel/Scholastic 1999, ISBN 0–439–13519–2

You may gain weight just by reading this one aloud because the illustrations are so realistic you can almost taste the chocolate. (We even scratched the pages to see whether they smelled.) Pallotta has taken all the fear out of learning about fractions with the simply delicious Hershey's Chocolate bar. In the book, the candy bar is used to illustrate the many ways you can create equivalent fractions. Then, he bumps up the pace by moving into adding fractions, all in one little book with one candy bar. How good is that for your budget?

Multiplication

Anno's Mysterious Multiplying Jar

Written by Masaichiro and Mitasumasa Anno
Illustrated by Mitsumasa Anno
PaperStar/Penguin Putnam 1983, 1999, ISBN 0–698–11753–0

Inside Anno's jar strange things begin to happen. Water turns into a wide, deep sea. Within the sea is one island and on the island are two countries. In those two countries, you find three mountains and on those mountains you find four walled kingdoms. And things just keep multiplying. Readers are introduced to the mathematical term *factorials*. The authors provide detailed algorithms at the end of the story to explain how factorials work.

The Best of Times: Math Strategies That Multiply

Written by Greg Tang
Illustrated by Harry Briggs
Scholastic 2002, ISBN 0–439–21044–5

The front flap tells readers that this author is on a mission to revolutionize the way children learn math. Greg Tang's *The Best of Times* shows children how to move beyond rote memorization to develop an intuitive understanding of how to multiply. Every page takes children on a journey that makes math much more meaningful and nonthreatening, even fun. The art is appealing and matches every poem to perfection. Here's a sample of what you can expect. The first page explains what happens each time you multiply with zero; it reads:

> *Zero is a cinch to do,*
> *The answer's right in front of you.*
> *For every problem it's the same,*
> *Zilch or zero is its name!*

Each Orange Had 8 Slices: A Counting Book

Written by Paul Giganti Jr.
Illustrated by Donald Crews
Greenwillow 1992, ISBN 0–688–13985–X

Don't let the title fool you. This is far more than a counting book. It opens with this problem. *On the way to the playground I saw 3 red flowers. Each red flower had 6 petals. Each petal had 2 tiny black bugs. How many red flowers were there? How many pretty petals were there? How many tiny black bugs were there in all?* The art illustrates every problem so vividly and in the typical style of Donald Crews. Each new page presents yet another problem. Giganti ends the book with a mathematical joke that may stump children. Be sure to keep the answer covered—it is upside down on the same page. Children will enjoy working with each of the pages as you read aloud to introduce multiplication.

The Hershey's Multiplication Book

Written by Jerry Pallotta
Illustrated by Rob Bolster
Cartwheel/Scholastic 2002, ISBN 0–439–25412–4

Before beginning this book to introduce multiplication, take a look at the front page and notice the map in the math teacher's classroom. Does it bring back memories of the presidential election of 2000? Pallotta and Bolster will always slip one in on you, so keep your eye out for their tricks. Pallotta shows children how to multiply using sections of the tasty Hershey's Chocolate bar once again. Remember his book about fractions? If not, check page 63.

The King's Chessboard

Written by David Birch
Illustrated by Devis Grebu
Puffin 1988 (Dial), 1993, ISBN 0–14–054880–7

> The King always liked to reward the people who did services for him. One day he calls the wise man to him and asks what he wants as a reward. The wise man wants nothing but the King insists. Finally, the wise man tells the King he will take a grain of rice for the first square of the King's chessboard, and with each succeeding square, the number of grains of rice is to double. The King thinks the wise man very simple for asking for such a small reward but it is the King who learns an important math lesson from this.

Minnie's Diner: A Multiplying Menu

Written by Dayle Ann Dodds
Illustrated by John Manders
Candlewick 2004, ISBN 0–763–61736–9

> You and your children will love reading this refreshing story about some hungry boys who go one by one to Minnie's Diner. Each boy orders more than the one before. Suddenly their father realizes the boys are missing, so he goes off in search of them. He finds them at the diner and tells them eating must wait until their work is done. But as he's leaving, his nose smells the food and says he'll take double of what the last boy ordered. The rhyming text is just delightful to read and Manders' art is equally pleasing.

Sea Squares

Written by Joy N. Hulme
Illustrated by Carol Schwartz
Hyperion 1991, ISBN 1–56282–520–8

> Introduce children to many math concepts with this rhyming story about the sea. Hulme takes readers from one to ten and demonstrates how to multiply using the animals of the sea. *Six six-pointed sea stars, with rays all around, turning seaside somersaults on the sandy ground. That's only 6 sea stars*

sprawling, but 36 arms crawling. Seven heavy pelicans diving for their dinner. Seven fish in every pouch can never make them thinner; 7 pouchy pelicans gulp 49 fish with fins. You and students will have a blast. Think of ways to extend the experience by creating a similar text using animals on land.

Subtraction

The Hershey's Kisses Subtraction Book

Written by Jerry Pallotta
Illustrated by Rob Bolster
Cartwheel/Scholastic 2002, ISBN 0–439–33779–8

Bring on the clowns and the candy kisses and this read-aloud and you are ready to teach children how subtraction works. What happens when a clown has seven pieces of candy on the back of his truck and hits a bump in the road? Well, wouldn't you know it, two pieces fall off and you have a subtraction problem. All along the way, Pallotta very carefully explains each of the steps taken during subtraction, and he gives the language needed to define the process. The book is very focused and delightful.

Rooster's Off to See the World (Counting and Addition)

Written and Illustrated by Eric Carle
Aladdin 1972 (Watts), 1999, ISBN 0–689–82684–2

When you open this book to the first spread, readers and/or listeners will be captivated by the colorful rooster covering the full two pages with his gorgeous feathers. *One fine morning, a rooster decided that he wanted to travel. So, right then and there, he set out to see the world. He hadn't walked very far when he began to feel lonely.* Then he meets two cats who join him on his travels. Next they meet three frogs, then four turtles, and finally five fish. On the top of the right page, Carle puts each animal in a separate box lined up under each other to give children a picture graph so that they can visualize the process of addition and subtraction. For example: One rooster on the top line, two cats in two boxes on the second line, three frogs in three boxes on the third line, and so on. Then the fish swim off and the pattern reverses to illustrate subtraction. This one is a favorite of ours; so, of course, we think it should be on your shelf too.

Percentage

Twizzlers Percentages Book

Written by Jerry Pallotta
Illustrated by Rob Bolster
Cartwheel/Scholastic 2001, ISBN 0–439–15430–8

If percentages have ever stumped your students, here's help for you. This book explains in clear terms, with illustrations, how to move from a fraction to a decimal and finally arrive at a percentage. You'll be saying, "Why didn't I think of this clever book before Jerry Pallotta did?" Jerry's words and Rob's helpful art make percentages easy to understand.

■ *Standard Two: Algebra*

Sorting

The Button Box

Written by Margarette S. Reid
Illustrated by Sarah Chamberlain
Puffin 1990 (Unicorn), 1995, ISBN 0–14–055495–5

Many children (and adults) are fascinated by buttons, but after this read-aloud, you will need a box of old buttons for children to practice sorting; better begin your collection now. In the story, a young boy enjoys visiting his grandmother because of the fun he has with *The Button Box*. The uses for this delightful read-aloud are endless—patterns, counting, sorting, and more. This book can also serve as a great story if you want to tell the history of your buttons.

Grandma's Button Box: With Fun Activities!

Written by Linda Williams Aber
Illustrated by Page Eastburn O'Rourke
Kane Press 2002, ISBN 1–57565–110–6

In this adorable one, Kelly and her cousins are visiting their Grandma. When Kelly tries to get Grandma's button box from the top shelf, the box falls and the buttons spill everywhere. When the cousins find all the buttons, they discover a real problem: How to sort them . . . by size . . . by color . . . or by shape? The back of the book suggests additional activities that focus on the concept the book has just helped you develop (sorting, in this case). This is one of many in a Math Matters Series from Kane Press. Other concepts featured in the series include addition, probability, place value, measurement, perimeter, fractions, counting, money, division, bar graphs, comparing, time, geometry, subtraction, estimation, liquid measurement, calendars, area, elapsed time, multiplication, weight, patterns, ordinal numbers, positional words, organizing data, and coordinating. Each of them is written with young children in mind.

Shoes, Shoes, Shoes

Written by Ann Morris
Photographs from various sources
Mulberry/Murrow 1995, 1998, ISBN 0–688–16166–9

Introduce sorting by reading this very simple book aloud. Most pages have only one phrase under a picture. Here are examples of the many ways you can sort shoes: old, new, work, play, school, dance, walking, riding, ice skates, snowshoes, rain, cloth, straw, wooden, and more. In addition, the shoes represent those worn in countries around the world. And as a social studies bonus, you will find an outline map at the back of the book that shows all the countries.

 *Comparisons*

Biggest, Strongest, Fastest

Written and Illustrated by Steve Jenkins
Houghton Mifflin 1995, 1997, ISBN 0–395–86136–5

This one by Steve Jenkins could fit in the science collection as easily as it fits here among math books. Immerse children in a read-aloud about animals that live all around us. Some of them are too small to see, while others are much bigger than a house. Along with the very short description of each animal, Jenkins provides additional information about their height, weight, and interesting facts. This added feature is located in the lower right corner of the pages.

Hottest, Coldest, Highest, Deepest

Written and Illustrated by Steve Jenkins
Houghton Mifflin 1998, 2004, ISBN 0–618–49488–X

Travel around the world with Jenkins as he invites children to explore the *Hottest, Coldest, Highest, Deepest* places on Earth. On every page, he provides the reader with something familiar to use as a basis for comparison. For instance, the Nile River, the world's longest and located in Africa, is compared to an outline map of the United States and the next three largest rivers. Lake Baikal, in Russia, is the world's deepest lake at 5,134 feet. For this comparison, Jenkins uses the Empire State Building (1,250 feet tall). Each page presents a new situation that will fascinate you as well as children.

A Pig Is Big

Written and Illustrated by Douglas Florian
Scholastic 2000, ISBN 0–439–35630–X

Using very simple text, Florian gives a clear explanation of size comparison; it is in a predictable format, with the size of each object named getting bigger. With only two words on the first page, it begins *What's big? . . . A pig is big. A pig is fat. A pig is bigger than my hat . . . What's bigger than a pig? A cow is bigger than a pig. A car is bigger than a cow. A truck is bigger than a car. A street is bigger than a truck.* And the pattern continues to a neighborhood, a city, the Earth's dimensions, and finally the biggest of all—the universe.

 *Patterns*

Lots and Lots of Zebra Stripes: Patterns in Nature

Written and Photographs by Stephen R. Swinburne
Boyds Mills 1998, 2002, ISBN 1–56397–980–2

Using dazzling photographs to illustrate the very simple text, Swinburne provides this outstanding example of patterns in nature. Many pages have numerous pictures to show patterns, but you will find only one sentence per page. This one will find its way onto your science bookshelf once you've read it aloud to introduce patterns.

Twizzlers: Shapes and Patterns

Written by Jerry Pallotta
Illustrated by Rob Bolster
Cartwheel/Scholastic 2002, ISBN 0–439–35796–9

Every inch on every page of this read-aloud can serve as a teaching tool for a math class. Pallotta uses *Twizzlers* to help him show children shapes and patterns. And if you know Jerry, you have come to expect a little something extra tucked in somewhere. Well, in this one, he cleverly brings in an architect, who is doing construction work on the school, to demonstrate lines, shapes, and angles. Use this one to demonstrate complex ideas in an engaging way.

■ *Standard Three: Geometry*

Geometry

Bigger, Better, Best! (MathStart Area)

Written by Stuart J. Murphy
Illustrated by Marsha Winborn
HarperCollins 2002, ISBN 0–06–02898-X

When Jill, Jenny, and their brother Jeff move into a new house, each of them will be getting a new room—one they do not have to share with each other. They immediately begin arguing about who will get the best and the biggest room. Once they chose their new rooms, the arguments continue. Mom and Dad offer advice: Take this pad of paper and cover your windows and the one that uses the most paper has the biggest window. After all three windows are covered, the children find out that even though each of their windows is different in shape, it took the same number of sheets of paper to cover them. The children then do the same with newspapers to see who got the biggest room. *Bigger, Better, Best!* is a great book to introduce the concept of area.

Cut Down to Size at High Noon: A Math Adventure

Written by Scott Sundby
Illustrated by Wayne Geehan
Charlesbridge 2000, ISBN 1–57091–168–1

> *At first glance, Cowlick looked like any other small frontier town. The people who lived there looked just like average, everyday folk. That is, until their hats came off. The person responsible was Louie Cutorze. . . . Louie's hair creations were the pride of Cowlick. The key to Louie's fantastic haircuts were scale drawings.* From this lead, Sundby and Geehan take you on a humorous trip that will leave you and students with an understanding of how mathematicians uses scale drawings to make very small things bigger and very big things smaller.

Grandfather Tang's Story: A Tale Told with Tangrams

Written by Ann Tompert
Illustrated by Robert Andrew Parker
Dragonfly/Crown 1990, 1997, ISBN 0–517–88558–1

> Tangrams come in seven pieces and, when placed together carefully, form a square. However, when they are rearranged, they can become many different things. In *Grandfather Tang's Story,* the tans are placed to form various animals as he tells his granddaughter Soo a story. While he tells the story, each of the animals is pictured using the tans. This one will fascinate students and ignite their curiosity as only a dedicated teacher and a good book can. And as a bonus, there is a pattern for tangrams at the end that you can trace and cut out of tagboard. Imagine having a set for every student the second time you read this book aloud.

The Greedy Triangle

Written by Marilyn Burns
Illustrated by Gordon Silveria
Scholastic 1994, ISBN 0–590–48991–7

> This outstanding book tells the story of one busy triangle that *spends its time holding up roofs, supporting bridges, making music in a symphony orchestra, catching the wind for sailboats, being slices of pie and halves of sandwiches.* One day the triangle becomes dissatisfied and wants more lines and angles added to make life more interesting. So, the shapeshifter transforms the triangle

into a quadrilateral, then into a pentagon, a hexagon, and finally a circle. But no matter what shape the triangle becomes, it finds reasons that don't please it. Finally, it realizes that and requests to be returned to its old shape. When once more in the shape of a triangle, it becomes very busy doing all the important things a triangle must do in our world. Burns, a renowned mathematics educator, makes this book an essential one for any math bookshelf.

Shape Up! Fun with Triangles and Other Polygons

Written by David A. Adler
Illustrated by Nancy Tobin
Holiday House 1998, 2000, ISBN 0–8234–1638–0

Adler takes geometry to another plane (no pun intended) with everyday objects that can't help but hook children. He invites them to take a toothpick and a piece of cheese. Then, following his simple instructions, they're to create a polygon. Then he explains the differences between triangles with additional pieces of cheese. Before the book ends, children will be finding polygons everywhere they look. A school tour will yield many new polygons and if you take a camera along, think of the new book your class can make—just like David A. Adler.

Sir Cumference and the Dragon of Pi

Written by Cindy Neuschwander
Illustrated by Wayne Geehan
Charlesbridge 1999, ISBN 1–57091–164–9

In this book, Sir Cumference is saved again by knowing how math works. This time while dining with his son, Radius, he eats something that makes him very sick. Radius runs back to the castle to get the doctor but finds him gone. When he returns, he finds a dragon in place of his father who is pleading with Radius to help rescue him. What's a boy to do? How can he save his father? How can he make the dragon turn back into his father? With his mother's help, young Radius solves the puzzle and comes up with the right formula by knowing the power of pi—π, the magic number that is the same for all circles.

Sir Cumference and the First Round Table: A Math Adventure

Written by Cindy Neuschwander
Illustrated by Wayne Geehan
Charlesbridge 1997, ISBN 1–57091–152–5

What's a king to do when, just to have his men hear him, he has to talk so loud that his throat gets sore? (It helps to know that they are sitting at a large rectangular table.) Each person begins to give King Arthur ideas about a solution. One suggests cutting the rectangle in half, thus making a square table. When that didn't work, Lady Di suggests cutting each of the squares diagonally to make diamonds. The suggestions go on until all shapes have been discussed and the king ends up solving his problem by making the table round.

Sir Cumference and the Great Knight of Angleland: A Math Adventure

Written by Cindy Neuschwander
Illustrated by Wayne Geehan
Charlesbridge 2001, ISBN 1–57091–169–X

Can Radius use a protractor to find his way through a maze of angles and earn his knighthood? Watch as he shows his knowledge about a right angle and then uses that skill to work his way through a maze. The same as with the raging success of Harry Potter, these books will be a hit in your classroom. They will whet children's appetite for math—you can bet on it.

Spaghetti and Meatballs for All: A Mathematical Story

Written by Marilyn Burns
Illustrated by Debbie Tilley
Scholastic 1997, ISBN 0–590–94459–2

Take children to a dinner party at Mr. and Mrs. Comfort's and join thirty guests as they are treated to spaghetti and meatballs. Mrs. Comfort carefully figures out the seating for the large crowd and has a seat for everyone. Her tables look lovely as they await her first guests. However, when they begin arriving, the guests also begin rearranging the tables. By the time all thirty guests have arrived, they finally realize that their arrangements won't work and in the end, the tables have to be put back in the original setup. The story is a delight to read and the math concept is so cleverly embedded that children will never believe you are about to introduce geometry.

What's Your Angle, Pythagoras? A Math Adventure

Written by Julie Ellis
Illustrated by Phyllis Hornung
Charlesbridge 2004, ISBN 1–57091–150–9

Pythagoras, who lives in ancient Greece, is a curious little boy whose curiosity seems to lead him into trouble. Yet, it also leads him to ask questions that yield important answers. Read this one to children and have them begin to notice how math is all around us in objects not normally thought of as mathematical. Let Pythagoras show children how to square a number. This one will find its way into the hands of many class members after one read-aloud.

 *Shapes*

Bear in a Square

Written by Stella Blackstone
Illustrated by Debbie Harter
Barefoot Books 1998, 2000, ISBN 1–84148–120–3

Each full page of colorful art is filled with various shapes, but the text asks the child to find a specific shape. Even though *Bear in a Square* was written for very young children, it could be used successfully for kindergarten and first-grade classrooms for buddy reading following your read-aloud.

A Cloak for the Dreamer

Written by Aileen Friedman
Illustrated by Kim Howard
Scholastic 1994, ISBN 0–590–48987–9

This is a lovely story about a tailor and his three sons. When the Archduke of the land orders three cloaks for himself and three dresses for his wife, the tailor knows he needs the help of his three sons if he is to complete the order in time for the Archduke's trip. He asks his three sons to complete one cloak each while he sews the dresses. The first son surveys the fabric and decides to use patterns of rectangles. The second son uses the colors of the Archduke's family crest that he cuts into squares. Later, because he likes his cloak so much, he repeats the plan but this time he cuts each square in half making triangles, which he quickly sews into another wonderful cloak. The third son, who longs to be a world traveler rather than a tailor, cuts his fabric into circles. Of course, circles simply won't do because even when sewn together, there are many holes. After seeing all the cloaks, the tailor finally realizes that his third son, whom he loves dearly, is not destined to become a tailor. Notes at the back of the book extend the use of the text for both parents and teachers. These explain that the book contributes to children's knowledge of geometry by presenting a context for thinking about geometric shapes and how they fit together.

The Shape of Things

Written by Dayle Ann Dodds
Illustrated by Julie Lacome
Candlewick/Harcourt 1994, 1996, ISBN 0–156–402698–1

> *A square is just a square, until you add a roof, Two windows and a door, Then it's much, much more!* And so begins this wonderful read-aloud that will heighten your youngest children's awareness of simple shapes. Dodds and Lacome present a clever way to explain these concepts. The text appears on the left page with the basic shape; on the opposite page, the shape becomes an object children will recognize. For example, a square becomes a house, a circle becomes a Ferris wheel, a triangle becomes a boat, and a rectangle becomes a train.

Shapes, Shapes, Shapes

Written and Photographed by Tana Hoban
Greenwillow 1986, ISBN 0–688–14740–2

> On the first page, Hoban features all the basic shapes for readers to search for in each of the photographs that follow. Every spread is filled from border to border with fabulous photographs simply brimming with various shapes. For example, the first page shows an adorable young boy in a lake with his floating sailboat. Of course, the sails are two triangles. The next page shows miniature dishes filled with different kinds of food. There are squares, rectangles, ovals, circles, and more. Young children will find this one truly fascinating, and they will learn to look for shapes in the world all around them.

Sir Cumference and the Sword in the Cone: A Math Adventure

Written by Cindy Neuschwander
Illustrated by Wayne Geehan
Charlesbridge 2003, ISBN 1–57091–601–2

> When King Arthur decides to choose a new heir, he calls all his knights together. He presents them with a puzzle about where he has hidden his sword.

He tells them that the one who solves the puzzle to locate his sword will be the new heir to his throne. Radius and Vertex are two of the knights who search for the sword. Travel throughout the land with the knights as they meet their math challenge when Vertex solves the puzzle. Spend some extra time with the last page and have children attempt to solve that puzzle.

A String of Beads

Written by Margarette S. Reid
Illustrated by Ashley Wolff
Dutton 1997, ISBN 0–525–45721–6

Beads come in all shapes, sizes, and colors and this book has them all—or at least it seems like it does! In the story, a grandmother and her granddaughter are bead makers. As they work throughout the book to create necklaces, the many shapes of the beads are discussed. Wolff's illustrations clearly show beads of all shapes, sizes, and colors.

So Many Circles, So Many Squares

Written and Photographed by Tana Hoban
Greenwillow 1998, ISBN 0–688–15165–5

This wordless book is a great "interactive-talk-aloud" (we made that word up, in case you're wondering). It is perfect for exploring the simple shapes of circles and squares. Hoban's photographs of everyday objects will have young children searching for squares and circles everywhere. It is amazing how this simple book will stimulate their thinking about shapes.

The Wing of a Flea: A Book About Shapes

Written and Illustrated by Ed Emberley
Little, Brown 2001, ISBN 0–316–23487–7

Displayed on a striking black background, Emberley presents several bright shapes in everyday objects that can be found all around us. He begins with the triangle and carefully weaves the story around that shape. *A triangle could be the wings on a flea or the beak on a bird, if you'll just look and see. A bandit's bandana, an admiral's hat, and, in case you don't know it, the nose on a cat.* Each phrase is illustrated, but then the text invites children to see how many triangles they can find in a full-spread illustration. Following the triangle, the author presents the rectangle and the circle.

When a Line Bends . . . a Shape Begins

Written by Rhonda Gowler Greene
Illustrated by James Kaczman
Houghton Mifflin 1997, 2001, ISBN 0–618–15241–5

Using rhyme, this text begins by defining all the things that appear as a line: a jump rope, ants in a row, a violin bow, a pole for fishing, a leash and a trail, a kite string, a shoelace, a whisker, and a tail. Then what happens when the line bends? Well, a square if formed or a rectangle, a triangle, a diamond, a circle, an oval, a star, and others. With each shape, the verse tells many of the things that shapes can make and the illustrations show that object. This lively read-aloud is as much fun to look at as it is to read. It is also a great springboard to get children looking for additional examples of all of the shapes.

■ *Standard Four: Measurement*

Calendars

The Official M & M's Book of the Millennium

Written by Larry Dane Brimner
Illustrated by Karen E. Pellaton
Charlesbridge 1999, ISBN 0–88106–071–2

We would not use this as a one-time read-aloud, but it does offer a wonderful literature resource to support the math curriculum. Brimner wrote this one to help teachers explain the millennium to children, and because of his excellent research, the book provides a lot of information to explain how our calendar works. Each of the book's subtopic is written in short segments with illustrations strategically placed to break up the amount of text on each page. The book is very reader-friendly.

One Lighthouse, One Moon

Written and Illustrated by Anita Lobel
Greenwillow 2000, 2002, ISBN 0–06–000537–8

This one is rich in concepts and is divided into short chapters to focus on each of those concepts. The first chapter (with seven sentences) focuses on developing the days of the week. The second chapter (with twelve sentences) is directed at developing the concept of the months of the year. The third and last chapter focuses on number sense with a sentence to pair with each of the ten pictures.

One Monday Morning

Written and Illustrated by Uri Shulevitz
Sunburst/Farrar, Straus and Giroux 1967 (Scribner's), 2003, ISBN 0–374–45648–8

Organized around the days of the week, a little boy is visited by a king, a queen, and a prince *One Monday Morning*. When they arrive, the little boy isn't home so the Prince tells his parents that they must come back the next day. On the subsequent days of the week, another member of the royal family is added, but the boy is always away from home. Finally, on Sunday, along with a knight, a royal guard, the royal cook, the royal barber, the royal jester, and a little dog, the royal family finds the little boy home and gets to say hello. On the last page of the book (with no words), you see the little boy with a deck of playing cards showing the royal family. What will children conclude? Did the royal family really visit or was the little boy simply using his vivid imagination? This one is a real treat.

The Very Hungry Caterpillar

Written and Illustrated by Eric Carle
Philomel 1969 (World), 1987, ISBN 0–399–20853–4

This timeless classic is a perfect book to introduce or reinforce the understanding of the days of the week. *In the light of the moon a little egg lay on a leaf. One Sunday morning the warm sun came up and—pop—out of the egg came a tiny and very hungry caterpillar. He started to look for some food. On Monday he ate . . .* The art on every page features the caterpillar's feast for that day with a hole strategically punched right through the page showing where the growing caterpillar has eaten through. When he has finally eaten enough, he wraps himself into a cocoon where he stays for two weeks. The cycle ends on Sunday when the reader turns the final page to reveal a beautiful butterfly.

 *Measuring*

Actual Size

Written and Illustrated by Steve Jenkins
Houghton Mifflin 2004, ISBN 0–618–37594–5

When you read this one, you'll wonder why you didn't think of this clever approach before Jenkins. We couldn't decide whether to put it on the Math or Science bookshelf. We finally settled for Math because of its size (no pun intended). However, don't use this book just to introduce measurement; use it for a study of insects and animals too. It will quickly become a favorite in any classroom.

Big & Little

Written and Illustrated by Steve Jenkins
Houghton Mifflin 1996, ISBN 0–395–72664–6

Oh my, what a treat this one will be for a read-aloud to support math concepts and for an earth science unit on animals. Jenkins uses scale drawings in cut paper collages to show which animals are comparable in size to other animals. For example, did you know that the smallest bird weighs just one-half ounce while the biggest one weighs almost 10,000 times more? Each page presents similar facts—facts that follow the shape of the animal leaping across the spaces. You'll need more than one copy because this one is bound to be a favorite of many students.

A Cake All for Me

Written by Karen Magnuson Beil
Illustrated by Paul Meisel
Holiday House 1998, ISBN 0–8234–1368–3

A Cake All for Me is simply adorable and will charm young children. Beil used the old nursery form to illustrate simple counting. Through the art, she illustrates many different forms of measurement. *Warm up the oven. Grease up a pan. I'll bake a big cake fast as I can. One, two, get out the moo. Three, four, open and pour. Five, six, sift and mix. Seven, eight, chop and grate. Nine, ten, eggs from the hen. Oh, a cake all for me, all for me!* The rhyme continues counting up to twenty. On every page, the art shows measuring cups and spoons of different sizes. The last few pages provide a graph of a lot of measuring instruments and several recipes.

The Giant Carrot

Written by Jan Peck
Illustrated by Barry Root
Dial 1998, ISBN 0–8037–1823–3

This humorous read-aloud will have children giggling as they watch when a family seeks to grow healthy carrots. Each member of the family dreams up what they want to do with the healthy carrots they will raise. However, it is little Isabelle whose unique talents actually raise *The Giant Carrot*. The math lesson comes following the read-aloud tale when you take carrots and measure other ingredients to make a carrot pudding. The recipe is given at the back of the book.

Hershey's Weights and Measures

Written by Jerry Pallotta
Illustrated by Rob Bolster
Cartwheel/Scholastic 2003, ISBN 0–439–38877–5

See summary on the Weight shelf (page 89).

How Tall, How Short, How Faraway

Written by David A. Adler
Illustrated by Nancy Tobin
Holiday House 1999, 2000, ISBN 0–8234–1632–1

Do you want to introduce children to the different measurement systems used in the world? Adler's clever presentation will have them wanting to measure everything they see. He very clearly explains how you can convert the US system of measurement into other systems and demonstrates both standard and nonstandard units of measure. The illustrations further extend the meaning of the words in this amazing book. A conversion table is given at the back.

Inch by Inch

Written and Illustrated by Leo Lionni
Mulberry/HarperTrophy 1960 (Scholastic), 1995, ISBN 0–688–13283–9

The irresistible Leo Lionni has provided another treasure featuring a little inchworm who measures animal after animal *Inch by Inch*. Finally, he is asked by a nightingale to measure his song. The inchworm wonders whether and how you measure a song, but the bird demands that he try or he will be eaten. The problem-solving inchworm tells the nightingale to sing while he measures inch by inch. And the inchworm measures and measures right out of sight.

Inchworm and a Half

Written by Elinor J. Pinczes
Illustrated by Randall Enos
Houghton Mifflin 2001, 2003, ISBN 0–395–82849–X

> The inchworm figures out how to measure by making loops around her vegetables and each loop equals one inch. However, she runs into problems when it doesn't take a complete loop to go around, so she must come up with another solution. She calls her solution a *fraction*. Along the way, she enlists the help of several other worms of different lengths and together they measure everything in the garden.

Is a Blue Whale the Biggest Thing There Is?

Written and Illustrated by Robert E. Wells
Albert Whitman 1993, ISBN 0–8075–3656–3

> From the back of the book: *A blue whale is big; it's the BIGGEST animal alive. But it isn't the biggest thing there is. After all, a blue whale would look small sitting on top of a mountain. And though a mountain is large, it's no more than a pebble in relation to the whole earth.* Every page of this wonderful book was designed and written to explain how one thing compares to another; it uses the blue whale as a starting point. The illustrations are outstanding and will help children visualize the things the story is using to show size and measurement. This book is truly worthy of a space on any math bookshelf.

Jim and the Beanstalk (Length and Proportional Reasoning)

Written and Illustrated by Raymond Briggs
PaperStar/Putnam & Grosset 1970, 1997, ISBN 0–698–11577–5

> Briggs has taken *Jack and the Beanstalk* and rewritten it for Jim. In this retelling, Jim climbs the beanstalk to find a giant who can't see to read anymore. Jim offers to help and with a very large gold coin, he slides back down to have some glasses made for the Giant. When they are delivered, the Giant now requests new teeth. Jim measures his mouth and with another very large coin, slides back down to have new teeth made. Now with new glasses and new teeth, the Giant wants a wig made. Jim measures his head and goes back to have a wig made. This time the Giant is so happy that he tells Jim to leave quickly and chop the beanstalk down once and for all. Jim does but not before a very large gold coin gets tossed down to him with a note telling him how happy he has made the Giant.

Measuring Penny

Written and Illustrated by Loreen Leedy

Henry Holt 1997, 2000, ISBN 0–8050–6572–5

> When her teacher gives the assignment to measure something, the little girl decides to measure her dog, Penny. When she gets home, she realizes there is so much about a dog you can measure: the length of the tail, the length of the nose, the width of a paw, the length of an ear. Her project becomes more interesting when she takes Penny to the park where there are many other dogs, so she begins to make comparisons between Penny and the others. It becomes even more interesting as the girl uses both standard (e.g., tape measure, scales, seconds) and nonstandard (e.g., dog biscuits, swabs) to measure various features of Penny. This one will make measurement an exciting invitation, so be prepared because students will want to measure everything in sight.

Millions to Measure

Written by David M. Schwartz

Illustrated by Steven Kellogg

HarperCollins 2003, ISBN 0–06–623784–X

> Schwartz and Kellogg have teamed up once again to provide a wonderful resource for the math classroom. This tale begins on the front endpapers and doesn't end until the back ones. Using an enlarged font and outstanding illustrations, this book will be invaluable as you introduce the many ways to measure things.

Twelve Snails to One Lizard: A Tale of Mischief and Measurement

Written by Susan Hightower

Illustrated by Matt Novak

Simon & Schuster 1997, ISBN 0–689–80452–0

> Milo the beaver realizes that the water is drying up and if he doesn't get his dam patched quickly, the pond will soon be gone. When he explains his confusion about measurement to Bubba Bullfrog, Bubba gets busy helping explain how you use inches, feet, and yards to solve Milo's problem. Before long, they get other animals involved in solving measurement problems and the pond is saved.

Money

Alexander, Who Used to be Rich Last Sunday

Written by Judith Viorst
Illustrated by Ray Cruz
Aladdin 1978 (Atheneum), 1988, ISBN 0–689–71199–9

When Alexander's grandparents visit and give him a dollar, he dreams about all the things he can buy. Slowly throughout the week, he spends his dollar little by little until finally he is broke. Now he wishes he had saved some of the dollar, so he tries to think of ways to earn more money. Everything falls through, however, and Alexander is left with some useless items that he spent his dollar on.

Benny's Pennies

Written by Pat Brisson
Illustrated by Bob Barner
Bantam 1993, 1995, ISBN 0–440–41016–9

With five pennies, Benny tries to decide what he will buy. His mom, brother, sister, dog, and cat all try to give him ideas of ways to spend his money. Then slowly he begins to spend his pennies. First he buys a rose for one penny. Then he spends another for a cookie. From Michael he buys a paper hat for another penny. Now with two pennies left, Benny buys a bone and then a fish with his last penny. Finally, he walks home and he gives everyone a present: a rose for his mom, a cookie for his brother, a hat for his sister, a bone for his dog, and a fish for his cat. The book is very simple and offers many places that invite children to join in with choral reading, and then to tell how much money Benny has left after he buys each of the gifts.

The Big Buck Adventure

Written by Shelley Gill and Deborah Tobola
Illustrated by Grace Lin
Charlesbridge 2000, ISBN 0–88106–294–4

What an adventure this little girl has on her very first shopping trip after her allowance is raised to one dollar. Will she spend her dollar on candy (Gill and Tobola list various types of candy for different amounts of money) or will she choose toys, food, or maybe a pet? The font is enlarged and the text is a joy to read. On the very last endpaper, the sheet is cut so that children can slip in four quarters and/or ten dimes. What a very clever way to end a book about a buck.

The Coin Counting Book

Written and Illustrated by Rozanne Lanczak Williams
Charlesbridge 2001, ISBN 0–88106–326–6

With tightly focused photographs of all the US coins, Williams adds verse, in an enlarged font, that invites children to join in as she counts pennies to make a nickel, nickels to make a dime, and dimes and a nickel to make a quarter. She groups them visually, in verse and in algorithms. This book is written in simple and clear language to explain a difficult concept for young children. A wise teacher could easily build many math lessons around this one book.

Follow the Money!

Written and Illustrated by Loreen Leedy
Holiday House 2002, 2003, ISBN 0–8234–1794–8

Once you spend some time reading this little, clever book, you won't ever teach the concept of money without using it. Leedy begins with the minting of a quarter and then the text follows it around to the various places money can be found. Every page is packed with information about money as the quarter passes through each of them.

The Go-Around Dollar

Written by Barbara Johnston Adams
Illustrated by Joyce Audy Zarins
Simon & Schuster 1992, ISBN 0–02–700031–1

This book has a two-layered text that begins with the front endpapers. There you will find two large one dollar bills; one shows the front view and the other shows the back view. Each view is carefully labeled to identify all the significant features found on US currency. Readers follow a dollar around town and experience how it changes hands in a variety of purchases and exchanges. Along the sides of every spread readers find facts about dollar bills. If your math curriculum includes the study of money, this book is a good one to use with all ages in the elementary school.

How the Second Grade Got $8,205.50 to Visit the Statue of Liberty

Written by Nathan Zimelman
Illustrated by Bill Slavin
Albert Whitman 1992, ISBN 0–8075–3431–5

A group of second graders must earn enough money to take a trip to New York to visit the Statue of Liberty, so they develop a plan and get to work. The unique story tells about each of the projects and how much money is made, but it also explains how much it cost to do the project. As a result, children have to add and subtract all the way through the story.

If You Made a Million

Written by David M. Schwartz
Illustrated by Steven Kellogg
Lothrop, Lee & Shepard 1989, 1994, ISBN 0–688–13634–6

Before beginning a unit about money, you may need to follow up a read-aloud by providing many copies of this one. The book is very detailed and gets rather advanced, so we suggest using small sections and making time for children to get knee-to-knee to talk about money with a copy handy. Kellogg's art is, as usual, truly spectacular and the placement of it on every page is in small chunks, but the concepts move rapidly.

Once Upon a Dime: A Math Adventure

Written by Nancy Kelly Allen
Illustrated by Adam Doyle
Charlesbridge 1999, ISBN 1–57091–161–4

Isn't this a clever title? *Once Upon a Dime* is a sneaky math book about Farmer Truman Worth, a very happy farmer. He works from sunup to sundown milking his cows, gathering eggs, feeding the pigs, and chasing after his sheep. With a cow named Moolly Pitcher, a rooster named Franklin D. Roostervelt, chickens named Lewis and Cluck, and pigs named William Muckinley and Dolly Madisow, you may wonder where the social studies leaves off and the math begins. Well, besides having lots of farm animals, Farmer Worth likes to grow things. Just wait until children hear about the money tree that continues to grow—first pennies then nickels, dimes, quarters, and finally dollars—year after year when he changes the way he fertilizes the plant. This one is a delight, and you will need more than one copy.

Penny: The Forgotten Coin

Written by Denise Brennan-Nelson
Illustrated by Michael Glenn Monroe
Sleepy Bear Press 2003, ISBN 1–58536–128–3

> From the author of *Buzzy, the Bumblebee* and *My Momma Likes to Say* comes another book that informs and entertains. Do you know the history of the penny? Do you know how many idioms there are about pennies? Readers will find these things, and more, cleverly embedded in a meaningful way.

Pigs Will Be Pigs: Fun with Math and Money

Written by Amy Axelrod
Illustrated by Sharon McGinley-Nally
Aladdin/Simon & Schuster 1994, 1997, ISBN 0–689–81219–1

> Like all pigs, Mr. and Mrs. Pig are hungry and there's no food at home for them. So they begin looking for enough money to go out and get something to eat. All the little piglets join them in their search for money. They find all kinds of money—dollars, quarters, dimes, a fifty-cent piece, a five-dollar bill, a twenty-dollar bill, and many pennies. Once at the restaurant, they read the menu (one with the cost of each dish is in the book) and decide to order the special. On the back page, there's a list of how much money the Pig family spent so that children can figure out how much they found.

The Purse

Written and Illustrated by Kathy Caple
Houghton Mifflin 1986, 1992, ISBN 0–395–62981–0

> *Clinkity clinkity clinkity clinkity* . . . Katie loves the way her box full of coins sounds as they bump around inside. But her sister Marcia talks her into spending her money for a purse rather than keeping her money in a box. The problem is that the new purse is empty and Katie doesn't like that. She wants money to put in her purse. Read this one aloud to find all the ways she earns money to put in her new purse. This one might give students ideas about doing things to earn money.

Sold! A Mothematics Adventure

Written by Nathan Zimelman
Illustrated by Bryn Barnard
Charlesbridge 2000, ISBN 1–57091–167–3

This is a charmer that will provide everyone with not a *mothematics* adventure but a mathematical adventure! Read to find out what happens when a dad takes his son to an auction (the book defines *auction* and how to bid on items). While he tries to catch a bothersome moth, the little boy finds he has bid on numerous items that will take his allowance for many weeks to come. Not only is the story highly engaging, but the art is also so pleasing it makes the story a wonderful addition to any math curriculum bookshelf.

Time

Chimp Math: Learning About Time from a Baby Chimpanzee

Written by Ann Whitehead Nagda
Photographs by Cindy Bickel, Denver Zoological Foundation, and various other sources
Henry Holt 2002, ISBN 0–8050–6674–8

We are absolutely sure children will want to take this little chimp home with them after they watch him grow from a tiny baby. The book will introduce the class to timelines, charts, clocks, and calendars as children keep track of baby Jiggs' growth. Nagda and Bickel pack lots of information into this read-aloud and use the various charts to demonstrate how helpful math can be in our world.

The Grouchy Ladybug

Written and Illustrated by Eric Carle
HarperCollins 1977, 1996, ISBN 0–06–027087–X

This now-classic book has helped us teach children what NOT to do. Unlike the ladybug, we want children to be kind and polite and civil. We want children to share and to live together peacefully. And, many teachers have used this delightful read-aloud as a means to introduce children to telling time. Oh, how clever Carle was to give us a humorous story that is such fun to read while giving students such support in so many different ways. In case you haven't noticed, Eric Carle is one of our favorites.

Just a Minute

Written by Bonny Becker
Illustrated by Jack E. Davis
Simon & Schuster 2003, ISBN 0–689–83374–1

How long is a minute? Why does it seem longer sometimes (when waiting) and shorter at others? When Johnny's mother takes him shopping with her and asks him to wait *Just a Minute* while she shops, he finds that minutes can seem like hours, days, months, and even years. Becker uses humor in this great read-aloud to introduce the concept of time. Davis adds to the humor with his cartoon-like illustrations that are certain to appeal to children.

Telling Time: How to Tell Time on Digital and Analog Clocks!

Written by Jules Older
Illustrated by Megan Halsey
Charlesbridge 2000, ISBN 0–88106–397–5

Older uses humor to help children build an understanding of the terms we use when talking about time and to understand the differences between types of clocks. Every page contains several illustrations to explain the concepts presented in the limited text. In addition, there are small pictures of children with speech bubbles to further explain concepts. The book makes a great curriculum connection between literature and math concepts.

Telling Time with Big Mama Cat

Written by Dan Harper
Illustrated by Barry Moser and Cara Moser
Harcourt 1998, ISBN 0–15–201738–0

This book is one you shouldn't miss when teaching children how to tell time. The text is written in very simple terms and the art is so splendid that you'll feel like you can reach out and stroke the cat shown on each page. The front cover folds out to reveal a manipulative clock that children can use to match the hands to both the text and the clock in each picture.

Volume

Capacity: Math Counts

Written by Henry Pluckrose
Photographs by Chris Fairclough, Betts Anderson, Tommy Dodson, and Unicorn Stock
Childrens Press 1995, ISBN 0–516–45451–X

Using pictures of everyday items, the short text simply explains *capacity* and how it takes the shape of a container. From a sand pail to more complex objects, Pluckrose seeks to show children the importance of being able to measure capacity.

 Weight

Hershey's Weights and Measures

Written by Jerry Pallotta
Illustrated by Rob Bolster
Cartwheel/Scholastic 2003, ISBN 0–439–38877–5

Pallotta and Bolster team up to show several different ways to measure, and they demonstrate math terms in a supportive and engaging way—with clowns and lots of candy. If readers aren't comfortable with terms, such as *kilometer* and other units of measure, that is no problem. Bolster's illustrations enlist a clown's help to carefully explain them.

Just a Little Bit

Written by Ann Tompert
Illustrated by Lynn Munsinger
Houghton Mifflin 1993, 1996, ISBN 0–395–51527–0

The opening page gives the story away when you see an irresistible elephant with his tiny mouse friend trying to swing. When both the slide and swing break under the elephant's weight, they decide to try the seesaw. Well, of course, nothing happens. Along comes giraffe who offers to help mouse. Nothing happens because elephant was still too heavy. Animal after animal joins mouse until finally elephant soars up into the air! This one is just perfect for a read-aloud and illustrates so clearly how a scale works.

Who Sank the Boat?

Written and Illustrated by Pamela Allen
Putnam 1982, 1996, ISBN 0–698–11373–X

Beside the sea, on Mr. Peffer's place there lived a cow, a donkey, a sheep, a pig, and a tiny little mouse. They were good friends, and one warm, sunny morning, for no particular reason, they decided to go for a row in the bay. Do you know who sank the boat? Allen places each animal in the boat using delightful rhymes. Then on the last page, just as the tiny mouse is stepping aboard, the boat sinks. *Who Sank the Boat?*

■ *Standard Five: Data Analysis and Probability*

Graphing

Berries, Nuts, and Seeds

Written by Diane L. Burns
Illustrated by John F. McGee
Garth Stevens 1996 (Northword Press), 2000, ISBN 1–55971–573–1

> This is a delightful little field guide to *Berries, Nuts, and Seeds*. With each species pictured, the text either tells or shows you what it looks like, where you can find it, what eats it, and many other interesting facts. Bring in a few samples of each and follow up with a graphing lesson that will snowball into a series of fascinating math lessons for many days. There are twelve books in this series, which will be equally at home in many science units: *Rabbits, Squirrels, and Chipmunks; Caterpillars, Bugs, and Butterflies; Trees, Leaves, and Bark; Birds, Nests, and Eggs; Tracks, Scats, and Signs; Seashells, Crabs, and Sea Stars; Snakes, Salamander, and Lizards; Frogs, Toads, and Turtles; Wildflowers, Blooms, and Blossoms; Ricks, Fossils, and Arrowheads; Planets, Moons, and Stars.*

The Great Graph Contest

Written and Illustrated by Loreen Leedy
Holiday House 2005, ISBN 0–8234–1710–7

> Here's a new one for you to teach everything you ever wanted to know about creating graphs to illustrate mathematical thinking. From simple yes and no graphs to pie charts and line graphs, from Venn diagrams and bar graphs to quantity graphs, Leedy and her little munchkins explain complicated mathematical thinking in a reader-friendly, simple cartoon format. At the back of the book, she defines the process with more details.

Tiger Math: Learning to Graph from a Baby Tiger

Written by Ann Whitehead Nagda
Photographs by Cindy Bickel
Henry Holt 2000, ISBN 0–8050–7161–X

> What better way to teach children about graphs than to introduce them to T. J., an orphaned Siberian tiger cub who has been hand-raised at the Denver

Zoo. Every page is filled with information that tracks his growth through written description and several types of simple graphs—pie, block, bar, and line—that explain the text. The photographs are sharp and tightly focused.

Two More Math Resource Books

The Book of Think (or How to Solve a Problem Twice Your Size)

Written by Marilyn Burns
Illustrated by Martha Weston
Little, Brown 1976, ISBN 0–316–11743–9

Do you want a few fresh ideas to use when getting children lined up? Would you like a short read-aloud about mathematical thinking? If so, then this may be the book for you. It is a "many day" mental math book that was developed to get children into thinking math. For example, try these: When you cross your arms, which one is always on top of the other? What color socks do you have on right now? Which sock do you always put on first? Imagine asking the questions while children are in their seats, then having them line up according to the answers. There are hundreds (hey, we're thinking math) of ways this book can be used in a classroom.

G Is for Googol: A Math Alphabet Book

Written by David Schwartz
Illustrated by Marissa Moss
Tricycle Press 1998, ISBN 1–883672–58–9

This one is a very sophisticated alphabet book for math. David Schwartz has developed one that deals in vocabulary that can support students through measurement, statistics, geometry, place value, shapes, patterns, and much, much more. In fact, this one may contain everything you ever wanted to know about math but were afraid to ask. The very extensive resources in this book will last all year as you support the math curriculum with history and interesting facts about all the math terms.

3

Picture Books and Read-Alouds to Support the Science Curriculum

SCIENCE EVOKES IMAGES of wonder and inquiry and invites the mind to question. Perhaps more than any other area of the curriculum, science begs us to pose problems, to pursue possibilities, and to probe with an open mind while remaining receptive to options while zeroing in on solutions. In this chapter we pull books from our shelves that open the world to readers, books that tickle the brain with new information, and books that tease the imagination with new questions.

As you consider these collections, there will be many opportunities for building text sets. One possibility is to select a topic from science and follow our suggestions from the introduction (where we chose a set of books that featured The Underground Railroad). Another way of organizing an inquiry with these books is to pull together a set on the basis of a specific topic. We have organized a few sets in this chapter that way as examples.

Suppose students have been engaged in a study of insects that sparked an interest in arachnids. So what next? Begin with brainstorming about the topic to generate all that is known or believed as truth within the learning community. As students begin sharing their knowledge and beliefs, chart the information on the board. Consciously organize what's known into clusters with like headings (e.g., habitat, diet/nutrition, mating/reproduction, physical characteristics). Don't name the categories during the brainstorming; just cluster the ideas and statements as if you are creating an index without headings.

As ideas begins to wane, ask your students to turn and talk about why information is clustered in this way. Remind the class that readers sometimes use only portions of a book to locate information to validate, extend, or negate their thinking. Introduce, or remind them of, the purpose of an index and ask students to think about words they would use to find more information for each cluster. Let those words become the names for the categories.

Present the books in the set that follows or use similar titles. Select one title from this list as a read-aloud. From this set we would use *About Arachnids*.

About Arachnids: A Guide for Children

Written by Cathryn Sill
Illustrated by John Sill
Peachtree 2003, ISBN 1–56145–038–3

Black Widow Spider: Habits and Habitat

Written by Nancy J. Nielsen
Illustrations from various photographers
Crestwood House 1990, ISBN 0–89686–513–4

Eight Legs

Written by D. M. Souza
Illustrations by various photographers
Carolrhoda 1991, ISBN 0–876–14441–5

The Fascinating World of Spiders

Written by Maria Angels Julivert
Illustrated by Marcel Socias Studios
Barron's 1992, ISBN 0–8120–1377–8

The Spider (Dimensional Nature Portfolio Series)

Written by Luise Woelflein
Illustrated by Tomo Narashima
Stewart, Tabori, & Chang 1992, ISBN 1–55670–254–X

Spiderology (Backyard Buddies Series)

Written by Michael Elsohn Ross
Photographs by Brian Grogan
Illustrated by Darren Erickson
Carolrhoda 2000, ISBN 1–57505–438–8

Spiders

Written and Illustrated by Gail Gibbons
Holiday House 1993, ISBN 0–8234–1006–4

Spiders

Written by Seymour Simon
Illustrated by various photographers
HarperCollins 2003, ISBN 0–06–028391–2

Spiders (AnimalWays)

Written by Marc Zabludoff
Illustrated by various photographers
Benchmark/Marshall Cavendish 2006, ISBN 0–7614–1747–8

Spiders (Eyes on Nature Series)

Written by Jane Parker Resnick
Illustrated by various photographers
Rourke 1996, 2001, ISBN 1–58952–205–2

Spider's Lunch: All About Garden Spiders

Written by Joanna Cole
Illustrated by Ron Broda
Grosset & Dunlap 1995, ISBN 0–448–40223–8

Spiders Near and Far

Written and Illustrated by Jennifer Owings Dewey
Dutton 1993, ISBN 0–525–44979–5

As you read, have students signal you when they hear anything that validates (thumb up), extends (palm up), or negates (thumb down) information. Every time you validate information, circle the item on the board. If something you read aloud extends a thought, circle it and write a bit more to show the new thinking. If a thought is negated, draw a single line through it and make a note of the new information. Recognize that one source may validate, another may stretch, and yet another may negate the same thought.

After the first book is read aloud, revisit the board and the clusters. Make a chart or transparency of the revised information. Some information will not have been addressed. There will be students who feel certain their information is correct even if it was negated by a single source. There will also be new thinking in the mix. At this point, now that there is more information, ask whether there are new questions that could be posed. Pose them in the appropriate cluster and challenge the community to help find answers.

We have found it helpful to give each group one cluster to focus on. This can rotate and escalate over a few days. For example, group one may take "physical characteristics" and find some answers, validate some information, and extend ideas a bit using a book they have. The next day they should keep the same resource and move on to another cluster. An alternate approach is to let the group keep the same cluster and rotate the books. Our preference is to have group members stay with one book and examine the same topic from several angles, as with the clusters. This seems to help learners recognize that one book may hold a wealth of information on some topics and very little on others. It also demonstrates the idea of "mining" a resource for all it is worth.

Each day as the groups conclude their work, revisit the class chart and layer in all new findings. Synthesize the information and lay out the next challenge. Continue this work for about four or five days so that each group can thoroughly examine two or three clusters of information within the same topic through a close study of one resource. As you conclude the cycle, come back together as a whole class and generate an opening paragraph about the topic. Then encourage each group to organize a short text using the information from their thorough investigation of one cluster.

Bring the reports together and read them as one cohesive text. Next, return to the separate written pieces and work together as a class to generate transitions between the sets of information and some concluding section for the whole. Place the combined text in a binder about the topic.

To extend this work, think about a follow-up for which every group takes a topic and follows the project cycle independently. That would mean that each group does its own brainstorming, clustering, and investigating in an entire set of books. As learners read and make notes, it may be helpful to organize information using headings such as these:

Cluster	Use the heading (physical characteristics)
Source	Bibliographic information
Assumption	Statements from brainstorming
Validation	Cite page and paragraph number to provide evidence
Extension	Citation plus additional information
Negation	Citation plus information

Another topic that could be studied is bats; books to use include the following.

Bats

Written and Illustrated by Gail Gibbons
Holiday House 1999, 2000, ISBN 0–8234–1637–2

Bats (Animals, Animals Series)

Written by Margaret Dornfeld
Illustrated by various photographers
Benchmark/Marshall Cavendish 2004, ISBN 0–7614–1754–0

Bats (Let's Investigate Wildlife Series)

Written by Nancy J. Shaw
Illustrated by various photographers
Creative Paperbacks 2001, ISBN 0–89812–318–6

Bat Loves the Night (Read and Wonder Series)

Written by Nicola Davies
Illustrated by Sarah Fox-Davies
Candlewick 2001, ISBN 0–7636–1202–2

The collection of books for this chapter was selected to address the strands in the science curriculum as described by the National Science Teachers Association (NSTA). Once again, think of these books as a starter set. We realize that we have only scratched the surface of what is available. However, our intention is to demonstrate that there are numerous picture books available to support various units of study and cycles of inquiry. The broad array of picture books in the market enables every teacher to make read-aloud a viable part of the instructional day. The following books are organized into shelves that will address many, although not all, of the areas of a school's science curriculum.

■ *Life Science*

Animals, Birds, Fish, Insects, Reptiles, and Amphibians

About Mollusks: A Guide for Children

Written by Cathryn Sill
Illustrated by John Sill
Peachtree 2005, ISBN 1–56145–331–5

> This science series (*About . . . Birds, Mammals, Reptiles, Amphibians, Insects, Fish, Arachnids, Crustaceans*) is an outstanding addition to any classroom, regardless of the grade level. Sill, a former elementary teacher, was so clever in the design of this series that she pulls even uninterested children into the subjects. Every book in the series follows a single simple format—large, bold print is always placed on the left page. The language is concise and clear usually one to two sentences defines what is pictured on the right. Words never describe more than a single concept, so it sometimes is limited to a phrase that will be continued when the page is turned. On the facing page, there is always a crisp full-color illustration created by the author's husband John. The illustrations are carefully presented so that the concept being featured in the language is obvious in the art. Once you read through to the back of the book, you will find what truly makes this series a rich treasure for science classrooms—the Afterword. Yes, you read right, the Afterword. Here each of the illustrations from the book appears again in a thumbnail-size print accompanied by elaborate text offering more in-depth information for the teacher to extend conversations and inquiry. Of course, more proficient readers will take advantage of this information on their own. In addition, you will find a bibliography of books on the subject and websites for further research.

All About Owls

Written and Illustrated by Jim Arnosky
Scholastic 1995, 1999, ISBN 0–439–05852–X

> This little book packs lots of information into a short text for an animal study unit. The illustrations are supportive of the facts presented in three to

five sentences per page. Every page will fascinate children as they explore the world of the owl. In addition, various species of owls are pictured and identified along with several facts about each. We've found all the books by Arnosky to be accurate and extremely reader-friendly. Children generally adore nonfiction when it is accessible, and you can trust this writer for your classroom.

Animal Dads

Written by Sneed B. Collard III
Illustrated by Steve Jenkins
Houghton Mifflin 1997, 2000, ISBN 0–618–03299–1

Dads do many things. They build us homes to live in. Presented in a smaller font and tucked away in a sidebar, Collard tells how the animal dad pictured on that page builds homes for his family. Jenkins gives us large collage animals throughout the book to illustrate the text that Collard provides. Here are a few brief examples: *They keep us snug and warm.* The words give examples of how the penguin dad keeps the babies warm and safe while the mother penguin goes off in search of food. *They bathe us.* Collard tells us how the prairie vole shares the responsibilities of raising their young with the mother. The very short and extremely well-crafted text makes this one an excellent fit for the science curriculum.

Around the World: Who's Been Here?

Written and Illustrated by Lindsay Barrett George
Greenwillow 1999, ISBN 0–688–15269–4

In the story, Miss Lewis, a teacher, writes a grant that would allow her to travel around the world with her camera and sketchpad to observe animals in their natural habitat. The entire book is in the form of letters back to her class telling them where she is and what she is seeing. In the last sentence of every letter, Miss Lewis gives the class clues about something a special animal has left for her to see. The letter always ends with *Who's Been Here?* Turn the page and there is the answer in a double spread of that animal. If you are not familiar with George's art, this will be a treat.

Beaks!

Written by Sneed B. Collard III
Illustrated by Robin Brickman
Charlesbridge 2002, ISBN 1–57091–388–9

Want to become a bird-watcher and learn how the birds use their beaks? If you don't have the time or the place with binoculars handy, just take this book and spend time lingering with each page to discover the many ways birds use their beaks. Beaks are shaped differently on different species of birds; therefore birds gather their food according to the shape of their beaks. Every page is short but very descriptive of the various types of birds and how they use their beaks. The last spread offers a test to see what you can recall and studies the shape of the beak and how it is used. The answers are given on the very last page but the print may require a strong light and a magnifying glass—well it did for us, but we are a bit older than most students.

Beatrice's Goat

Written by Page McBrier
Illustrated by Lori Lohstoeter
Atheneum 2001, ISBN 0–689–82460–2

Beatrice lives with her mother and five brothers and sisters in a mud hut in Africa. Beatrice wants to go to school so badly, but her family does not have the money to pay for school. So she spends her time helping her mother earn a living. One day the family is given a good-luck gift—a goat. Beatrice isn't excited because she can't imagine how the goat can help improve their standard of living. But once the goat arrives, Beatrice loves it. Life with the goat is only the beginning of a life change for the young African girl. The story is touching and will introduce students to a life style that is far different from the one they live. It will also help children understand how life is so dependent on many other factors in our world.

Beaver at Long Pond

Written by William T. George and Lindsay Barrett George
Illustrated by Lindsay Barrett George
Greenwillow/HarperTrophy 1988, 2000, ISBN 0–688–17519–8

This book is extraordinarily beautiful in both the visual presentation and the lovely way the authors craft the language to tell the story of the life of the beaver. When most other animals go to sleep, the beaver begins his hunt for food. If the sky is still too light, he eats from the pond until he feels safe. The beaver is a cautious animal who is always looking out for danger. The font is enlarged with minimal text on every page. The story is circular as it ends with the beaver arriving back home, smelling around for danger, and once satisfied, diving down and entering his tunnel for another day of sleeping.

Big Blue Whale

Written by Nicola Davies
Illustrated by Nick Maland
Candlewick 1997, 2001, ISBN 0–763–61080–1

This message sets the stage for another of Davies' outstanding read-alouds:
For every blue whale alive today there were once twenty. People hunted and killed so many of them that fewer than 10,000 remain. Now blue whales are protected and hunting them is banned, so in some places their numbers are growing—very, very slowly. Still, you could sail the oceans for a year and never see a single one. Each page makes you feel as if you are surrounded by the sea as you explore the world of the blue whale. The font changes and flows along with the whale through the sea. Facts float beside, around, and out of the pictures, yet the book still reads like a beautiful narrative. At the back is an index to help readers quickly locate specific information. For additional books by Davies, which are just as outstanding, see: *Bat Loves the Night* (2004), *One Tiny Turtle* (2002; reviewed on page 109), and *Surprising Sharks* (2003).

The Bird House

Written by Cynthia Rylant
Illustrated by Barry Moser
Blue Sky Press/Scholastic 1998, ISBN 0–590–47345–X

This lovely book has so much to offer—homelessness, loneliness, love, a fairy tale, an introduction to various types of birds! With books like this available for use to support curriculum, children will never moan regardless of what area you are beginning to study. In the story, a young homeless girl discovers *a bright blue house standing beside a river.* As she watches in fascination, many birds—sparrows, swallows, wrens, hummingbirds, nuthatches, and a great barred owl—begin flying by. She returns over and over to watch the birds until one day they discover her and bring her to the attention of the old woman who lives alone in a bright blue house. As is characteristic of all fairy tales, this one ends happily with the girl making her home with the old woman.

Birds Build Nests

Written by Yvonne Winer
Illustrated by Tony Oliver
Charlesbridge 2002, ISBN 1–57091–501–6

This one is truly a masterpiece. The combination of the beautiful language and the crisp and vivid art will simply take your breath away. The words are delicate as they weave—like a bird building a nest—the story of the many ways and places birds build their homes. A reading of this beautiful text is a science lesson at its very best. *Birds build nests secret and deep, in holes in old trees or banks that are steep. That's where birds build their nests.* Every page begins and ends with the same phrases but caressed within those repetitive phrases are the various spots on earth birds build their nests. Don't miss this one. For additional books that are equally as beautiful and well-written see *Spiders Spin Webs* (1998), *Butterflies Fly* (2001), *Frogs Sing Songs* (2003; reviewed on page 106), and *Carry Me!* (2005; see next page).

In the Blink of an Eye

Written and Illustrated by Dieter Wiesmüller
Walker Books 2003, ISBN 0–8027–8854–8

This book's structure presents you with an eye that covers the full left page. There is text to describe the behavior of the creature whose eye is featured. That eye and the text are the only clues you get to guess the identity. Each turn of the page provides the reader with another eye and new clues. Not until the very end can you check your predictions. This one is a great introduction to the art of careful observation and a science unit on animals.

Carry Me!: Animal Babies on the Move

Written and Illustrated by Susan Stockdale
Peachtree 2005, ISBN 1–56145–328–5

When it is time to launch an animal unit, pull children close and open this treasure for a wonderful and successful beginning. The book has a very simple text that will have you scrambling to find more to satisfy the appetite of the children. The text describes the many different ways animals carry their young but doesn't give you their names. Children will be able to identify many of them while others may provide a mystery to be solved and a springboard for you.

Castles, Caves, and Honeycombs

Written by Linda Ashman
Illustrated by Lauren Stringer
Harcourt 2001, ISBN 0–15–202211–2

We adore this carefully crafted book about all the different types of homes that exist in our world. The art is a perfect balance to the quiet language featuring the habitat of the animal or insect whose home is introduced to the reader. This title is a simple text that will be useful to you as a curriculum connection and as a demonstration text for young writers.

Chameleon, Chameleon

Written by Joy Cowley
Photographs by Nic Bishop
Scholastic 2005, ISBN 0–439–66653–8

You simply must read the message about how the photographs were taken and the method Bishop had to use to capture the pictures. This information will make the book even more captivating for children. It will also help you introduce this amazing creature into your science curriculum. A picture walk will take much longer than the short read-aloud, but the text is essential to understanding the life functions of the chameleon. Together Cowley and Bishop have produced a dynamic must-have nonfiction book on this clever creature.

Chicks & Chickens

Written and Illustrated by Gail Gibbons
Holiday House 2003, ISBN 0–8234–1700–X

This text describes the complete life cycle of the chicken from eggs to embryos to hatchlings and on to adult chickens. We cannot imagine a classroom today providing any science lesson without the support of the all the quality literature available. We have decided that Gail Gibbons must have the course of study for many states on her shelves because her many, many books cover such a wide variety of subjects. We have come to trust Gibbons and her tried-and-true books. As with her many other titles, you can trust *Chicks & Chickens* to be factually based and well researched. She is a master at providing just enough text without overpowering young readers. Every page is carefully laid out with a balance of words and labeled illustrations. In addition to using Gibbons' books to support your science curriculum, you can also turn to them to demonstrate how to read and create diagrams, captions, and labels with illustrations.

Eaglet's World

Written by Evelyn Minshull
Illustrated by Andrea Gabriel
Albert Whitman 2002, ISBN 0–8075–8929–2

> *Where Eaglet was . . . was cozy. It was dark and damp and warm.* These words
> launch an informative story about how the eaglet begins his life and eventu-
> ally soars off into the sky. Many facts are embedded in a well-crafted narra-
> tive that is charming, yet informative. Gabriel's striking art extends the story
> so nicely. An Author's Note provides even more information about the bald
> eagle is at the back of the book. This one will have children eager to hear and
> see more.

At the Edge of the Forest

Written by Jonathan London
Illustrated by Barbara Firth
Candlewick 1998, ISBN 0–7636–0014–8

> If you love Jonathan London's work as we do, this one won't disappoint you.
> It is truly a lovely fictional account of a family of sheep farmers who experi-
> ence the presence of a coyote and the loss of a sheep. The young boy doesn't
> want his dad to kill the coyote, but the dad must protect the sheep. Read
> with tenderness in your voice when the father discovers that the coyote is
> part of a den and rejects the idea of shooting it. You and your students will
> be surprised by the measures he takes to protect his sheep while not killing
> the coyote. Firth's art is soft and the perfect fit to the tone of this story.

The Emperor Lays an Egg

Written by Brenda Z. Guiberson
Illustrated by Joan Paley
Henry Holt 2001, ISBN 0–8050–6204–1

> This will be one of the most unusual books you will read to build under-
> standing about this fascinating bird. Most children know penguins are black
> and white, covered in thick feathers, and that their natural habitat is
> Antarctica. When you read this one aloud, students will sit wide-eyed as they
> learn that the mother penguin lays her egg and the father immediately
> scoops it up on his feet and tucks it into his pouch to keep it protected and

warm. Then, the mother, who has not eaten for more than a month, sets off on a journey for food. It is very typical for a mother penguin to travel as much as a hundred miles just to find food. Meanwhile, the father penguin stands very still for the first three weeks because the egg is so fragile. During this time, the father goes without food while the egg is incubating. In sixty-five days, the baby penguin hatches. Where is the mother? When does she see her baby? When does the father eat? In this very short, but totally amazing book, you will find all the answers and more.

Exploring Ants: Amazing Facts About How Animals Adapt

Written by Joanne Settel, Ph.D.
Atheneum 1999, ISBN 0–689–81739–8

Scan the contents and you'll know you've found a book children are going to love. The first section is all about why some animals do gross things. Settel uses a "textbook" format but provides short little snippets about each of the tiny chapters. In addition to the gross things, there are chapters on . . . fooled ya; invasion of the body snatchers; swelling, expanding, and exploding bodies; dog mucus and other tasty treats; sucking blood; getting it down; the mating game. The book also has a glossary, an index, and suggestions for additional reading.

Faces Only a Mother Could Love

Written and Illustrated by Jennifer Owings Dewey
Boyds Mills 1996, ISBN 1–56397–046–5

If your curriculum includes a study on animals, this would be an appealing selection to begin with. As you know, children love unusual things and this book will fit the bill. Dewey shows us a wide range of animals, and she cleverly puts a baby with the mother so that we can see what the baby will look like all grown up. Along with the pictures, she gives a brief description of each of the animals. Every section is short and will easily hold the attention of students.

Families of the Deep Blue Sea

Written by Kenneth Mallory
Illustrated by Marshall Peek III
Charlesbridge 1995, ISBN 0–88106–885–3

This one is not to be missed. Take a visual walk through the book first because the illustrations are a treat that deserve time before the words are spoken. Now begin the reading and linger with the language that is equally well crafted. Mallory and Peek take the reader deep into the sea to discover and investigate many of the animals that exist there. Every spread features the life of a different animal. Read to find out how the walrus mother protects her young pup and how they stay warm in the winter. Turn the page to discover how the crocodile family lives. Move next to the South Pole and read about the emperor penguins and how the sea plays a major role in their survival. By the end of this delightful book, you will not want to put it down. Children will be calling, "Read it again." Just buy several copies because this one won't stay on your read-aloud shelf if you don't.

Fireflies, Fireflies, Light My Way

Written by Jonathan London
Illustrated by Linda Messier
Viking 1996, ISBN 0–670–85442–5

London tells the reader he was inspired to write this poetic story by a lullaby from the Mesaquakie tribe who lived in the Great Lakes region during the seventeenth and eighteenth centuries. Later the tribe moved to a settlement along the Iowa River in Iowa. In the story, London follows the fireflies as they explore and visit all the inhabitants of the forest. This pattern in the text— *Fireflies, fireflies, light my way. Lead me to the place . . .*—moves the reader from page to page. Every turn of a page brings you to the habitat of another animal: the turtles, the bullfrogs, the beavers, the catfish, the wood duck, the muskrats, the raccoons, the crawdads, the otters, and the alligators. Look closely and see whether you can find the tiny fireflies that Messier painted everywhere.

Fish Faces

Written by Norbert Wu
Photographs from the Scripps Institute of Oceanography
Owlet 1993 (Henry Holt), 1997, ISBN 0–8050–5347–6

With thousands of fish to choose from, Wu selected some of the most unusual to feature in this short book. Outstanding pictures illustrate the very minimal text with only one or two sentences per page. If you are preparing for an ocean unit, a study of sea life, or just have a student interested in fish, this delightful book will fill the bill. While the text is extremely short, it can easily be used with older children because the photographs are so gorgeous and unusual that they will fascinate all ages. Notes at the back of the book identify all the fish pictured in the text.

Frogs Sing Songs

Written by Yvonne Winer
Illustrated by Tony Oliver
Charlesbridge 2003, ISBN 1–57091–549–0

This one is so gorgeous you will want to spend some time with the picture walk. Once your eyes have been satisfied, the gentle text will teach much about frogs in a narrative that is so poetic and pleasing to the ear as the words are put into the air. *Frogs sing their songs from the lakes to the trees. Rattles and croaks create sweet melodies. That's how frogs sing songs.* Each page follows a predictable pattern with new information about how frogs can make all the delightful sounds they make.

The Good Luck Cat

Written by Joy Harjo
Illustrated by Paul Lee
Harcourt 2000, ISBN 0–15–232197–7

Everyone has heard that cats have nine lives. In this story, a young Native American girl is ready to go to the powwow and wants to take her cat, Woogie, along. But Woogie is nowhere to be found. The young girl worries that she has already used up eight of her lives so her aunt takes the girl all around the neighborhood. They put out signs and knock on doors, but Woogie isn't found. As the young girl worries, readers hear about each of the eight events that Woogie has already survived. Then, on the fourth night the cat is missing, the sad little girl puts meatloaf and Woogie's favorite toy out on the porch just hoping to entice her to come home. The next morning Woogie is curled up by her dish with half of an ear missing. The art captures the tone and emotion of the young girl in her heartfelt search.

The Grouchy Ladybug

Written and Illustrated by Eric Carle
HarperCollins 1977, 1996, ISBN 0–06–443450–8

This classic of Carle's is reviewed in the math chapter (see page 87) because of the references throughout the narrative to the time on the clock as the grouchy ladybug bullies her way through the day. This one can also be used to introduce many different animals and insects: aphids, yellow jackets, stag beetles, praying mantis, sparrows, lobsters, skunks, boa constrictors, hyenas, gorillas, rhinoceros, elephants, and finally whales.

I Am the Dog / I Am the Cat

Written by Donald Hall
Illustrated by Barry Moser
Dial 1994, ISBN 0–8037–1504–8

This is a great book to demonstrate point of view for your writer's workshop. The story will let children see the world from two different sets of eyes as they discover what it's like being a cat and what it's like to be a dog. The simple text offers lots of possibilities as a springboard to future studies about other animals.

Ice Bear: In the Steps of the Polar Bear

Written by Nicola Davies
Illustrated by Gary Blythe
Candlewick 2005, ISBN 0–7636–2759–3

Davies once again provides us with a book filled with beautiful language that informs the reader all about the majestic life of the polar bear. With the gentle prose, she takes us right into the frigid world of this very large bear who is unlike his nearest relatives—brown and grizzly bears. Readers will learn that large polar bears have a layer of fat that is *four fingers deep* to protect their body heat. The fur that covers the entire body, except the tip of the nose and the bottom of each paw, is so thick that the bear's black body can stay warm in temperatures that drop lower than −40 degrees Fahrenheit. Blythe's art is a perfect complement to Davies work. If your science class calls for studying the habits and habitats of polar bears, this one is a must-have to support your study.

I Didn't Know That Crocodiles Yawn to Keep Cool

Written and Photographs by Kate Perry
Illustrated by James Field and Jo Moore
Alladin 1998, ISBN 0–7613–1015–0

Did you know that crocodiles eat only twice a year or that an alligator can leap up into the air? This amazing little book will provide many other interesting animal facts and very likely a few surprises. The facts are given in short segments that won't overwhelm listeners. The illustrations are extremely well done. Once used as a read-aloud, leave this one lying around on a table near your shelf and magic will happen—it will disappear.

Lizards, Frogs, and Polliwogs

Written and Illustrated by Douglas Florian
Harcourt 2001, ISBN 0–15–202591–X

Use this book as a delightful way to extend a study of reptiles and amphibians. Every poem in this focused collection is filled with facts, presented in playful rhyme, and supported by Florian's equally playful and child-friendly art. And if you like this one, you'll want to pull a few selections from Florian's earlier book, *Insectlopedia* (Harcourt 1998, ISBN 0–15–201306–7).

Mothers Are Like That

Written by Carol Carrick
Illustrated by Paul Carrick
Clarion 2000, ISBN 0–395–88351–2

A very short, simple, gorgeous, and delightful book about how animal and human mothers care for their babies. The first few spreads begin with some task that mothers do. The art shows that animal doing something paired with the words . . . *Mothers are like that.* When the art shows the mother hen sitting on her eggs and the mother pig feeding her babies, the pattern of the text changes with the mother cat; on each page the mother is *cleaning* (cat), *keeping close* (sheep), *safe from harm* (geese), *finding them in a crowd* (cow) followed by *Mothers are like that.* On the very last page, you see a human mother tucking her baby in for the night followed by . . . *Mothers are like that!*

Night Rabbits

Written by Lee Posey
Illustrated by Michael G. Montgomery
Peachtree 1999, ISBN 1–56145–164–9

If you think that fiction plays no role in building background to introduce a science unit, then you need to spend some time with this jewel. Even though it is fiction, this book provides all sorts of information about rabbits, and it does so in beautifully lyrical language. Readers learn about rabbit habits from eating grass, to leaping as soft as shyness, to darting as quick as moon-beams, to jumping to the music of the crickets. In this lovely story, the little girl loves watching the rabbits play and doesn't want her dad to harm them. She finally comes up with a plan so that everyone can enjoy the lawn, including her lovely rabbits. Place this one on your shelf because you are likely to read it again and again.

No One Told the Aardvark

Written by Deborah Eaton and Susan Halter
Illustrated by Jim Spence
Charlesbridge 1997, ISBN 0–88106–871–3

This is an adorable read-aloud that invites children to compare the tasks they have to do with the ones animals don't have to do. For instance, when the little boy is told to use a spoon rather than his fingers, he wonders why chimpanzees get to use their fingers and their toes as well. Why do horses have their shoes nailed on when little boys have to tie their shoes? Think about all the warnings about hurrying up to get to school on time, when the snail can take three hours just to cross the road. The book follows a predictable pattern with what the boy is asked to do at the top of the pages and his comparisons to the animals written in italics along the bottom of the pages. This is a charming way to let children explore the habits of animals and learn about comparisons at the same time. Spence's art is very crisp and child-friendly, which makes the book even more appealing.

One Tiny Turtle

Written by Nicola Davies
Illustrated by Jane Chapman
Candlewick 2001, ISBN 0–7636–1549–8

Davies is one author we have come to trust. When we see her name, we just put the book in our stack and head for the checkout counter. After you read this book to your class, you'll be a fan for life too. From the front endpapers to the last punctuation mark, her books are so well designed you'll forget you are reading an informational text. The art is skillfully matched to the concepts of the text and does an equally fine job of enhancing the language. For this book, the front endpaper shows a turtle swimming deep in the sea with a brief *About Turtles* floating along. The font is enlarged to begin our journey out to sea. *Far, far out to sea, land is only a memory, and empty sky touches the water. Just beneath the surface is a tangle of weed and driftwood where tiny creatures cling. This is the nursery of a sea turtle.* And from there, it only gets better. As is the case with all Davies' books, this one provides an index that even young children can understand. What a jewel this book will be in your classroom collection.

A Pinky Is a Baby Mouse and Other Baby Animal Names

Written by Pam Muñoz Ryan
Illustrated by Diane deGroat
Hyperion 1997, 1999, ISBN 0–7868–1144–7

> *Baby pigs are piglets wallowing in the pen.*
> *Kids are baby goats ramming now and then.*
> *Baby pigeons are squabs perched near the windowpane.*
> *I am a baby mouse. Tell me, what's my name?*
> With its delightful rhyming text and deGroat's outstanding art, this little book will introduce children to the names of several baby animals. Before you get to the end of it, we expect that even you will find some new information. This very clever presentation is one to layer in to any collection.

Prehistoric Actual Size

Written and Illustrated by Steve Jenkins
Houghton Mifflin 2005, ISBN 0–618–53578–0

> If you think you don't like history or science or unusual facts, maybe you shouldn't seek this book out! But if you choose not to, you will miss the opportunity to investigate another of Steve Jenkins' gifts to children. In this treasure chest, he reveals the actual size of a baby (back cover) as well as an adult (cover) protoceratops, a velociraptor, a sea scorpion, and even a tiny protozoan. There are many other strange and unusual animals that students will rave over for weeks to come. Once *Prehistoric Actual Size* is introduced, it will become an absolute favorite for all ages.

Shark in the Sea

Written by Joanne Ryder
Illustrated by Michael Rothman
HarperCollins 1997, ISBN 0–688–14909–X

From the first line, the reader is led to believe this will be a fictional account of a young boy diving into the sea. But then the text begins *imagine*. . . . Then as he glides through the water, he becomes bigger and stronger and then there is the shark in all its glory. From that point on, the great white shark takes readers deep into the sea to reveal life there among other sharks. You will read about their habits of seeking food and about loosing teeth as they tear into that food, and about an extra set of teeth waiting to replace the lost ones. The art gets fairly graphic before the ending when the young boy glides back up to the surface.

Ten Flashing Fireflies

Written by Philemon Sturges
Illustrated by Anna Vojtech
North-South Books 1995, 1997, ISBN 1–55858–674–1

This lovely read-aloud could be used with young children learning to count. It is also very descriptive of the behavior of fireflies that are such a joy to ob-serve on a summer night as they flash off and on—twinkling in the growing darkness. In this book, the children catch fireflies one by one and place them in jars only to let them go at the end of a night of play.

The Whale: Giant of the Ocean

Written by Valerie Tracqui
Photographed by L'Agence PHO.N.E
Translated by Randi Rivers
Charlesbridge 2004, ISBN 1–57091–625–X

There are several books in the science Animal Close-Ups Series published by Charlesbridge; those sampled in this section should give you insight into what is available. Based on our review of four, we recommend without reser-vations the others; they all follow a predictable basic text format that is bro-ken up into short factual descriptions along with many crisp, full-color photographs of the animal in various situations. The books have a layout similar to a textbook, but without the concept density and overwhelming number of pages. Each title maintains a tight focus enabling readers to delve into a topic without searching through dense volumes. In addition, the pic-tures are more numerous and are far richer in detail than you would gener-ally find in a standard science textbook. So, consider using the following three in addition to *The Whale.*

The Cheetah

Written and Photographed by Christine and Michel Denis-Huot
Translated by Randi Rivers
Charlesbridge 2002, 2004, ISBN 1–57091–626–8

The Dolphin: Prince of the Waves

Written by Renée Lebloas-Julienne
Photographs by the PHO.N.E Agency
Charlesbridge 2004, ISBN 1–57091–627–6

The Penguin: A Funny Bird

Written Beatrice Fontanel
Photographs by Andrâe Fatras
Translated by Elizabeth Uhlig
Charlesbridge 2004, ISBN 1–57091–628–4

Turtle in July

Written by Marilyn Stinger
Illustrated by Jerry Pinkney
Harcourt 1989, 1991, 1995, ISBN 0–153–05588–X

> *Turtle in July* is a wonderful book of poems that spotlights animals and their habits during the four seasons. The one constant is a poem about the Bullhead fish whose habitat is described in all the seasons. Other animals featured include the deer, the owl, and the deer mouse in winter. The spring poems feature the bear, a dog, and the warbler. In the summer poems, you hear about a cow, a turtle, and a dragonfly. Autumn poems describe the rattlesnake, the Canada goose, the beaver, and the cat. This one will appeal to animal lovers of all ages.

Walk with a Wolf (Read and Wonder Series)

Written by Janni Howker
Illustrated by Sarah Fox-Davies
Candlewick 1997, ISBN 0–7636–1872–1

> *Walk with a wolf in the cold air before sunrise. She moves, quiet as mist, between spruce trees and birches. A silent gray shadow, she slides between boulders and trots over blue pebbles to the edge of the lake.* Every page reads with this

same grace, gently informing the reader about the daily life of a wolf in the far north known as the Yukon Territory.

Whale Passing

Written by Eve Bunting
Illustrated by Lambert Davis
Blue Sky Press/Scholastic 2003, ISBN 0–590–60358–2

> Bunting is at her best as she skillfully tells the reader about the orca whales (killer whales) as observed by a young boy and his dad. As they observe the whales at play, their conversation provides the reader with many details about the patterns of the whales' lives. Midway through the book, Bunting shifts the point of view to that of the whales as they watch the young boy and his father watches them. The enlarged font makes this an especially appealing book to read to young children. Following the read-aloud, the illustrations deserve spending many moments of lingering with the mystery of the whales. A bonus feature is the Author's Note at the back of the book offering offers many additional facts about orca whales.

What Do You Do When Something Wants to Eat You?

Written and Illustrated by Steve Jenkins
Houghton Mifflin 1997, 2001, ISBN 0–618–15243–1

> In his distinctive style, Jenkins has created another remarkable book that belongs in your science collection. This terrific read-aloud will strengthen your resources for the study of animals. In the wild, animals have to do many things to avoid being eaten by their many predators. For example, *when an octopus is threatened, . . . it squirts a thick cloud of black ink into the water, confusing the attacker.* Another example: *The glass snake is really a lizard without legs. When it is grabbed by the tail . . . its tail breaks into many small, wriggling pieces.* This fascinating collection of information will engage readers and listeners as they enter into a study about animals.

Where Butterflies Grow

Written by Joanne Ryder
Illustrated by Lynne Cherry
Penguin 1989 (Puffin), 1996, ISBN 0–14–055858–6

> *This is a growing place*
> *Green and warm and bright.*

Lift up a leaf
and you may find
someone ready to be born.
Lift up a leaf
and imagine . . .

At Reba's school, Woodmeade Elementary, the second graders participate in a butterfly unit for which they watch the entire process this book describes so beautifully. Ryder explains the miracle of the butterfly's birth. Her crystal-clear words are enhanced by Cherry's extraordinary art. Don't miss this exceptional read-aloud to extend your science curriculum.

When Hunger Calls

Written and Illustrated by Bert Kitchen
Candlewick 1994, 1996, ISBN 1–56402–971–9

This startling book features twelve predatory animals and tells how they succeed at the very daunting task of obtaining food. Every page is revealing and sometimes shocking but will certainly grab the interest of children. Just to give you a sneak preview, one of the twelve animals featured is the African rock python. It can grow to be twenty feet long and is one of the biggest snakes in the world. The python can overpower and swallow a whole swift gazelle. When he is ready to strike, the African rock python must be fast enough to grab the gazelle with his jaws before wrapping his long body around the animal to squeeze it to death. The python's jaws unhitch and, using the elasticity of his throat, he is able to swallow a much bigger animal such as the gazelle. If you find this gross, well get ready because this is only one feature of this very fascinating book on animal behaviors. And this one is the third in a series (*Somewhere Today* and *And So They Build*) by Kitchen that focuses on animal behavior.

Whose House?

Written by Barbara Seuling
Illustrated by Kay Chorao
Gulliver/Harcourt 2004, ISBN 0–15–216347–6

Who would have ever thought you could teach science with such a wonderful read-aloud about a little boy who tries to imagine himself living in the same type home as all the animals he is reading about in a book? Well, this one shows us just how far books have come in making curriculum connections for children in such a pleasing way. The little boy discovers that beavers live in a lodge of twigs, while frogs live in a nice hollow log and, of course, both are fine for them *but not for me!* Each time the young boy reads about where the animals live, he imagines their homes and knows that is fine for them but not for him. The pattern of the text remains the same throughout the book until, at the end, he remembers all the reasons his house is just right for him. Don't miss this precious little book that teaches far more than science.

Wiggling Worms at Work

Written by Wendy Pfeffer
Illustrated by Steve Jenkins
HarperCollins 2004, ISBN 0–06–028448–X

If worms make you squeamish, you may get a bit of an upset stomach at the thought of what worms are doing in the soil. But, children will delight in this eyewitness account of a day in the life of a worm. The book is filled with information about the good things worms do for the soil. Children will be fascinated with this one because there is little text on each full-color spread. Jenkins' art completes the story in a simple collage style.

Will We Miss Them? Endangered Species

Written by Alexandra Wright
Illustrated by Marshall Peck III
Charlesbridge 1991, ISBN 0–88106–488–2

This is a science read-aloud you will not want to miss. The text was written when the author was only eleven years old, no kidding! That is enough to entice most students to take a look and check this one out. In addition, the artist's presentation of each of the endangered animals is a visual treat. Every full spread begins with the words *Will we miss the . . .* Then young Alexandra Wright provides you with many facts about the featured animals: the bald eagle, the African elephant, the blue whale, the panda, the Galapagos tortoise, the mountain lion, the whooping crane, the grizzly bear, the manatee, the muriqui, the rhinoceros, the mountain gorilla, and the crocodile. At the end of the double spreads about the animals, Wright shows an outline map to identify the natural habitat of all the featured animals.

Wonderful Worms

Written by Linda Glaser
Illustrated by Loretta Krupinski
Millbrook/Harcourt 1992, 1994, ISBN 1–562–94730–3

> *Earthworms are fat and wiggly like my fingers and toes. They live where it is cool and dark and damp, where roots spread out like underground trees.* Each page has only one sentence with illustrations filling the spread to extend and illuminate the sentence that describes another aspect of the world of a worm. The text is simple enough to use with young children who will find the subject fascinating.

In the Woods: Who's Been Here?

Written and Illustrated by Lindsay Barrett George
HarperTrophy 1995 (Scholastic), 1998, ISBN 0–688–16163–4

> As two children walk though the woods, they find various natural habitats and wonder who lives in them. When you turn the page, you find out. *They walk under an old cherry tree. They see an empty nest. Who's been here?* (turn page) *A northern oriole.* This book is another resource for the study of animals and their habitats.

■ *Earth Science*

Landforms

The Forest in the Clouds

Written by Sneed B. Collard III
Illustrated by Michael Rochman
Charlesbridge 2000, ISBN 0–88106–986–8

> After reading this book about a tropical forest high up in the mountains of Costa Rica, we became fascinated with its existence and wanted to learn how the ecosystem there is being threatened. In fact, Collard tells us this cloud-filled landform is the most threatened area on Earth. The detailed artwork of Rochman visually depicts the story as it unfolds page by page. You will meet animals you've never heard of that make their homes in the mountains. A glossary at the back will help you understand this unique environment. This

is one for your science shelf that you don't want to miss. You can launch an extensive study of caring for the Earth and protecting our environment by reading this one.

At Home in the Tide Pool

Written by Alexandra Wright
Illustrated by Marshall Peck III
Charlesbridge 1993, ISBN 0–88106–482–3

> If you aren't sure what a tide pool is or where to locate one, then this little book will clarify any misunderstandings on the very first page. A tide pool is formed along the seashore among the rocks by water left behind following a high tide. It usually exists until the tide comes in again to wash it out to sea. Within it is an ecosystem that is brimming with life. This picture book examines life in the tide pool and provides outstanding illustrations. An interesting tidbit for students—this text was written when the author was only thirteen years old.

Our Natural Homes

Written by Sneed B. Collard III
Illustrated by James M. Needham
Charlesbridge 1996, ISBN 0–88106–928–0

> From the tundra to the tropical rain forest, Collard takes readers on an adventure exploring each of the biomes of the Earth to discover which one we live in. Every spread investigates one of the biomes with a description of the land, the plants found there, and many of the animals that call that area home. A large map will make this book even more meaningful for a science study. Each page brings a new land area and a new set of questions to pursue.

The Seashore Book

Written by Charlotte Zolotow
Illustrated by Wendell Minor
HarperTrophy 1992, 1994, ISBN 0–06–443364–1

> A young boy wonders what the seashore is like because he lives in the mountains and has never experienced the joys of walking along the sand and finding the treasures left by the ocean. So his mom tells a story while they

pretend to be there alongside the gulls scooping up shell after shell. This one has such beautiful language you might choose to read it simply because you want the words floating and drifting through the air. But it should also be read when your class is studying the ocean. And as a bonus, Wendell Minor's sumptuous art will have you feeling the sand between your toes in no time.

Tundra Discoveries

Written by Ginger Wadsworth
Illustrated by John Carrozza
Charlesbridge 1999, ISBN 0–88106–876–4

This insightful book features the life of thirteen animals living at the northern tip of the world. Carrozza adds dimension to the language by putting a thermometer on every page to show the reader the average temperature during the month being featured. Opposite the thermometer is a calendar that shows the number of daylight hours for that season. In addition, each page poses a simple math problem that can be solved by counting the animals of the tundra. The book is filled with facts to extend a study.

Why Do Volcanoes Blow Their Tops?: Questions and Answers About Volcanoes and Earthquakes

Written by Melvin and Gilda Berger
Illustrated by Higgins Bond
Scholastic 1999, ISBN 0–439–14878–2

This is not a book you would want to read aloud for enjoyment. It is, however, one to read in sections as you build background and interest in the topic. This title is one of a series of question-and-answer books that we have found to be an outstanding resource for any library. Every section is short with a photo to expand understanding. The authors present, in a very concise manner, at lot of information about what causes a volcano to erupt. The following are the others in the series.

> *Can It Rain Cats and Dogs?*
> *Can You Hear a Shout in Space?*
> *Did Dinosaurs Live in Your Backyard?*
> *Do All Spiders Spin Webs?*
> *Do Stars Have Points?*
> *Do Tarantulas Have Teeth?*
> *Do Tornadoes Really Twist?*

Do Whales Have Belly Buttons?
How Do Flies Walk Upside Down?
What Makes an Ocean Wave?
Why Don't Haircuts Hurt?

Water Forms

Atlantic

Written and Illustrated by G. Brian Karas

G. P. Putnam's Sons 2002, ISBN 0–399–23632–5

If you are about to introduce young students to the continents and oceans, you need to find this book. It is so clever in the way it explains the power and ever-changing state of the mighty Atlantic Ocean. The illustrations are playful yet do not detract from the facts embedded within the pages. The text is short, which makes it very appealing for children. To make the book even more attractive as a read-aloud, Karas changes the text structure often throughout the book: at times it looks like a poem; sometimes you find only one sentence on a page; and for one spread, the playfulness of the text follows the shape of the waves.

The Deep-Sea Floor

Written by Sneed B. Collard III
Illustrated by Gregory Wenzel

Charlesbridge 2003, ISBN 1–57091–402–8

With crisp descriptions and simple sketches, this one provides a study to show children how the bottom of the ocean floor looks. Key words appear in bold print much the same as in a textbook. But that's where the similarities end. The book is very child-friendly, offering detailed information without overtaxing its intended audience. The pages that offer you vivid pictures of the sea life found on the very bottom of the ocean. Finally, the last pages provide readers with images and information about the many pieces of equipment used by scientists to explore and study the ocean floor. The book also has a glossary at the back.

Into the Sea

Written by Brenda Z. Guiberson
Illustrated by Alix Berenzy

Henry Holt 1996, 2000, ISBN 0–8050–6481–8

Tap, tap. Scritch. begins the story of how the tiny sea turtle, only the size of a bottle cap, begins the journey from the safety of her nest across the sandy beach to be carried out to sea by the waves. If you are studying sea life, this is a must-read. It gives you the complete life cycle of the sea turtle in a narrative text that entertains and informs. In addition, Guiberson provides an Author's Note that will help readers build background information. Berenzy's art is exceptional, providing another layer to the telling of the story. Read this along with *One Tiny Turtle* by Nicola Davies.

The Mighty Mississippi: The Life and Times of America's Greatest River

Written by Linda Vieira
Illustrated by Higgins Bond
Walker Books 2005, ISBN 0–8027–8943–9

With marvelous drawings that extend the meaning of the text, you won't know whether to use it in science or social studies. We suggest both! Not only do the story and illustrations show the reader how the river was formed, they also explain the history of all the people who lived and explored the river thousands of years before the Europeans settled in the region. The book is fascinating for adults and children, so don't hesitate to use it with all ages. The text is rather lengthy and contains many facts that will take you off into another direction of study; therefore settle in for a period of time to preview so that you can make this one a treasure for students.

Mississippi

Written by Diane Siebert
Illustrated by Greg Harlin
HarperCollins 2001, ISBN 0–688–16445–5

I am the river, deep and strong. I sing an old, enduring song with rhythms wild and rhythms tame, and Mississippi is my name. Siebert is well known for her use of personification to tell the story of landforms and regions and other natural features. In this one, she writes in the voice of the mighty Mississippi River. Readers begin with the river telling of its origin from melting glacial waters and travel through thousands of years and across miles and miles, existing alongside the changes brought by the presence of humans and technology and war and industry and pollution and more. As readers, we hear the river tell how the first Native Americans lived on her banks and ate from her bounty. We move along with the river into the era when European settlers moved to her banks for the fertile soil that produced large harvests. Decades later, we watch as steel bridges cross the breast of the river to join one side of the country to the other. We travel with the mighty river as she flows around bends to rush toward the Gulf of Mexico where she empties. *I am the river, wide and deep, whose restless waters never sleep. And as I move with currents strong, I sing an old, enduring song, with rhythms wild and rhythms tame, and Mississippi is my name.*

Our Wet World

Written by Sneed B. Collard III
Illustrated by James M. Needham
Charlesbridge 1998, ISBN 0–88106–268–5

The opening page alone is worth the price of this wonderful read-aloud, but don't stop there. Every page is a new adventure and is filled with information waiting for the reader to discover and question and delve into. Readers will leave this one buzzing with questions to their friends in other classes: Did you know that our bodies are made up of 70 percent water and that we need two quarts of water every day to survive? Had you thought about the fact that all living plants and animals need water to survive? This book invites students to put on a snorkel and dive right in to investigate other ecosystems in the watery world. The pages are visually stimulating and explore another water world with short snippets of interesting facts about each. The text is in tight, very reader-friendly little boxes on each page.

Out of the Ocean

Written and Illustrated by Debra Frasier
Voyager/Harcourt 1998, 2002, ISBN 0–15–216354–9

Oh my, if you love the ocean as much as we do, you must own this book. Frasier is at the top of her game as she takes the reader on a walk along the sandy beach to discover all the treasures left behind by the ocean's tide. Her art is distinctive because she uses photographs embedded in collages. Those who decide to join her on this stroll along the shore can't wait to turn the page to see what treat Frasier will have for them next. At the end of this lovely book are six pages of very informative text about the many treasures that can be found on the beach. Oh, and the endpapers are breathtaking.

River Discoveries

Written by Ginger Wadsworth
Illustrated by Paul Kratter
Charlesbridge 2002, ISBN 1–57091–419–2

> *Water from rain and melting snow runs over rocks and down tiny gullies high*
> *in the mountains. These little streams join together to form a river . . . the river*
> *widens and slowly winds across open lands. Streams and other rivers flow into*
> *the main river. . . . Hundreds of miles later, it empties into a lake or ocean.*
> Wadsworth's words pull the reader, like the current of flowing water, into
> discovering life on and around a river. She uses the clock to move the story
> along, beginning with early morning when the moose comes to graze along
> the banks, then on to the raccoon who comes out only at night to fish for
> tadpoles, crayfish, or other slow-moving fish. As readers move along with the
> author, they discover thirteen different animals that depend on the river for
> sustenance. Wadsworth provides a one-page description of each animal.

A River Ran Wild

Written and Illustrated by Lynne Cherry
Voyager/Harcourt 1992 (Gulliver), 2002, ISBN 0–15–216372–7

> Always devoted to environmental issues, Cherry provides another outstand-
> ing read-aloud that could as easily be used in a social studies unit as in a sci-
> ence unit. The story begins many years ago (six centuries) when the Nashua
> River in Massachusetts ran wild and was free of pollution. It was a time
> when fish and wildlife roamed in a healthy environment and the river left the
> ground surrounding its banks full of fertile soil. The history of the river re-
> gion is traced through its settlement by Native Americans to the English set-
> tlers and finally to the era of factories built directly along the river. With the
> building of the factories, the water became so polluted that animals could no
> longer live near the river. This book is a powerful look at what many people
> call "progress" while others point out how natural resources have been dam-
> aged and destroyed.

River Story

Written by Meredith Hooper
Illustrated by Bee Willey
Candlewick 2000, ISBN 0–7636–0792–4

This lyrical text informs readers about rivers while filling their ears with beautiful language. The book begins on the front flap with a brief list of facts about rivers nestled in a watercolor illustration. The text describes how rivers are formed high up in the mountains from puddles of melted snow before flowing into small streams, eventually being fed by other streams before joining together to create the racing river. Willey's art is truly a masterpiece and worth the price of the book; when coupled with the information provided by Hooper, it is a definite keeper.

A Sea Within a Sea: Secrets of the Sargasso

Written and Illustrated by Ruth Heller
Grosset & Dunlap 2000, ISBN 0–448–42417–7

Have you ever heard about the sea that lies in the middle of the Atlantic Ocean? The *sea within a sea in the northern cold Atlantic that is as warm as tepid tea?* The sea that has an abundance of seaweed that blankets the surface and a mysterious calmness that causes *ships to become becalmed and then disappear.* Heller weaves a story that combines fact with fantasy to bring readers this astonishingly beautiful book that will interest even the most reluctant scientists. If you are familiar with Heller's work, you won't be disappointed in this one because in it she even weaves science into her characteristic poetry. Read this one aloud and launch an inquiry into separating fact from fantasy.

Plants

Dandelions

Written by Eve Bunting
Illustrated by Greg Shed
Voyager/Harcourt 1995, 2001, ISBN 0–15–200407–7

Dandelions could be placed on our Curriculum Connection Bookshelf, and it could just as easily be placed on the Family Bookshelf because of the strong story about a young family who travels by wagon during the Westward Movement. But we chose to place it in this section to honor people who have shown so much commitment to making the world a better place by tending the soil. When this one is pulled out, it will take many weeks before it finds its way back to the shelf. Children are just mesmerized by it. All of us who are accustomed to dandelions will find this book's theme amusing, plus it simply helps us to better understand the period of time in which Zoe and her family lived. Shed's art on canvas gives a texture to the pictures that makes the book even more engaging.

Down to Earth: Garden Secrets! Garden Stories! Garden Projects You Can Do!

Created by Michael J. Rosen with 41 children's book authors and illustrators
Harcourt 1998, ISBN 0–15–201341–5

Forty-one of the world's best-known authors and illustrators share stories of remembrances about gardening. Sometimes the stories are about parents or others who made an impression with their love of making things grow. This book is special because it gives readers insights into the thoughts, memories, and feelings of our most beloved authors and illustrators. In addition, there is stunning art on every page that nestles in with those memories. This book could have been placed on any number of shelves; for example, it would be great to use during an Author Study or when beginning a study of plants. The Author' s Note at the back tells of the mission of Share Our Strength— an organization formed to help raise money to feed communities through-out the world.

Flower Garden

Written by Eve Bunting
Illustrated by Kathryn Hewitt
Voyager/Harcourt 1994, 2000, ISBN 0–15–202372–0

This is another book that is so beautiful you must take children for a slow walk through the gorgeous pages of art before putting the language in the air. The words are equally delightful, taking the reader along to shop with a little girl who is buying a tray of potted plants to make a flower garden in a window box. Once the plants are bought and carried home, the little girl and her dad plant them for her mother's birthday present. The text is short with enlarged font that helps make this one a must-read for young children.

The Growing Up Tree

Written and Illustrated by Vera Rosenberry
Holiday House 2003, ISBN 0–8234–1718–2

With a similar focus on the relationship between a boy and a tree, *The Growing Up Tree* reminds us of Shel Siverstein's *The Giving Tree*. However, this one shows the complete life cycle of both the tree and the boy. The tree is planted by the boy's mother when he is just a baby. As the story unfolds, readers witness the boy and the tree growing old together. This one is sure to be a favorite. The text is short with a playful font. Every colorful page contains only a few sentences, which makes it an easy read-aloud for young children.

Miss Rumphius

Written and Illustrated by Barbara Cooney
Puffin 1982 (Viking), 1985, ISBN 0–14–050539–3

Miss Rumphius is the neighbor we all need for our classroom communities. She grew up wanting to travel and see the sights of the faraway world and to live by the sea. Her grandfather told her that there was a third thing she must do—make the world more beautiful. As a grown-up, she did both of the things she had longed to do but the thing her grandfather wanted of her, left her puzzled. What could she do to make the world a better place? Read to discover how she, like Johnny Appleseed, answered that question. Share this one with your budding community and perhaps a caring project will sprout from the ensuing conversations.

The Moonflower

Written by Peter Loewer
Illustrated by Jean Loewer
Peachtree 1997, ISBN 1–56145–138–X

The back cover offers a lovely way to introduce this book: *When the sun sets and the moon glows bright, the night comes alive with all sorts of wonderful creatures. And at the center of this mysterious world, the night-blooming moonflower twines its way toward the sky.* Each page of this beautifully written book will provide a description of the after-sunset activity of various plants and insects and animals. *When the sun has set in the west . . . but the sky is still too bright for most stars to shine, the buds on the moonflower vine are closed tight. A bumblebee that cannot find the way to his underground home curls up in a flower to wait for dawn.* Included on the right edge of each spread is a sidebar that provides additional information about the insect, animal, or plant discussed (bumblebee, bats, fireflies, moonflower, moths, owl, pollen, and other nocturnal animals). For an added treat, at the back of the book, the author provides information about how to plant and take care of a moonflower. The art perfectly extends this science text offering a visual depiction of each insect, animal, or plant mentioned in the language.

A Packet of Seeds

Written by Deborah Hopkinson
Illustration by Bethanne Andersen
Greenwillow/HarperCollins 2004, 0–06–009090–1

> This is the story of one of the hardships experienced by one early pioneer family who left all that was safe and familiar to move West in hopes of a better life. Momma was so homesick that when she has a baby, she is too depressed to name the baby girl. Little Anne's heart is weighed down by her Momma's depression and she wants desperately to help. When she remembers how much Momma loved her garden back home, she sets out with the help of her young brother to cut through the sod to dig her Momma a garden. This is a heartwarming story of what love can mean in a family even in the harshest of times. Every page has full-color art with the words framed in a text box. Andersen chose to use very soft colors to set the tone for this tender story of love.

Pick, Pull, Snap!: Where Once a Flower Bloomed

Written by Lola M. Schaefer
Illustrated by Lindsay Barrett George
Greenwillow 2003, ISBN 0–688–17834–0

> Here is another one you need to take a picture walk through before reading because it offers an art gallery with the turn of every page. All the full-page art folds out to provide even greater detail for close-up study. The book is truly delightful. Don't worry though; Schaefer's language is the music for the pictures. She has crafted a remarkable story about the cycle of seeds that become flowers and produce even more seeds. Throughout the book, she follows a single pattern to introduce a variety of different plants and seeds. Be sure to read the opening flap because it is significant to the pattern. This one belongs in your hands when you begin a unit about plants.

The Reason for a Flower

Written and Illustrated by Ruth Heller
PaperStar/Putnam 1983 (Grosset & Dunlap), 1999, ISBN 0–698–11559–7

All of us are fascinated by how flowers are pollinated by bees, butterflies, wind, and birds. Heller shows readers how this occurs, then she moves into all the parts of the flower with very simple text. This one is beautiful to look at, but don't let the art fool you into thinking the combination of image and very short sentences is not a teaching text. This one belongs on your shelf if you're teaching about flowers.

Seeds

Writing and Photographs by Ken Robbins
Atheneum 2005, ISBN 0–689–85041–7

If your curriculum calls for a study of plants, this one is too good to miss with its crisp photographs and very short explanations. Not only does it inform children about what a seed needs to grow, but it also presents various kinds of seeds. While some of the seeds will be very familiar to most children, there will be a few new discoveries for them to make.

The Story of Johnny Appleseed

Written and Illustrated by Aliki
Aladdin 1963, 1971, ISBN 0–671–66746–7

Making the world a better place must include a story about Johnny Appleseed—that is, John Chapman, a frontiersman from Massachusetts. There are many versions of this story, so choose one and enjoy; this one is told by Aliki. Throughout his life, John went around the countryside with a large sack on his back filled with apple seeds. During his journeys across America, he sometimes stayed in an area for weeks at a time to help the pioneers settle the land. Wherever he went, he always planted apple seeds. However, his mission did not keep him in one place very long. Johnny made friends everywhere he traveled. He worked for peace between the Native Americans and the pioneers.

Tops and Bottoms

Adapted and Illustrated by Janet Stevens
Harcourt 1995, ISBN 0–15–292851–0

On the front flap, Stevens tells readers that this tale was blended from European folktales and stories from the time of slavery in the American South. While this gives you the history for the story, you may be wondering why we would choose to put a fiction story in with nonfiction books. The answer is simple: It is too good to miss as an introduction to a study of plants. In story form, the book provides readers with an exceptional and entertaining introduction for a plants unit. A short recap of the tale reveals a clever, yet poor, Hare who lives near a lazy, yet rich, Bear. Hare offers to provide all the labor to produce food for both of them from a garden they will share. One reading will lead to an understanding of plants that produce edible products above the ground in contrast to those that produce food below the ground (i.e., tops and bottoms).

Rain Forest

Here Is the Tropical Rain Forest

Written by Madeleine Dunphy
Illustrated by Michael Rothman
Hyperion 1994, 1997, ISBN 0–7868–1212–5

This book belongs on many of our shelves—beautiful language, curriculum connection, and supporting the writing workshop. And, if we had a shelf for luscious art, this one would belong there as well. The diversity of the rain forest is described in this cumulative story. You will love the language and the information it imparts about the inextricable links that exist between life in the rain forest, the health of the world's environment, medicines, and more. The Author's Note at the back provides additional facts. There is also a contact for even more information about the endangered rain forest with its abundant species that are doomed to extinction if human activities do not stop there.

At Home in the Rain Forest

Written by Diane Willow
Illustrated by Laura Jacques
Charlesbridge 1991, 1992, ISBN 0–88106–484–X

This text is so lush and full of information about life in the rain forest that you will want to spend more than one read-aloud session with it. The book simply has too much for one sitting even though the text is relatively short. Many of the full-page illustrations are labeled, which makes the book even more helpful to build background understanding of this valuable resource of the world.

The Living Rain Forest: An Animal Alphabet

Written and Illustrated by Paul Kratter
Charlesbridge 2004, ISBN 1–57091–603–9

> The introduction to the book gives a brief background of how the rain forest is being threatened every day by the people of the earth. *In the past 200 years, we've lost over half of the earth's rain forests.* With this loss, *many animals have become extinct.* This treasure of a read-aloud will provide children with a visit into the vast and beautiful world they must grow to respect and help to protect. Every spread follows the same pattern. The left page, proceeding in alphabetical order, gives a brief description of the animal; the opposite page offers the reader a delightful picture of the animal along with its scientific name and size. If the description gives unusual words, the definition of them is generally below the text.

Red-Eyed Tree Frog

Written by Joy Cowley
Photographs by Nic Bishop
Scholastic 1999, ISBN 0–590–87175–7

> In the rain forest, the red-eyed tree frog sleeps all day and travels at night in search of food. During this search, he has to be very careful not to become food himself for the various animals he encounters. The text is very short and focused. The photographs alone are worth the price of the book.

Welcome to the Green House

Written by Jane Yolen
Illustrated by Laura Regan
PaperStar/Putnam & Grosset 1993, 1998, ISBN 0–698–11445–0

> Don't let the charming way Yolen leads you into these pages make you to think this one is just a poetic narrative. Every powerful sentence is woven together to tell the reader the story of the rain forest, and it is loaded with fact after fact. Together with the very green illustrations you have a perfect read-aloud to support a study of the mysterious rain forest.

Trees and Forests

A Grand Old Tree

Written and Illustrated by Mary Newell DePalma

Arthur A. Levine 2005, ISBN 0–439–62334–0

> This is a "grand old book" for the beginning of a plant unit. Written in very simple phrases that will appeal to even the youngest children, the book tells about the life cycle of the tree through the many seasons of its life. From the front flap, the flavor of this delightful book reads: *This is the tale of a grand old tree, whose roots ran deep, and whose arms reached high. For years and years she flowered and spread. She grew and shed many millions of leaves. And her children grew tall beside her.*

Sky Tree (Seeing Science Through Art Series)

Written and Illustrated by Thomas Locker

HarperCollins 1995, ISBN 0–06–024883–1

> Locker takes us on a tour of the seasons and the effects those seasons have on a single tree. He provides a rare perspective as he paints the tree and the sky that both complements and frames the changing seasons. As adults, we found the perspective to be unparalleled. If you are familiar with Locker's work, you know how spectacular his art is; this book will live up to your every expectation.

Seasons

Arctic Lights / Arctic Nights

Written by Debbie S. Miller

Illustrated by Jon Van Zyle

Walker Books 2003, ISBN 0–8027–8856–4

> This book helps to explain how the amount of light varies significantly with each of the seasons in the vast areas in the state of Alaska. From the introduction, you learn that there are regions that experience continuous light in the summer for eighty-four days. Yet, in the winter, the same regions experience no light for more than sixty days. This book is a great way to introduce seasons and to explore how the Earth's tilt and rotation impact exposure to

the sun. In addition, running across the top of every page are facts about the time of sunrise and sunset along with the average temperature for the day. This text will deepen everyone's understanding of life in our forty-ninth state.

The First Day of Winter

Written and Illustrated by Denise Fleming
Henry Holt 2005, ISBN 0–8050–7384–1

With repetitive text that reflects the structure of *On the first day of Christmas my true love gave to me,* Fleming has gifted young children with a text that will make you long for a red wool cap and mittens. The snowy pages are fluffy with new snow as the snowman is built article after article. First comes the *red cap with a gold snap,* next comes *the bright blue mittens.* While you are filling the air with the carefully chosen words, let Fleming pack into the little ears of children additional practice on the sequence of numbers . . . *first, second, third, fourth, fifth, sixth, seventh, etc.* On the last page, you will find the completed snowman in all the splendor of a well-dressed piece of art!

Here Comes the Year

Written by Eileen Spinelli
Illustrated by Keiko Narahashi
Henry Holt 2002, ISBN 0–8050–6685–3

I am the January dark,
dappled and deep,
teasing you, easing you
out of your cuddle-down sleep,
announcing it's morning,
having a bit of fun
staying up way past my bedtime,
replacing the sun.

Spinelli and Narahashi have teamed up to provide a read-aloud that features rich descriptions and soft watercolors for each of the twelve months. On every spread there is one lovely sentence in beautiful poetic language to usher in each month. Read this one with poetry or read it with curriculum, or even read it with beautiful language—just be sure to read it aloud and let the music fill the space you share with children.

The Months of School

Written by Margie Sigman
Photograph (see credits at the back)
Harcourt 2005, ISBN 0–15–340896–0

> The opening spread shows the four seasons in spectacular color. Every spread describes the months in order from September through June. When the month is named, a short description of associated activities and clothing follows. This one is a simple, yet wonderful addition to your bookshelf for when you are working with primary children.

The Shortest Day: Celebrating the Winter Solstice

Written by Wendy Pfeffer
Illustrated by Jesse Reisch
Dutton 2003, ISBN 0–525–46968–0

> When we said earlier that picture books are available to teach every concept you must teach, we weren't kidding. Here is an outstanding one that explains so well why the days grow shorter during the winter. The concept is so comfortably discussed that we wouldn't hesitate to read it with children in any grade level for which the study of weather is in the curriculum. Reisch's art makes such wonderful use of color that children will delight in a simple picture walk through the pages before you begin to read.

 *Weather*

Cloud Dance

Written and Illustrated by Thomas Locker
Voyager/Harcourt 2000, 2003, ISBN 0–15–204596–1

> The next time you are ready to begin a study of clouds and cloud formations you will definitely want a copy of this book in your possession. Locker gifts us with an astonishingly beautiful book that combines his art and poetic language in a tightly focused exploration of clouds. The sumptuous art falls across the spread, working from a one-sentence description. As an added bonus, Candace Christiansen provides a spread with very interesting information and a page of labeled clouds.

Hurricane!

Written by Jonathan London
Illustrated by Henri Sorensen
HarperCollins 1998, ISBN 0–688–12977–3

> Children won't believe it's science class when you read Jonathan London's account of the time a hurricane hit his family's home in Puerto Rico. When he and his brother came up from snorkeling, the sky had already become dark and threatening. Throughout the remainder of the pages, London does an exceptional job of describing the feel, the sounds, and the sights of living through a hurricane. Sorensen's art perfectly reflects the text and makes you "feel" the ominous weather.

I Call It Sky

Written by Will C. Howell
Illustrated by John Ward
Walker & Company 1999, ISBN 0–8027–8677–4

> This book on the atmosphere reads almost like a poem; it is so descriptive and beautifully written. Howell's ability to weave a story around a concept like air will enchant readers while making them aware of our dependence on the atmosphere. His words inform us that while air is everywhere, it reacts differently at times and changes with the seasons. Ward does an equally fine job with the illustrations making this one very appealing.

It Is the Wind

Written by Ferida Wolff
Illustrated by James Ransome
HarperCollins 2005, ISBN 0–06–028191–X

> A little boy is awakened during the night by a sound that shakes him. He begins to question what it could be . . . an owl who whispers *hooo,* the dog who howls *oooh,* the gate that creaks on its hinges with a *groan,* the swing that sways and clunks in the wind; maybe it is the calf who calls out *waaah,* or the toad that splashes in the pond; maybe it's the cat in the woods who hollers *yeeow;* or just maybe it could be the hare that thumps and bumps with each jump. No, it is the bugs that stir and crick and the sheets that rustle, swish, and twish in the wind. Finally, he decides that it is only the wind that

is sighing *good night* to him right there in his room. The language is wonderful and the pattern is predictable; the discussion that can follow about the power of the wind is only the beginning of the connections you can make.

Weather Forecasting

Written and Illustrated by Gail Gibbons
Aladdin 1987, 1993, ISBN 0–689–71683–4

Most children, well most of us for that matter, have grown up turning to the weathercaster on the radio or television to find out what the weather might be for the day. This interesting work of nonfiction will take readers into a weather station and explain how forecasters do their work to keep the rest of us informed. As with each of her books, Gibbons writes in language that is informative and factual without being overwhelming. Consistent with the style we have come to expect from her, illustrations are labeled and support every page of information.

■ *Space Science*

The Universe with Its Planets

Destination: Mars

Written by Seymour Simon
Photographs from various US observatories
HarperTrophy 2000, 2004, ISBN 0–06–054638–7

With incredible photographs to support every page of information on Mars, Simon does a fine job of describing everything that is known about the red planet, from its history to what life is like on its surface. If your curriculum includes a study of the planets, consider using this author because he has one on all of them. Each book is well-written and the photographs are exceptional. (In case you need the photo credits: Richard Dreiser, The Yerkes Observatory; National Space Science Data Center; The Mars Global Surveyor Project; The Planetary Data System; Malin Space Science Systems/NASA; and the Jet Propulsion Laboratory.)

Earth: Our Planet in Space

Written by Seymour Simon
Photographs from NASA and Chris Van Hans
Simon & Schuster 1984, 2003, ISBN 0–689–83562–0

> *You live on Earth. You may live in a city or in the country. You may live where snow falls or where it never snows at all. But wherever you call home, you live on Earth.* With these words, Simon brings into your classroom a fresh look at planet Earth. Along with well-crafted language, the photographs are truly outstanding. The book is well worth your time as you begin a unit of study. (*See also The Moon and Our Solar System by Simon.*)

Footprints on the Moon

Written by and photographs collected by Alexandra Siy
Charlesbridge 2001, ISBN 1–57091–409–5

> Twelve men have left footprints on the moon and this is their story. How did those men get there? Why did they go? What did they hope to accomplish? This book explores the first studies of the moon as well as early space travel. Siy collected numerous pictures that help to tell the story of getting those twelve men to the moon and home again. Midway through the book, you will find the words and pictures made by Michael Collins of Armstrong's and Aldrin's walks on the moon. His words are powerful and the photographs are memorable. This book may take several days to complete if you choose to present the entire text; perhaps you'll want to feature only special sections, such as the one just mentioned, to support a curriculum connection. Either way, this one will be an added resource in any classroom collection.

Living in Space

Written by Katie Daynes
Illustrated by Christyan Fox and Alex Pang
Usborne Books 2003, ISBN 0–794–50301–2

> Young children will be fascinated with this minitextbook about what happens to astronauts when they go into space. With very simple straightforward language, the book explains gravity, what training is required to become an astronaut, and how astronauts spend time in space. Daynes does an amazing job of getting a lot of information into such a condensed format.

Night Wonders

Written and Illustrated by Jane Ann Peddicord
Charlesbridge 2005, ISBN 1–57091–878–3

> *Beside a dark and quiet sea*
> *Beneath a starlit canopy,*
> *I shone my light upon a star*
> *And wondered, What is out that far?*
> *Ascending high across the sky*
> *As if inviting me to fly,*
> *The light escaped the Earth's embrace*
> *And soared away through open space.*

With this lead, you may be wondering whether this can truly be a nonfiction book. Let us assure you that it is. Each spread offers a rich description of one aspect of the universe (e.g., stars, moon, sun, planets, Milky Way, nebulae, galaxy). Peddicord has two texts running on each page. The prominent part reads almost as poetry and the second, in smaller print at the bottom of the page, is a set of interesting facts about the topic. The opposite page presents a full-page, outstanding illustration of the topic. If this topic is needed for your curriculum, you won't go wrong with this book.

Saturn

Written by Larry Dane Brimner
Photographs by Corbis-Bettmann, Finley Holiday Films, NASA, Cassini/Huygens, Jet Propulsion Laboratory
Photo research by Lynette Cook and The Planetary System
Children's Press/Grolier 1999, ISBN 0–516–26501–6

Brimner has given us books in a series about the planets that look like mini-textbooks for younger readers. This one has a table of contents, an index, a vocabulary list, and wonderful resources for further research at the back.

Starry Skies: Questions, Facts & Riddles About the Universe

Written by Mike Artell
Photographs from various sources (see credits on copyright page)
Good Year Books 1997, ISBN 0–673–36350–3

Your children will adore this book, and once it has been introduced, you won't find it on your shelf again. It contains facts in a colorful cartoon on one page and a realistic photograph on the next. There are riddles, jokes, and tongue twisters right alongside facts. Artell even provides pictures of the planets that can be cut out and made into a mobile for your classroom. This single book could serve as a textbook for the study of the universe. Don't miss it!

The Sun Is My Favorite Star

Written and Illustrated by Frank Asch
Gulliver/Harcourt 2000, ISBN 0–15–202127–2

We have grown to expect a certain kind of text from Frank Asch, and he has not let us down with this charming one about the sun. He has magnificently slipped an abundance of information into a narrative that can and should be used with small children. With limited words on every page, he lets the child tell you the role the sun has in life on Earth. From waking you up with its light and drying up the morning dew, the sun stays busy all day as it follows children everywhere. But sometimes the sun goes away for a day, but it always comes back with a big bouquet . . . a rainbow. What a treat for young readers.

Sun, Moon and Stars

Written by Stephanie Turnbull
Illustrated by Kuo Kang Chen and Uwe Mayer
Usborne Books 2003, ISBN 0–794–50485–X

This lovely little book is part of a series written for young children that will be an excellent resource for a study of the universe. The format is very friendly, with an enlarged font with small snippets of information on every page. Turnbull places well-crafted pieces of news there too to make the information easy for children to relate to: *The Moon looks small, but it would take about four days to drive all the way around it.* The series has books for all the areas of a school's science program.

Notes of Interest About Three Authors' Books for the Science Classroom

Gail Gibbons has written dozens and dozens of books that range from earth science to life science to space science. The format for her nonfiction books is meant for younger students, but they also provides information that older readers will find appealing. Each of her books illustrates the importance of labeling. By the way, Gail does all her artwork.

Jerry Pallotta, the prolific "alphabet man," has produced many excellent resources to spice up a study of earth and life sciences in the classroom. While following the structure of the alphabet, Jerry packs a lot of information into each twenty-six-page picture book. The tone is entertaining and he often finds ways to surprise readers; all ages will adore his books. The illustrators often embed additional surprises into the artwork.

Seymour Simon has written more than 150 award-winning books to support the science curriculum. Each one is a minitextbook with incredibly stunning pictures and outstanding writing. His books address concepts in each of the three science areas: earth, life, and space.

4

Picture Books and Read-Alouds to Support the Social Studies Curriculum

THROUGHOUT HISTORY, story has been one of the primary means of passing all that is important to families and communities and cultures from one generation to the next. Story has helped us develop a sense of who we are and where we come from. Story has helped us come to know ourselves in relation to others. It has been through story that we begin to understand times past and begin to shape our hopes for the future. The social studies curriculum is rich with opportunities to mine the treasures in literature; story is therefore a natural vehicle in this rich and robust curriculum.

The collection of books presented in this chapter includes many stories—ones about people, places, and events that made history. There are stories that lead us to pause and reflect on events of the past. There are stories about moments so near to the present that we can hardly take them in. And there are stories that cause us to look to the future and say, "I can make a difference. I can be like that. I can."

The National Council for the Social Studies (NCSS) has delineated ten thematic strands that form the basis of the social studies standards. These broad strands have helped to shape, though have not limited, our search for titles to include in this chapter. We hope you will take the time to visit the website of the NCSS at www.socialstudies.org/standards/strands for a more in-depth look at the strands.

Books in this collection have been organized into sets by broad topics and then subdivided into smaller sets by categories that we are calling bookshelves. Each bookshelf is presented in alphabetical order, but the titles on any shelf can be easily organized into a text set, as described in the introduction to this book. Each collection can be used to introduce, extend, or enrich a unit of study.

Every bookshelf can also be the foundation for a close study of related novels. For example, the bookshelves making up the collection on civil rights could form a foundation—vocabulary, concept, image—for a study of novels such as *Roll of Thunder, Hear My Cry; The Well; Mississippi Bridge;* or *The Watson's Go to Birmingham, 1963.* So, as you peruse our shelves, we hope you will be thinking of the connections you could make to your units of study and to the bridges you could build across the curriculum with these picture books and selected opportunities for read aloud in the social studies class.

■ *Building Background for a Study of Civil Rights*

For this section, we selected a few books on each of several topics to create "starter sets" that can help launch different studies. We hope that you will consider each of the sets as a beginning point and that you will continue adding to each of them as you make read-alouds a vital part of the curriculum areas across the day. The books in this particular collection are intended to extend those presented in our companion book, *Learning Under the Influence of Language and Literature: Making the Most of Read-Alouds Across the Day* (2006).

Civil Rights Bookshelf One: In the Time of Slavery

Christmas in the Big House, Christmas in the Quarters
Written by Patricia C. McKissack and Fredrick L. McKissack
Illustrated by John Thompson
Scholastic 1994, ISBN 0–590–43028–9

The McKissacks provide the stark contrast between the events of "Big Times" (Christmas) in the plantation owner's big house and those of the slaves who lived in the quarters. The hauntingly beautiful language richly describes the traditions and scenes of the holidays in the mid-1800s. This is not a one sitting read-aloud so plan for a few installments. Take your time and savor the beautiful art that so aptly brings the story alive.

Lest We Forget: The Passage from Africa to Slavery and Emancipation

Written by Velma Maia Thomas
Crown 1997, ISBN 0–609–60030–3

> This is a three-dimensional book containing photographs and documents from the Black Holocaust Exhibit. With its many interactive pages (e.g., fold-outs, removable letters in pockets, pullouts), this book is an unbelievable resource for older readers. It will support hand-in-hand the reading of *From Slave Ship to Freedom Road* as it tells the story of Africa before people were sold into slavery. Each double page deals with another area of the timeline through emancipation and every one has a special feature that invites the reader to interact with the text in some way to extend meaning. This is an excellent resource to bring an additional dimension to a study of this period of history.

Nettie's Trip South

Written by Ann Turner
Illustrated by Ronald Himler
Aladdin 1987, 1995, ISBN 0–689–80117–3

> Through a child's eyes, slavery is observed and truth is sought by Nettie who lives up North and has never seen the South or a slave. She longs to see both before the war, which would prevent her trip, breaks out. When she arrives in the South for her first stay in a hotel, she meets the first person she has ever known who has only one name. On Nettie's first trip around town, the adventure turns out to be very upsetting—she witnesses her first slave auction. As she watches, two young children are sold; she becomes so heartsick she throws up. The book is sketched in black and white to embrace the harshness of the theme of the story. It provides a different perspective to bring into the discussion.

No More! Stories and Songs of Slave Resistance

Written by Doreen Rappaport
Illustrated by Shane W. Evans
Candlewick 2002, ISBN 0–7636–0984–6

> Rappaport explains in an Author's Note that she did extensive research to trace the history of the *courageous struggle waged by enslaved Africans from the time they boarded the first slave ships heading for the New World to*

emancipation with the ratification of the Thirteenth Amendment. This reference book, with many illustrations, will appeal to older students. The language while accurate can be disturbing for younger children. (The opening poem by Phyllis Wheatley could be read after sharing *A Voice of Her Own*.)

Civil Rights Bookshelf Two: Escape from Slavery and The Underground Railroad

Aunt Harriet's Underground Railroad in the Sky

Written and Illustrated by Faith Ringgold
Dragonfly Books 1992, ISBN 0–517–88543–3

> This book was the recipient of the Coretta Scott King Award and was named a Caldecott Honor Book. Ringgold tells the story through the eyes of young Cassie whose baby brother, Be Be, escapes her care to soar through the sky. Cassie follows him. On their trip, they meet Harriet Tubman who sends them on the same journey escaped slaves took during the late 1800s. The slave escapes are described in simple terms that young children can understand. In addition, the Author's Note and map at the end of the book provide additional support for developing insight. Some children may question the veracity of the story when the characters begin to soar through the night sky, so be prepared to help them focus on the true power of this book, which lies in the story of all the many struggles faced by escaping slaves. We recommend that this book be paired with *Minty*.

Barefoot: Escape on the Underground Railroad

Written by Pamela Duncan Edwards
Illustrated by Henry Cole
HarperTrophy 1997, 1999, ISBN 0–06–443519–9

> *The Barefoot didn't see the eyes watching him. . . . His breath came in great gasps . . . , he had traveled faster and farther than ever in his life. He was fearful of what lay before him. He was terrified of what lay behind.* With these words, Edwards begins a journey that takes you running right alongside this barefoot slave running for his life. The story is told through the eyes of all the forest animals who have witnessed many barefoot slaves running through their woods over the past several months. Some succeeded while others had

been captured and led off in ropes. Cole's dramatic art features dark tones and shadows and embeds images of the events on every page.

Escape North! The Story of Harriet Tubman

Written by Monica Kulling
Illustrated by Teresa Flavin
Random House 2000, ISBN -0–375–80154–5

> This short forty-eight-page chapter book can easily be read in one sitting. Yet it could be used in short segments to support your study. The story begins with Harriet Tubman when she became a conductor for The Underground Railroad. As the story continues, readers discover that during her years of leading slaves to freedom, she never lost a single life and made more than nineteen trips over the dangerous route from the South to the free states of the North. The book is very specific about terms and is a worthy resource read-aloud for the classroom.

Follow the Drinking Gourd

Written and Illustrated by Jeanette Winter
Dragonfly Books/Knopf 1988, ISBN 0–679–81997–5

> This book is easily a cornerstone for the beginning of your study on the importance of The Underground Railroad in the mid-1800s. Jeannette Winter, in her Author's Note, gives readers a frame of reference with a brief history at the beginning of the book. The story is written in clear and simple terms that reveal critical information explaining how The Underground Railroad worked and how critical each step of the journey was for the safety of the escaping slaves. This one is essential for any collection on the topic.

Journey to Freedom: A Story of the Underground Railroad

Written by Courtni C. Wright
Illustrated by Gershom Griffith
Holiday House 1994, 1997, ISBN 0–8234–1334–0

> Help students imagine what it was like for children to travel The Underground Railroad for many days, cold, hungry, weary, and scared. The journey begins in Kentucky with Harriet Tubman leading the group to Canada and freedom. The book is very descriptive of the trip as families face harsh

weather without the clothes and shoes needed to endure waist-deep snow. Despite injuries and fear, they do not turn back. Finally, after many nights of walking fifteen miles, the family reaches Canada. The story is realistic and makes you feel like the fifth member of the family facing the hardships of the journey.

Sweet Clara and the Freedom Quilt

Written by Deborah Hopkinson
Illustrated by James Ransome
Dragonfly/Knopf 1993, ISBN 0–679–82311–5

Young Clara is sold as a field hand before she is twelve years old. She is so sad she can't even eat. A woman at the plantation takes her in and teaches her to sew so that she can begin to work in the Big House rather than in the fields. Once she becomes a seamstress, Clara begins to hear about The Underground Railroad and wants very badly to be reunited with her mother and to run for freedom. Yet, to find her way safely, she knows she will need a map. By listening to many people, she soon develops symbols for a quilt that would reflect the journey slaves have to take to get them to the Ohio River. Once the quilt is complete, she follows it first to her Momma then on to freedom.

Civil Rights Bookshelf Three: Emancipation

Free at Last!: Stories and Songs of Emancipation

Written by Doreen Rappaport
Illustrated by Shane W. Evans
Candlewick 2004, ISBN 0–7636–1440–8

This excellent resource is the second in a series of three books and follows *No More: Stories and Songs of Slave Resistance* (2002). Like the other two books, this one cannot be read aloud in one sitting. Instead, the set makes an excellent resource library for deeper study of many of the topics, questions, and wonderings that will be sparked by many of the other books on this shelf. One way you might choose to use this set is to select segments to give another perspective alongside a picture book about the same time period or character. Or you may find it appropriate to mark selections from this set to accompany specific titles you do choose to read aloud. Place the marked se-lections on an easel or book stand and leave it out for independent or group study to follow the read-aloud book.

Walking the Log

Written and Illustrated by Bessie Nickens
Rizzoli 1994, ISBN 0–8478–1794–6

> Nickens was born in the early 1900s and lived throughout the South with her parents as they moved from state to state looking for work. Each page-long vignette can be read as a stand-alone story. Each of these memories layers more and more background for understanding this period of history. Turn the pages and jump rope with the young children (since there were few toys), walk across the log in the forest to explore, attend church every Sunday, or help do the laundry on laundry day as story after story reveals the simple life in the rural South. The art is very primitive and colorful.

Civil Rights Bookshelf Four: The Struggle for Civil Rights in the United States

The Bus Ride That Changed History: The Story of Rosa Parks

Written by Pamela Duncan Edwards
Illustrated by Danny Shanahan
Houghton Mifflin 2005, ISBN 0–618–44911–6

> If you are a fan of Pamela Duncan Edwards' work, you are in for a surprise with her newest gift to readers. In this one, she deals with a serious historical event that truly changed the face of America. That day occurred in 1955 in Montgomery, Alabama, when a tired seamstress named Rosa Parks refused to give up her seat to a white man. Edwards and Shanahan give children a for-mat that looks almost like a simplified comic book with only one sentence per page. The speech bubbles provide additional support for the story line, which tells a complex story in easy-to-follow short sentences. Every page ends with bold letters that say *which was overturned because one woman was brave*. An introduction is provided that gives a summary of Rosa Parks' life and her role in history.

The Civil Rights Movement for Kids: A History with 21 Activities

Written by Mary C. Turck
Illustrated by actual photography
Chicago Review 2000, ISBN 1–55652–370–X

If you teach the civil rights movement in your classroom, this one will become a wonderful resource beginning with the 1948 to 1968 timeline at the front of the book. It is structured in chapter format much like a textbook but each chapter reads like a narrative. This title also includes an extensive list for suggested readings.

Dear Willie Rudd

Written by Libba Moore Gray
Illustrated by Peter M. Fiore
Aladdin 1993, ISBN 0–689–83105–6

This story unfolds slowly and clearly reveals the shameful customs of the 1950s when housekeepers were most often black women who helped raise the children and kept house for white homeowners. This warm and sensitive story introduces Elizabeth, one of those children who grew up being held and rocked by Willie Rudd, a black woman who worked for Elizabeth's family. At that time Willie wasn't allowed to walk through the front door, ride in the front of the bus, or even share a meal in the family dining room. Now many years later, Elizabeth writes a letter to her beloved Willie Rudd telling her how life would be different if they could rewrite their memories together. At the end, Elizabeth attaches the letter to a kite and lets it drift up to Willie Rudd. The book is poignant and beautifully written.

Grandmama's Pride

Written by Becky Bertha
Illustrated by Colin Bootman
Albert Whitman 2005, ISBN 0–8075–3028–X

This book is sure to become one of the staples for your study of civil rights. It's told through the eyes of a six-year-old Sarah Marie who, with her family, travels to the South in 1956 to visit her Grandmama. On the bus ride, they sit in the back of the bus *because Mama says it is more comfortable.* When it's time to have lunch, instead of going into the café, they eat a picnic lunch *because Mama says a picnic lunch is better.* When they arrive at Grandmama's, she is waiting for them standing rather than sitting *because it is better to stand than to sit.* All summer long, they don't ride the bus to town *because according to Grandmama when you have two good legs, it is better to walk than to ride.* When Sarah Marie learns to read during the summer, she suddenly understands all the signs posted around town that forbid her family from doing things the white children are doing. The dignity and strength of both Grandmama and Mama are so powerfully woven throughout the story as Bertha reveals historical events of the 1950s in the narrative. Bootman's watercolor art strongly reflects the story line with stunning work. The cover alone is worth the price of the book.

Ma Dear's Aprons

Written by Patricia C. McKissack
Illustrated by Floyd Cooper
Aladdin 1997, ISBN 0–689–83262–1

This is one you don't want to miss because it provides insight into the timeline that African Americans traveled to obtain equal rights as citizens. In the 1900s, life after slavery was still difficult for most black families. In *Ma Dear* (shortened for Mother Dear), we read about a mother and son who live each day by the kind of chores they must do to make enough money. It is important to note that all the tasks are ones completed in the service of rich white folks who live on the other side of town. Every day Ma Dear wears a different color apron depending on the job she must do. As she interacts with her son, David Earl, readers will see a goodness shining through her character, a trait to emulate. Cooper's remarkable art graces each page with softness and shades of amber.

Momma, Where Are You From?

Written by Marie Bradby
Illustrated by Chris Soentpiet
Orchard 2000, ISBN 0–531–30105–2

When a young girl inquires about her mother's roots, Momma tells of her childhood in a different era. Bradby's poetic prose creates sensory images for readers as we travel back to an earlier time when black women cleaned the houses of white families and took in their laundry and when schools were divided by color. Soentpiet's crisp, detailed art captures the loving relationship between this storytelling Momma and her little one. Read this once and the story will linger long after the book is closed.

Rosa

Written by Nikki Giovanni
Illustrated by Bryan Collier
Henry Holt 2005, ISBN 13: 978–0–8050–7106–1

This powerful and moving tribute to Rosa Parks captures the quiet strength of the woman who refused to give up her seat on the bus, which helped set America on a course of action leading to the events known as the civil rights era. Giovanni's words and Collier's watercolor and collage illustrations ground readers in the realities of the time. Giovanni artfully weaves in references to historic events, including the 1954 *Brown vs. the Board of Education* decision and the heinous murder of fourteen-year-old Emmett Till. The portrayal of Mrs. Parks as a gifted seamstress, a devoted daughter, and a loving wife only magnify her humanness, helping readers recognize the need to come to know others heart to heart. Though she is presented as a great American hero, readers cannot fail to see the peaceful dignity and quiet resolve of this great lady in the words and images presented in this beautiful work.

Civil Rights Bookshelf Five: Honoring the Lives of African Americans Who Led the Way to Equal Rights

Bill Pickett: Rodeo-Ridin' Cowboy

Written by Andrea D. Pickney
Illustrated by Brian Pickney
Voyager/Harcourt 1996, 1999, ISBN 0–15–202103–5

In 1881, black cowboys were not allowed to ride in the rodeo in any of the western states. However, there is one young boy, the son of a former slave, who loves being a cowboy and wants to be the best cowboy he can possibly become. As he watches the older men rope and wrestle steers to the ground, he decides he can do it better. With his roping method, Bill Pickett becomes the talk of the town and, while working for his dream, forges the way for others who want to be all they can be despite the color of their skins.

Black Cowboy, Wild Horses: A True Story

Written by Julius Lester
Illustrated by Jerry Pinkney
Dial 1998, ISBN 0–8037–1787–3

> Long before the world heard about the Horse Whisperer, former slave Bob Lemmons could track a wild horse and lead it into doing whatever he wanted. Julius Lester does a remarkable job of describing how Lemmons and his horse Warrior round up the wild herd. Pinkney's art is spectacular and every page is a visual delight.

Her Stories: African American Folktales, Fairy Tales, and True Tales

Written by Virginia Hamilton
Illustrated by Leo and Diane Dillon
Blue Sky Press/Scholastic 1995, ISBN 0–590–47370–0

> *Her Stories* is a history book that can serve as a read-aloud for many different events and can also be used as a reference book. Hamilton's dedication clearly reveals the importance of knowing and holding on to the history of those who came before us: *To our mothers and grandmothers, aunts and great-aunts. To all the women who stood before us, telling us about where they came from, what they saw, did, and imagined. Talking, they combed our hair, rocked us to sleep, sang to us, told us tales of then and now—and tomorrow. They worried about us. They hoped for us and showed us the way. They cared.* Following each of the different stories, Hamilton provides a comment section that gives additional background about the story or tale.

Langston's Train Ride

Written by Robert Burleigh
Illustrated by Leonard Jenkins
Orchard/Scholastic 2004, ISBN 0–439–35239–8

> Langston Hughes was raised by his grandmother after his daddy left the family. Without a lot of money and support for his talent, it was up to Langston to believe in himself . . . to believe enough to work to develop his talent. This book was written by Burleigh to *serve as a beacon to other young people with a dream.* One day, after Langston became successful, he was walking to a celebration party and his mind drifted back to the time when he was only eighteen years old riding the train to Mexico to visit his daddy. When the train crossed the mighty Mississippi River, the experience made the words of

Langston's most famous poem flow. That experience gave us *The Negro Speaks of Rivers.*

Martin's Big Words: The Life of Dr. Martin Luther King, Jr.

Written by Doreen Rappaport
Illustrated by Bryan Collier
Jump at the Sun/Hyperion 2001, ISBN 0–7868–0714–8

> Launch your reading of this title with the Author's and Illustrator's Notes at the beginning of the book. Only then will readers have the lens needed to truly appreciate this insightful portrayal of the life of Dr. King. The presentation of the words will move you. This is one book that could be used with a wide range of ages and interests and will certainly help build a background for understanding the powerful role of this man in this turbulent time in US history.

More Than Anything Else

Written by Marie Bradby
Illustrated by Chris Soentpiet
Orchard/Scholastic 1995, ISBN 0–531–09464–2

> In this lovely story, Bradby takes us into the childhood of Booker T. Washington who, along with his brother and Papa, leaves long before daybreak heading to work in the salt mines. We listen as young Booker T. talks about how empty his stomach is because there was no food for breakfast. We ache right along with this young boy when his arms ache from shoveling salt until it's too dark to work longer. But our spirits soar when, despite all these hardships, what Booker wants *More Than Anything Else* is to learn to read. And we celebrate with him when he meets a man who helps him unlock the secret of written language. Soentpiet's art captures the angst and the joy in the life of a remarkable American who is portrayed during his childhood.

Salt in His Shoes: Michael Jordan in Pursuit of a Dream

Written by Deloris Jordan with Roslyn M. Jordan
Illustrated by Kadir Nelson
Simon & Schuster 2000, ISBN 0–689–83371–7

> If there's ever been an exquisite ballplayer, it would have to be Michael Jordan. Who can ever forget how he crossed that centerline and with a simple flick of his wrist, the ball would sail as if it were a magnet toward the goal?

But for every shot he made that thrilled millions of sport fans, there was one time he practiced alone and shot after shot did not sail straight to the goal. This charming book written by his mother and sister tells of a young Michael who worried he'd never be tall enough to play. Like many children, he became discouraged and wanted to quit. What made the difference for young Michael? Pick this one to inspire children to stick with their dreams and to reach their goals through dedication to a vision and a lot of hard work.

Satchmo's Blues

Written by Alan Schroeder
Illustrated by Floyd Cooper
Bantam/Random House 1996, ISBN 0–440–41472–5

From an early age, it was quite clear to all who knew young Louie that he had music flowing through his veins as surely as his blood flowed. Living in New Orleans, jazz was heard on every street corner. Young Louie would often peek under the doors just to watch and listen as jazz filled the air. His Mama was so poor, Louie often went to bed without food and they certainly couldn't afford to buy him a horn. Walk the streets with young Louie as he keeps his dream alive and continues to believe in himself. Watch as he becomes the most famous trumpeter in the history of music.

Visiting Langston

Written by Willie Perdomo
Illustrated by Bryan Collier
Henry Holt 2002, ISBN 0–8050–6744–2

This glimpse into the life of Langston Hughes is told through the voice of a young poet (like the ones in your classroom) who is visiting the home of this renowned poet for the first time. The rhythmic text is presented in very simple language. As Perdomo's words paint pictures of Hughes' life, Collier embeds images of many famous people, important objects, and places into the illustrations that help tell this story.

"Wanted Dead or Alive": The True Story of Harriet Tubman

Written by Ann McGovern
Illustrated by R. M. Powers
Cover art by Brian Pinkney
Scholastic 1965, 1991, ISBN 0–590–44212–0

This short chapter book describes how Harriet Tubman came to be one of the leaders of The Underground Railroad. It shows life on a plantation and tells how Harriet is sold away from her family when she is only seven years old. Eventually she is taken back because she becomes sick and can't work. Later, Harriet runs away again but she continues to return to lead others to freedom. Although the story provides a rich description of the life of a slave, it may be disturbing to many children. However, it is interesting reading for background information.

And One Final Title for the Collection . . .

The last book we include here belongs in a grouping all its own. It would easily fit on any of two or three bookshelves within the collection, but we reserved it for the final book. Jacqueline Woodson's *Show Way* traces her own family across seven generations ending with her daughter. This beautifully crafted and artfully formatted book should be the piece that weaves the separate fibers into the story of one family. And in so doing, Woodson lets her readers see the injustice, the struggle, the sacrifice, the pain, and the great joy that love will endure to make a better life for those who follow.

Show Way

Written by Jacqueline Woodson
Illustrated by Hudson Talbott
Putnam 2005, ISBN 0–399–23749–6

Woodson is at her all-time best in this beautiful story that recounts her history for seven generations. Each of the brave women, several of whom were sold from their family as slaves, began a tradition that Woodson continues today—quilting. As you read it aloud, children will discover how Big Mama raised a seven-year-old who came to her after being sold away from her own family. Watch as Big Mama teaches her to quilt and how the seeds of desire for freedom are planted in her young heart. That little girl was the first of the seven generations that led to Jacqueline Woodson. Talbott's art only adds to the power of this unforgettable story of courage and love. Every spread enriches and illuminates Woodson's astonishing recount of history. Don't miss this one. It is indeed a treasure that will linger with both you and children forever.

■ Building Background for a Study of the Holocaust

The books in this set were selected to support and extend a study of the Holocaust, whether it is included as a portion of a study of war or of US history or of European history or as a study unto itself. These books can be read aloud to build background (concepts, images, vocabulary) for the novels most often read in association with the topic including, but not limited to, *Number the Stars, The Devil's Arithmetic, The Diary of Anne Frank, The Upstairs Room, Behind the Bedroom Wall.*

The Butterfly

Written and Illustrated by Patricia Polacco
Philomel 2000, ISBN 0–399–23170–6

> This story is told by Monique, a young girl who lived during the French Resistance. The strong message is presented with childlike sweetness and innocence. Monique lives in a French village during the war while Nazis march everywhere in town. One night when Monique wakes up, a strange little girl is sitting on the foot of her bed, looking out her window and petting her cat. Her mother tries to tell her it is just a dream, but Monique doesn't think so. By the time her family has to flee their home, Monique has become friends with the little girl and is very sad when she has to leave her home and friend. During this stressful time, Monique is in her garden watching a butterfly when a soldier reaches over the fence and crushes it. The following spring many new butterflies come back to the garden and Monique feels it was a sign from her friend that they are safe.

The Cats in Krasinski Square

Written by Karen Hesse
Illustrated by Wendy Watson
Scholastic 2004, ISBN 0–439–43540–4

> All those cats in Krasinski Square used to belong to someone, but now they wander the square in search of mice; they belong to no one. The narrator, a Jewish girl living in Warsaw during the time of Nazi occupation, becomes their friend. She and her sister, Mira, are all that is left of their family and despite that, she must play the part of being a loyal Polish citizen. They are so

poor that they must work to smuggle extra food into the ghetto. What happens when the Gestapo discovers their plan? Will the cats be able to help them? This important book allows us to see the innocence and sheer courage of children who faced a life of horror and sadness. Hesse provides an Author's Note and an historical context that connect the facts and fiction in this account. Watson's art in pencil, ink, and watercolors captures the period look of the 1940s. And just so you know, even the text type was designed and cast by a Polish typographer, Adam Jerzy Poltawski, in the late 1940s.

The Children We Remember

Written by Chana Byers Abells
Photographs from the archives of Yad Vashem, The Holocaust Martyrs' and Heroes'
Remembrance Authority, Jerusalem, Israel
Greenwillow/HarperTrophy 1983, 2002, ISBN 0–06–443777–9

This book's modest text and black-and-white photographs convey the stark reality of the lives portrayed, clear evidence that the Holocaust happened to real people—many of whom were small children. The text is very simple, often with only one sentence per page, but it will create an interest in learning more and form a beginning for a study of the subject.

Don't Forget

Written by Patricia Lakin
Illustrated by Ted Rand
Aladdin 1994, 2002, ISBN 0–689–84809–9

This one deals with a difficult subject in a loving, yet respectful way. Young Sara is baking her mother's birthday cake, the very first one she has baked. She goes down through her small town picking up all the ingredients she will need but she doesn't want to go to the Singer's store because of the numbers they have on their arms. However, she must go in if she is to get everything she needs. Once in the Singer's store, her eyes are drawn to the numbers and she mumbles "I'm sorry." Mrs. Singer quickly reassures her that the past should never be forgotten because if it is the mistakes could happen all over again. Sara ends up staying with Mrs. Singer to bake her cake. You must read the dedication page; its essence pulses through every line of this wonderful book.

Erika's Story

Written by Ruth Vander Zee
Illustrated by Roberto Innocenti
Creative Editions 2003, ISBN 1–56846–176–3

You will want to read this unforgettable book again and again, for yourself and your students. It is a true story told to the author who met Erika quite by accident while touring Europe with her husband in 1995 on the fiftieth anniversary of the end of World War II. Erica, a Jewish baby born around 1934, was aboard a cattle car on the train with her parents and many other Jews who were traveling to a concentration camp. The conditions aboard the train were horrible and the parents could only imagine what their future held. During the long ride as they were crushed together, they made a heart-wrenching decision to attempt to give their tiny baby a better chance for survival. They bundled the baby as tightly as they could and when the train slowed down in a village, they tossed her out into a patch of grass. A kind woman rescued her and raised her as her own. The book contains the details of her life that Erika told to Ruth Vander Zee on that day in 1995. The art is done in muted tones of gray with only a touch of color (e.g., the tiny bundle is pink) in most illustrations. There is full color as Erika's story draws to the present and she explains that her star still shines through her children and the hope for the life of her people. This touching book makes the atrocities of this era personal and real for readers.

The Flag with Fifty-Six Stars: A Gift from the Survivors of Mauthausen

Written by Susan Goldman Rubin
Illustrated by Bill Farnsworth
Holiday House 2005, ISBN 0–8234–1653–4

This significant picture book will make an important addition to your shelf of books used to build background for a study of the Holocaust. Mauthausen was one of the infamous Nazi camps; it was built to house the men who would be used as slaves to mine granite for the Germans. The camp was kept a secret from the world because it was one of the worst of all of them. Despite the inhumane treatment and the starvation experienced, many men's spirit survived the conditions. As the war raged, just the sounds of the planes brought hope. As their hopes increased, the men felt they must do something to symbolize their faith in the troops and in their future. From memory, they pieced together a crude US flag with fifty-six stars (one extra row). The flag later flew over the camp as an incredible symbol of the courage these men showed in making it. The text is rather long for a picture book, but it could be read to any age group as you begin a unit of study.

Forging Freedom: The True Story of Heroism During the Holocaust

Written and Illustrated by Hudson Talbott

G. P. Putnam's Sons 2000, ISBN 0–399–23434–9

This outstanding chapter book with pictures explains the situation described in Eve Bunting's *Terrible Things* (see page 159). Jaap Penraat lives in Amsterdam when it is taken over by the Nazi soldiers. He is not Jewish, but many of his friends are and they are being targeted for removal. As his city becomes a death trap for all Jews, Jaap (unlike the animals in *Terrible Things*) knows he must do something to help his friends. He knows he must be very courageous and much smarter than the Nazi soldiers or they will kill him along with all his friends. This book takes readers through the development and implementation of Jaap's plan in eleven short chapters. Readers will see reproductions of many forged documents drawn from a museum display in Amsterdam.

The Harmonica

Written by Tony Johnston

Illustrated by Ron Mazellan

Charlesbridge 2004, ISBN 1–57091–547–4

This story, inspired by the life of a Holocaust survivor, is retold in gentle prose by Tony Johnston. The young narrator recalls life before the war reached his home in Poland. His family's house was filled with the sounds of Schubert drifting from the neighbor's gramophone while his parents waltzed across the wooden floors. And though he knew the family was too poor, he dreamed of a piano and learning to make the music himself. His father knew of that dream and brought home a harmonica, the only instrument he could afford. Soon our young narrator finds Schubert in the harmonica and his parents dance and the war moves closer and closer. When the Nazi soldiers arrive, they take him to one concentration camp and his parents to another. *Like a length of kindling, in one stroke, they split our family."* In his darkest and loneliest moments, he finds comfort in the harmonica and in Schubert. The commandant of the camp hears the music and seeks him out. Every night as the commandant dines, he sends for the boy and demands that he play. Every night at the end of the meal, the commandant tosses the boy crusts of bread. The boy is conflicted with knowing that someone so ugly and cruel could understand something as beautiful as Schubert. He is riddled with guilt over eating the crusts of bread while others around him slowly starve. Yet he is comforted in the dark of night when someone whispers, *Thank you for Schubert.* From that night on he plays, not for the commandant, but for all those who take comfort from the beauty of the music and for his parents whom he never sees again. Mazellan's art, which is done in mixed media on illustration board using dark hues of browns, blues, golds, and clay, perfectly completes the tone and intensity of the text. We believe Johnston is at her very best in this tender and soulful story.

. . . I Never Saw Another Butterfly

Children's drawings and poems from Terezin Concentration Camp, 1942 1944
Expanded Second Edition with Foreword by Chaim Potok
Schocken/Random House 1959, 1978, 1993, ISBN 0–8052–1015–6

The note on the back provides a brief history of the 15,000 Jewish children who passed through the Terezin Concentration Camp; only a hundred of them survived the ordeal. This collection of drawings and poems done by the children while in the camp gives readers an unprecedented view of life through their eyes. Terezin was known as a "model ghetto" and as the "Führer's gift to the Jews." You will be deeply moved and stunned when you read the insights of these children. This book is powerful and will have to be used with care.

Let the Celebrations Begin!

Written by Margaret Wild
Illustrated by Julie Vivas
Orchard 1991, ISBN 0–531–07076–X

Miriam can remember life before the concentration camp. She can recall her own room and all her toys; yet her young friends, Sarah and David, think they have always lived here. Sarah and David relish the stories Miriam can tell about toys and beg for her to tell them again and again. Miriam enlists the aid of all the women in the camp to gather bits of cloth, buttons, scraps, and even pieces of their own clothing to help make toys for the children. In this moving account, the stark reality of the horror is tempered by the soft watercolor art. Julie Vivas reveals the situation in images that capture the tenderness of the human heart to care so deeply even in the face of tremendous atrocities. In the concentration camp, the women's heads are shaved and they wear very shabby clothing, but Vivas reveals the situation in a style that is not frightening for younger listeners. In the end, the British soldiers arrive to liberate the captives who are given soup and the children get their first toys. The celebration begins.

The Lily Cupboard: A Story of the Holocaust

Written by Shulamith Levey Oppenheim
Illustrated by Ronald Himler
Charlotte Zolotow/HarperTrophy 1992, 1995, ISBN 0–06–443393–5

In 1940, Germany occupied Holland and sent many Jews living there to concentration camps where they were put to death. Miriam's parents begin to fear for the safety of their family. The decision is made to hide Miriam with farmers, who aren't Jews, living in the countryside. There, though Miriam misses her parents, she does her best not to show how homesick she is. This gentle story is a safe one to begin a study of the Holocaust because the horrors of the time are only alluded to.

The Number on My Grandfather's Arm

Written by David Adler
Photographs by Rose Eichenbaum
URJ Press (formerly UAHC Press) 1987, ISBN 0–8074–0328–8

If you know other books by David Adler, you will appreciate this work of nonfiction supported with black-and-white photographs. In it, a little girl visits with her grandfather and often asks questions about when he was younger. Grandfather always wears long sleeves, even in the summer, but one night while he is sitting with his granddaughter, he rolls up the sleeves to help wash dishes. This is the first time she has seen the numbers on his arm and, of course, she asks about them. Grandfather reluctantly tells about his life in a concentration camp during the war. Through his story readers discover that all of his family and friends died there.

One Candle

Written by Eve Bunting
Illustrated by K. Wendy Popp
HarperTrophy 2002, ISBN 0–06–028115–4

This loving story tells of a Jewish family in America celebrating Hanukkah. At this holiday, the family lights candles in the menorah, but in the center of the table, there is one lone potato amidst all the wonderful trays of brisket, gravy, latkes, sour cream, and applesauce. At the end of the meal, the grandmother and her sister, Ruth, take the potato and grandmother slowly carves out the inside as she begins to tell the story of when she and Ruth were separated from the rest of their family and taken to different concentration camps. Continuing an annual tradition, she tells her family of the horrors they suffered in the camp. She tells them that as Hanukkah approached, she slipped a potato and a pat of butter out of the kitchen where she worked as a cook for the soldiers who ran the camp. The one lone potato with the pat of butter inside the carved out shell provided the women in their building that night with a simple menorah—an important symbol in the Jewish faith. This one act helped give them the strength and courage not to give in to the brutality they suffered every day. Popp's finely detailed art captures the mood of the story in somber tones.

Rose Blanche

Written and Illustrated by Roberto Innocenti
Creative Editions 1985, 2003, ISBN 15–6846189–5

While this is a picture book, it is very disturbing. After the Nazi soldiers take over her town, Rose Blanche gradually discovers the concentration camp and soon witnesses all the hunger of the people there. In an effort to help, she begins visiting every day after school to bring food, which she hands through the barbed wire fence. One day she sees truck after truck rushing out of town and wonders what has happened to all the people at the camp. When she gets there, it is empty. But she is also discovered by the Nazi soldiers and shot. We would suggest using this book with much older students.

Terrible Things: An Allegory of the Holocaust

Written by Eve Bunting
Illustrated by Stephen Gammell
Jewish Publication Society 1980, 1989, 1993, ISBN 0–8276–0507–2

When the *Terrible Things* come to visit the clearing of the forest and blot out the sun, the first thing they tell the animals is that they have come for every animal with feathers on its back. The squirrels, frogs, porcupines, rabbits, and even the fish immediately tell them they don't have feathers. Even though the birds fly high up into the sky, the Terrible Things use large nets and gather all the birds and carry them away. The other animals become nervous and begin talking about all the things that bother them about the birds anyway. The other animals think they are safe even though no one stands up to help the little birds. After all, the Terrible Things only want animals with feathers. Not long after, they come back. This time the Things want all the bushy tailed creatures. Over and over again the pattern is repeated until the only animals left are the rabbits. Finally, the Terrible Things come for the white creatures. All are captured and taken away except for one little rabbit who hides among the rocks. Too late, he realizes that all the animals should have stood together against the power of the *Terrible Things*. If you are going to study the Holocaust, this book is a must. Use it to build an understanding of the horrible misuse of power exercised by one group of humans over another. It helps develop an understanding of the fear, and perhaps the complacency, the people of Europe felt when the Nazi armies marched through their countries gathering up all the Jews.

The Secret Seder

Written by Doreen Rappaport
Illustrated by Emily Arnold McCully
Hyperion 2005, ISBN 0–7868–0777–6

During the years Hitler was rounding up Jews across Europe, young Jacques and his family move to a small village where they hope to avoid being sent to the concentration camps by pretending to be Catholics. However, when it is time to celebrate Passover, his mother begins secretly teaching Jacques all the rituals involved in the Jewish faith. When the day comes for the secret seder, Jacques and his dad slip out into the night to meet other Jewish men in the mountains. There, despite the dangers, they hold the ceremony. McCully's art reflects the emotions so evident in Rappaport's words.

Who Was the Woman Who Wore the Hat?

Written and Illustrated by Nancy Patz
Dutton/Penguin 2003, ISBN 0–525–46999–0

This simple, thoughtful book is a series of questions and wonderings about the life of a woman the author never even knew. Patz toured the Jewish Historical Museum in Amsterdam and saw a simple hat on display there that had been worn by a woman. The display and its simplicity caused her to begin thinking about the woman. Truths of the Holocaust era are woven like golden threads throughout the text as Patz imagines the life of the woman who wore the hat, the life she lived before the Holocaust, and the day she was taken from her home.

The Yellow Star: The Legend of King Christian X of Denmark

Written by Carmen Agra Deedy
Illustrated by Henri Sørensen
Peachtree 2000, ISBN 1–56145–208–4

Begin your read-aloud of this story with the Author's Note at the end of the text. The king of Denmark is loved by all for his wisdom and leadership. When the Nazi army rides into town, they place a Nazi flag on top of the palace. When King Christian X hears of it, he has it taken down. A soldier arrives the next day to tell the king another will be placed that very day. When King Christian tells the soldier it will be removed as well, the soldier threatens to shoot the man sent to remove the Nazi flag. The king tells that soldier to be prepared to shoot him that day. The Nazi flag never flew over the palace again. When the announcement comes that all Jews are to wear the yellow star on all their clothing, the king has to decide what to do to keep all his people safe. After a night of reflection and deep thought, King Christian decides to hide the Jewish subjects among all other Danes. To share his plan, he rides through the streets the next morning with a yellow star clearly embroidered on his jacket. By the next day everyone is wearing the yellow star, and no one can tell one Dane from another.

■ *Building Background for a Study of Immigration to the United States*

Many children have no sense of their families' history, where their ancestors came from before they arrived in this land to start a new life. Some know stories handed down at family gatherings such as reunions and holidays and birthdays and weddings and funerals. The sharing of stories is one way of holding on to the threads we use to weave our scattered lives into that tapestry we call "family." Some know the traditions and customs of the old country because their families have made it a point to keep those traditions alive. Some know their ancestors were here first and know stories of their struggles to maintain a certain way of life. Some think of the United States as the only home their families have ever known. Others have never even given a thought to the idea that their families may have their roots in other parts of the world.

To truly understand the vision of the founding fathers—the vision of a nation such as ours—children should hear a collection of stories that feature the struggles and successes of those who came before all of us. They should know the vision and drive that brought various people here. They should know that the lives we live are the result of those who came before us. They should know that we, in return, now help those who flee to this country in search of the same dreams. This collection of books will help students build a stronger, more solid background as they enter into any study for which immigration is an aspect.

Immigration Bookshelf One: Making a New Life in a New Land

The Butterfly Seeds

Written and Illustrated by Mary Watson

Tambourine Books/HarperCollins 1995, ISBN 0–688–14132–3

The Butterfly Seeds is the story of Jake's family as they leave their homeland and their grandparents behind to immigrate to America. Knowing he will miss his Grandpa, Jake doesn't find any excitement in the journey aboard the big ship. On their last visit together, Grandpa gives Jake some seeds to carry with him to America that will bring hundreds of butterflies to the plants. When Jake arrives in New York to live in an apartment, he has to be creative about planting them but with the help of several merchants, he plants the seeds in a window box that eventually brings Grandpa's butterflies for all the children in the apartment to see.

Dreaming of America: An Ellis Island Story

Written by Eve Bunting
Illustrated by Ben F. Stahl
Troll/Bridgewater 2000, ISBN 0–8167–6520–0

Have you ever wondered about the very first immigrant to pass through the Ellis Island checkpoint? Well Eve Bunting, an Irish immigrant herself, tells this wonderful story about Annie Moore who, on her fifteenth birthday, was the very first. The year is 1892 and Annie is bringing her two brothers over to join her parents in New York. The back of the book includes additional information telling us that a statue of Annie was erected in Ireland as a reminder of all the immigrants who left their homeland. And a second statue has been erected on Ellis Island where her journey ended. While the text is rather long, it contains many details about the journey. It stands out among immigration stories because layered in among Stahl's art are photographs of Annie, the ship she traveled on, and Ellis Island. These images extend the meaning of the story, lending it authenticity for students.

Grandfather's Journey

Written and Illustrated by Allen Say
Scholastic 1993, ISBN 0–590–48864–3

In *Grandfather's Journey,* Say gives us a lovely tribute to his grandfather's life as he moved from Japan to America with a poignant account of his love of both countries. His paintings are very supportive of the story and in fact educate us further about two other cultures. Most children feel this tug between homes when they have to move, so the core of this wonderful family story will be meaningful.

Hannah Is My Name

Written and Illustrated by Belle Yang
Candlewick 2004, ISBN 0–7636–2223–0

The front flap says it best: *The United States has long been a place of refuge and opportunity for immigrants . . . the destination for millions. . . . This book celebrates . . . hope by telling the story of a little girl . . . waiting for her green card and who meanwhile must adjust to a new language, a new school, a new way of life . . . even a new name.* While this is in picture-book format, it does have lots of text. The story is told by a little girl who takes the American name of Hannah. Because the story comes from a young girl, the concept of immigration will be more real and personal for students.

A Picnic in October

Written by Eve Bunting
Illustrated by Nancy Carpenter
Harcourt 1999, ISBN 0–15–201656–2

Come along and sail up to Ellis Island on a cold, breezy October day with one family as they go to celebrate Lady Liberty's birthday. Tony doesn't think a picnic in October is a very good idea until he is told of the important role Lady Liberty played in the life of his grandmother on the day she immigrated to America. The statue, the tiny island, the nation all take on new significance for Tony, and perhaps for all who read this memorable story infused with history.

Shutting Out the Sky: Life in the Tenements of New York, 1880–1924

Written by Deborah Hopkinson
Illustrated with actual photographs
Orchard 2003, ISBN 0–439–37590–8

This is not a cover-to-cover read-aloud but is a tremendous resource for selected parts to support a unit of study. It is a powerful source to show children the difficult times immigrants had just to be in the free world—the United States of America. There is a lot of text, but it is broken up by many pictures of the tenements of that time. Freedom comes with a great price . . . *we must cherish it.*

We Are Americans: Voices of the Immigrant Experience

Written by Dorothy and Thomas Hoobler
Actual photographs
Scholastic 2003, ISBN 0–439–16297–1

All Americans are immigrants or descendants of immigrants. Our ancestors came here from all over the globe. . . . But immigrants have always had a dream to guide them—the dream of America. . . . To many, freedom was what the United States was all about. This is another resource book that you can choose to read aloud selected parts that support or extend the background for understanding this area of the curriculum. The pictures cover many areas and many countries, and the quotes used make this book more significant.

■ *Building Background for a Study of the United States*

This is such a broad topic. There are so many books that can be used as various lenses for zooming in on the United States of America. This collection features a wide range of subjects, including famous Americans, significant events in US history, patriotic songs and symbols, landmarks, voting, and even the presidency. Our hope with this shelf is that you will find a few books to launch or extend your curriculum. We selected books that captured interesting facts or profiled significant people or places or events with an engaging slant. We hope you and your students find them helpful.

America Bookshelf One: The First Americans— Native Americans

Between Earth & Sky: Legends of Native American Sacred Places
Written by Joseph Bruchac
Illustrated by Thomas Locker
Voyager/Harcourt 1996, ISBN 0–15–202062–4

> *The landscape of North America is filled with places that hold deep, sacred meaning to the native people. Some are locations where special ceremonies took place. Other places are related to stories from long ago.* The story within the covers of this gorgeous book tells you about the Seven Directions Native American tribes observed. The Author's Note at the front provides additional information for children. In the story, Old Bear is describing for his nephew, Little Turtle, all the sacred places in their world. He begins with the sacred place found east of them. Each succeeding page takes another direction and describes for Little Turtle what can be found there. The map at the back of the book identifies many Native American tribes who call the North American continent home.

A Boy Called Slow
Written by Joseph Bruchac
Illustrator by Rocco Baviera
Philomel 1994, ISBN 0–399–22692–3

> This picture book is better suited for older children due to its lengthy text. It is the story of a Lakota warrior who, as a youngster, was named Slow. As the story unfolds, readers (listeners) discover the Lakota tradition of naming a child based on his characteristics. Although the name hurt, it molded Slow into a young boy determined to overcome obstacles. By the seventh winter

(age seven), Slow begins to show the characteristics of the brave Indian warrior that he will become. Only on the last page do you learn this is the story of a journey toward greatness—the story of the legendary Lakota warrior, Sitting Bull.

Buffalo Woman

Written and Illustrated by Paul Goble
Aladdin 1984, 1986, ISBN 0–689–71109–3

> This is a Native American legend about a young warrior who aims his arrow at a buffalo drinking water; it suddenly turns into a woman he knows he must marry. After the birth of their first son, *Buffalo Woman* returns to her people in the Buffalo Nation because the tribe has never accepted her. The young hunter is heartbroken, so he follows her against warnings. Each time he finds his wife and son, she again warns him not to follow because she fears her people will kill him because his tribe was unkind to her. Read to discover how the young son helps his father as the day of reckoning arrives.

Cheyenne Again

Written by Eve Bunting
Illustrated by Irving Toddy
Clarion 1995 ISBN 0–396–70364–6

> *Cheyenne Again* is a very sensitive story that tells of the suffering of Native American people in the late 1880s with an historical note at the back of the book that explains the events of the time. Young Bull, a young Cheyenne boy, is taken from his home and placed in a boarding school against his wishes. He endures much sadness and loneliness as he is forced to live like the white man. He has to leave behind all his customs, and the familiar things from his past can only be kept alive through his memories.

The Earth Under Sky Bear's Feet: Native American Poems of the Land

Written by Joseph Bruchac
Illustrated by Thomas Locker
PaperStar/Putnum & Grosset 1995, ISBN 0–698–11647–X

> This book is a series of twelve poems from different Native American tribes that reflect their deep respect and appreciation for the land. Each poem, told from the viewpoint of the Big Dipper as it revolves around the Earth, focuses

on the sights and sounds experienced on each of its trips. The art is simply stunning! A note of interest included in the book is that Native Americans called the Big Dipper *Sky Bear* and used it to guide their journeys, while the escaping African Americans called it the Drinking Gourd and also used it to guide their journeys.

Gift Horse: A Lakota Story

Written and Illustrated by S. D. Nelson
Harry N. Abrams 1999, ISBN 0–8109–4127–9

This must-read has history about the Lakota tribe woven into a suspenseful story. Readers learn about the Lakota custom of a father giving his young son a special horse to ride him from boyhood into manhood. The special horse in this story is named Storm. Together the horse and the young boy roam the fields and ride like the wind. People in his community begin calling the boy Flying Cloud because of the dust he and the horse leave behind them. As the story unfolds, the rituals and customs of moving into manhood are revealed. The story reaches a pinnacle when the Crow tribe rides into the Lakota camp and captures all their horses, including Storm. Following this event, Flying Cloud completes the final step to becoming a Lakota warrior. Nelson's art is colorful and invites readers into the culture and traditions of the day. The Author's Note at the back gives additional information that shouldn't be missed.

The Gift of the Sacred Dog

Written and Illustrated by Paul Goble
Aladdin 1980, 1987, ISBN 0–02–043280–1

The Author's Note at the beginning of the book gives you information to build background before reading about the Sioux tribe that was starving as they hunted for buffalo. One day after hearing his younger brothers cry from hunger, a boy tells his parents he is going into the hills to pray for help from the Great Spirit. There on the mountain, he is not sure whether he fell asleep but out of the clouds appears a rider on a magnificent Sacred Dog. The dog tells him it will carry his people faster than they can imagine in their hunt for buffalo. On his way back to tell the tribe of his dream, a whole herd of Sacred Dogs (horses) follow him. The warriors knew, when they saw the herd, that they must take good care of the Sacred Dogs because they in turn would always help them.

How the Robin Got Its Red Breast: A Legend of the Sechelt People

Illustrated by Charlie Craigan
Nightwood Editions 1993, ISBN 0–88971–158–5

> *In the beginning when the world was young and some of the first Sechelt people were living in a cave, many things were different than they are today.* One of these was the robin. According to this legend handed down generation to generation, the robin of that day was grey and dull while robins today have beautiful red breasts. The Sechelt people lived in caves and were close to nature. One day all the men and boys have to go out into the cold forest to gather wood and food, leaving all the women and children with one old man. He refuses to go to sleep for fear the fire will go out, so he sits day after day without sleep. But one day sleep takes over and the fire is slowly going out. Just before it is only a spark, a robin flys into the cave and begins flapping his wings to relight the fire. He flaps so furiously that his breast begins to reflect the embers. As the legend goes, that is how robins got their red breasts, which are still seen today. The black-and-white art is reflective of the Sechelt culture.

How the Stars Fell into the Sky: A Navajo Legend

Written by Jerrie Ougthton
Illustrated by Lisa Desimini
Houghton Mifflin 1992, ISBN 0–395–58798–0

> Oughton provides us with a retelling of an old Navajo legend explaining how the stars were placed in the sky to form the patterns we see every night. Each is carefully placed by the first woman until one day a coyote comes by and wants to help. She allows him to do so but he soon grows tired of the careful placement and flings a bunch of them out into the sky where they fall at random never to be corrected. The art is very simple and is the perfect support for this tale.

Maple Moon

Written by Connie Brummel Crook
Illustrated by Scott Cameron
Stoddart Kids 1997, 2000, ISBN 0–7737–6098–9

> Rides the Wind is an eight-year-old boy who injures his leg and limps badly enough that he can't play with the other children who taunt him by calling

him Limping Leg. One brutal winter, the tribe becomes very hungry because of the deep snow. One afternoon when he can't dance with the other children, Rides the Wind sadly walks out into the woods and leans against a maple tree. While leaning against the tree, he watches a squirrel as he nibbles and drinks from the tree. Rides the Wind teaches all the men from his tribe how to drain the sweet water from the maple trees. This discovery keeps the tribe from starving that winter. The chief gives him the name Wise Little Raven because of his discovery. Cameron's stunning art is a beautiful match for the story. From this tale, readers will discover that maple syrup is produced only in North America; Native Americans taught white men about this sweet water, which kept many of them from starving; and Native Americans call the season when the sap runs the Maple Moon. *Note:* This one could also fit into a unit on taunting and teasing.

A Rainbow at Night: The World in Words and Pictures by Navajo Children

Written by Bruce Hucko
Illustrated by Navajo children
Chronicle 1996, ISBN 0–8118–1294–4

This book celebrates the art and culture of the Navajo. The colorful art alone would make this a must-have. Yet, when paired with the many details and insights offered by the words of Bruce Hucko and these children, the book becomes all the more powerful. We suggest getting a copy as a gift for the art teacher in your school. It could lead to an exploration of art techniques and an extension of the projects children have created.

Raven: A Trickster Tale from the Pacific Northwest

Written and Illustrated by Gerald McDermott
Voyager/Harcourt 1993, 2001, ISBN 0–15–202449–2

This Caldecott Honor book features the Raven, a central figure in many of the myths and tales told by this Native American tribe. The Author's Note at the beginning of the book explains the many different characteristics that the Raven has in these traditional tales. It also tells the reader that the Raven is often found carved or painted on totem poles and is featured in jewelry and baskets. In this tale, *Raven* is searching for the sun because the world is so dark and he realizes that light is needed. This is a well-written book and the art is truly magnificent.

The Story of Jumping Mouse: A Native American Legend

Written and Illustrated by John Steptoe

Lothrop, Lee & Shepard 1984, ISBN 0–688–08740–X

This legend will become a favorite of yours as you journey with a little mouse who wants so badly to see the faraway land he has only heard about in stories. Even though everyone warns him against making such a dangerous trip, the little mouse believes he will always regret it if he never sees the glory of that faraway land. So one morning he sets out. The little mouse soon realizes he has to overcome many obstacles. His first hurdle is the big river. On the bank of the river, he meets a Magic Frog who becomes his friend and passes along some magic powers saying, *You will reach the far-away land if you keep hope alive within you.* All along the journey the little mouse meets others who need help and each time he remembers the frog's advice. Being the kind of mouse he is, he never refuses. Each animal in need is given magic powers by the mouse. But he loses something very important in giving to each of them—his sight and his hearing and finally his ability to smell. Because of his goodness and his determination, the Magic Frog arrives just as each of the other animals helps little Jumping Mouse reach the faraway land. When Magic Frog realizes how generous the mouse has been, he gives little mouse another magic wish and the little Jumping Mouse spends the remainder of his days soaring over the Earth as an eagle.

The Story of the Milky Way: A Cherokee Tale

Written by Joseph Bruchac and Gayle Ross

Illustrated by Virginia A. Stroud

Dial 1995, ISBN 0–8037–1737–7

When people work together, they can solve most any problem. In this story people work together to solve the problem of a giant spirit dog who is stealing their supply of cornmeal. This Cherokee story tells how the entire community joined together to chase the spirit dog away. According to the legend, as the dog ran off into the dark sky, a band of stars was left behind in its path. Thus the Milky Way was formed as a reminder to the Cherokees of the power of working together for the good of all. The art was painted by Stroud, a Cherokee-Creek artist. Notes from all three contributors give additional information about how the story came to them.

Thirteen Moons on Turtle's Back: A Native American Year of Moons

Written by Joseph Bruchac and Jonathan London
Illustrated by Thomas Locker
PaperStar/Putnam & Grosset 1992, 1997, ISBN 0–698–11584–8

Locker's luscious art provides the backdrop for this historical Native American tale about the use of the thirteen moons to tell the seasons. The story begins with a grandfather carving a turtle and explaining to his grandson that the turtle also has thirteen scales matching the thirteen moons. The authors take you through each of the moons beginning with the first moon named Northern Cheyenne, which signifies the bitter cold usually felt during that moon. The final or thirteenth moon, Abenaki, is the time when the circle of seasons is complete. The Authors' Note tells us that different tribes of Native Americans have various names for the moons and some even divide the year up by the seasons.

Two Pairs of Shoes

Written by Esther Sanderson
Illustrated by David Beyer
Pemmican 1990, ISBN 0–921827–15–6

This is one of those must-read stories for everyone. The gentle advice from this Native American author is an important reminder to us all. She tells us that little ones of one nationality living in another nation or culture must learn when and how to wear each "pair of shoes." The *shoes* are, of course, a metaphor for knowing how to live in the world without letting go of core values and traditions—without losing yourself and where you have come from. With support in launching the discussion, children will get the message packed into this short, yet powerful book.

Where Did You Get Your Moccasins?

Written by Bernelda Wheeler
Illustrated by Herman Bekkering
Peguis 1986, 1995, ISBN 1–895411–50–5

This story begins when a classmate arrives at school and all the other children are curious about his new moccasins. Following a cumulative, repetitive pattern (e.g., the one in the *House That Jack Built*), the young boy explains that his Kookum (Grandmother) made his moccasins. Readers quickly pick up the pattern as he tells that she made the moccasins from treated leather from a deer hide that his dad had gone hunting for. The pattern breaks on the last page when the little boy explains that the beads that decorate the toes of his moccasins came from a store.

America Bookshelf Two: Famous Americans

Abe Lincoln: The Boy Who Loved Books

Written by Kay Winters
Illustrated by Nancy Carpenter
Simon & Schuster 2003, ISBN 0–689–82554–4

> *In the wilds of Kentucky, 1809, a boy was born. His mother called him Abraham, his last name, Lincoln.* And what follows is a charming story of how Abe Lincoln grew up to love books and learning. Readers discover how, without pen and paper, he used any surface to practice his letters. Both of his parents were storytellers but neither of them had an education, yet their stories made Abe yearn for more. *The books he read changed his life while his life changed the world.*

Abe Lincoln Remembers

Written by Ann Turner
Illustrated by Wendell Minor
HarperCollins 2001, ISBN 0–06–027577–4

> Using facts taken from history, Turner has woven an insightful fictional account of Abe Lincoln growing up. She stays true to the characteristics of Lincoln as history has recorded them. He grew up very tall, shy, and very poor. Yet his ambition and drive were strong and he was determined to make a difference in the world. The enlarged font and short passages on every page make this one an engaging read-aloud. Many of the pages bear an enlarged copy of President Lincoln's signature. Turner's work is outstanding and is sure to be read every February as your classes celebrate the life of Abraham Lincoln.

Abraham Lincoln

Written by Amy L. Cohn and Suzy Schmidt
Illustrated by David A. Johnson
Scholastic 2002, ISBN 0–590–93566–6

From the front flap: *This passionate portrayal of one of America's greatest presidents explores Abraham Lincoln's life and the many facets of his unique personality—his intelligence, his tenacity, his compassion, and his wonderful quirky sense of humor.* The story in the book lives up to this build-up and then some. With wonderful crafting of words, these authors bring Lincoln to life, from the baby born on a cornhusk mattress to the man who would become president. As the words tell of his concern over the divided nation, they let you feel his anguish. Only five days following the end of the war, as Lincoln was watching a play, his life ended. *A train slowly carried Mr. Lincoln home to Springfield. . . . More people stood along the tracks, silent and solemn, as the barefoot, backwoods boy—now grown, now gone went past.* The soft hues of Johnson's watercolors are moving. This one is a definite keeper.

Amelia and Eleanor Go for a Ride

Written by Pam Muñoz Ryan
Illustrated by Brian Selznick
Scholastic 1999, ISBN 0–590–96075–X

Amelia and Eleanor were birds of a feather. Eleanor was outspoken and determined. So was Amelia. Amelia was daring and liked to try things other women wouldn't even consider. Eleanor, of course, was Eleanor Roosevelt, a former first lady of the United States, and Amelia was Amelia Earhart, the first female pilot to fly solo across the Atlantic. At a 1933 dinner in the White House, Eleanor is truly in awe of Amelia's flying because she has never flown. Before the night is over that changes when the two of them slip off to fly over Washington to see the Capitol by air. Eleanor describes her experience as *sitting on top of the world.* The art is reflective of the time and was completed in black and white, rendering a book that is quite dramatic and lovely.

Caesar Rodney's Ride: The Story of an American Patriot

Written by Jan Cheripko
Illustrated by Gary Lippincott
Boyds Mills 2004 ISBN 1–59078–065–5

This account of the events surrounding the signing of the Declaration of Independence is told through the eyes of Caesar Rodney, the representative from Delaware. The text is rather long; however, the art is so outstanding and the retelling so rich you won't mind the length of this picture book. As the story goes, Caesar must ride overnight from Delaware back to Philadelphia in order to be one of the signers of the Declaration. As Cheripko unfolds the story, he layers in tiny bits of history about events that were taking place at the same time the thirteen colonies were trying to make the important decision about independence. You must read the Author's Note at the beginning to understand Caesar's role and to realize how courageous and determined he was to make that grueling eight-mile ride for freedom.

Dangerous Crossing: The Revolutionary Voyage of John Quincy Adams

Written by Stephen Krensky
Illustrated by Greg Harlin
Dutton 2005, ISBN 0–525–46966–4

So often we think of our forefathers as grown men, not young men who had fears and illnesses. This book invites children to look at John Quincy Adams as a ten-year-old and at his forty-year-old father as they cross the Atlantic to enlist help from France in the colonies' fight against England. Readers journey with them through the storms at sea and through encounters with the English boats determined to prevent their safe arrival. The Author's Note at the end provides a brief history of what was in store for these future presidents following their successful landing in France.

Eleanor

Written and Illustrated by Barbara Cooney
Puffin 1996, 1999, ISBN 0–14–05583–8

Shortly after Eleanor's eighth birthday her mother dies. Her father had left home much earlier and died when she was nine. Now she has to go live with her grandmother who is not the typical loving grandmother. Because Eleanor is not a pretty child, she withdraws from the world and is painfully shy. Not until she leaves America to attend school in England does she begin to move beyond a small circle of people. The words of Eleanor's grandmother to the headmistress of the school in England reveal much about her feelings toward her own granddaughter: *Eleanor is a good girl but sadly unattractive and full of fears. Sometimes she is afraid to tell the truth and has headaches and sleepless nights.* In England with the guidance and love of the headmistress, the world opens up to Eleanor and she becomes the grand lady we now read about in history books.

Franklin & Eleanor

Written and Illustrated by Cheryl Harness
Dutton 2004, ISBN 0–525–47259–2

The Author's Note at the front deserves to be read and savored to make this book even more of a treasure for you and children: . . . *Franklin and Eleanor were complicated people who overcame many sorrows and used their partnership and their lives, lived in the best and worst of times, to forever change the relationship between the citizens of the United States and their government.* Although the text is long, it is a part of history that deserves to be put out into the air for children to hear. Plan on using it as you would a chapter book, but with this one, there is the added pleasure the illustrations bring to extend the meaning of the text. Harness has done an excellent job of filtering down the enormous amount of material written about the Roosevelts to bring readers this treasure.

George Washington's Teeth

Written by Deborah Chandra and Madeleine Comora
Illustrated by Brock Cole
Farrar, Straus and Giroux 2003, ISBN 0–374–32534–0

This entertaining story will get children giggling with the rhyme and rhythm of language revealing how George Washington lost all his teeth. Just as the story ends, the next two full spreads describe the major events of Washington's life. This is followed by a list of the resources that can be used to support the events of the story. A simply delightful book.

Houdini: World's Greatest Mystery Man and Escape King

Written by Kathleen Krull
Illustrated by Eric Velasquez
Walker Books 2005, ISBN 0–8027–8953–6

Houdini has never lost his allure and appeal to people who grew up reading about his magic and incredible ability to escape from unimaginable situations. After reading and rereading this new one, we cannot imagine a group of children who would fail to find this masterfully written account of Houdini's life fascinating.

How Ben Franklin Stole the Lightning

Written and Illustrated by Rosalyn Schanzer
HarperCollins 2003, ISBN 0–688–16993–7

> If you want to make history come alive for children, then this is the book for you. When you finish reading it, they will know the life of Ben Franklin as they would never know him from time spent with a history textbook. They will discover, for example, that Ben could swim faster than any of the other boys his age; that he was a very good writer; and that he was a musician, a printer, a cartoonist, and a world traveler. Children often associate him with electricity but he also helped write the Declaration of Independence and the US Constitution. The book is jam-packed with interesting tidbits of history that will change how children remember this renowned American. And chances are that you will learn a few new tidbits yourself. We certainly did.

I Could Do That! Esther Morris Gets Women the Vote

Written by Linda Arms White
Illustrated by Nancy Carpenter
Farrar, Straus and Giroux 2005, ISBN 0–374–33527–3

> This is a book about US history that your class shouldn't miss. It is loaded with historical events about an incomparable woman who believed in herself and in her ability to accomplish anything she set her sights on. From learning to make tea like her mother at six to opening her own store when she was nineteen, Esther was only in training for what she was to do in her future that still affects us today. As the reader turns each page, Esther grows up and reaches new goals that lead to her desire to get women the right to vote. She accomplished that goal in 1869 when the governor of Wyoming signed voting rights for women living in that state into law. The delightful art makes the reading of this kind of history book such a treat.

If I Only Had a Horn: Young Louis Armstrong

Written by Roxane Orgill
Illustrated by Leonard Jenkins
Houghton Mifflin 1997, ISBN 0–395–75919–6

Louis Armstrong was born in New Orleans where music floated in the air for more hours than not. As a young boy, Louis longed to play a horn like all the other jazz players down in the quarter, but his family was so poor that many nights there was not enough money for food and certainly not enough for a horn. One night he pulls a gun and fires it into the air when some boys begin bothering him and his friends. A policeman hears the gun shots and Louis is arrested and sent to a home for boys. After many months at the home, he discovers a band and, with his talent for music, a career was born—he was destined to become one of American's greatest talents.

Mr. Lincoln's Whiskers

Written and Illustrated by Karen B. Winnick
Boyds Mills 1996, ISBN 1 56397 805 9

Long before women were given the right to vote, little Grace Bedell knew that the country needed Abe Lincoln to be elected president. However, when she looked at his picture, she thought he would be more appealing to women if he would grow some whiskers. If he appealed to women, she reasoned, they could get their husbands to vote for him. She felt so strongly about it that she wrote to him to express her thoughts. This enchanting story tells how after being elected president, Lincoln's train stopped in the town where Grace lived so that he could meet the little girl to see whether she approved of his whiskers. At the back of the book is a copy of the letter Grace wrote to Lincoln and the endpapers include a copy of the letter written by President Lincoln to Grace Bedell.

Odd Boy Out: Young Albert Einstein

Written and Illustrated by Don Brown
Houghton Mifflin 2004, ISBN 0–618–49298–4

Many things we take for granted today can be traced back to the thinking of Albert Einstein. This story shows children what life was like for the young Einstein whose thought processes often got him into trouble. Albert was born in Germany in the late 1800s and did not talk until he was three and then he never stopped talking and asking questions. At four, he was allowed to wander the streets unattended. People did not like Albert and he became the *Odd Boy Out*. When he went to school, he was very good in subjects he liked and he just didn't bother with the ones he didn't like. His teachers thought he'd never amount to anything. He married in the early 1900s and suddenly became known as the great thinker because he ignored everything he wasn't interested in. He eventually won a Nobel Prize. As an adult, he moved to America where he died in 1955. This story reveals the child Albert Einstein once was and will be a comfort to many young readers who find themselves the "odd one out."

Remember the Ladies: 100 Great American Women

Written and Illustrated by Cheryl Harness
HarperTrophy 2001, 2003, ISBN 0–06–443869–4

> We've included this wonderful book because we believe it is an indispensable resource. It was clearly not written to be read aloud from cover to cover. Rather, this resource book deserves a prominent place on your bookshelf so that you can refer to it often and offer up a brief profile or encourage individuals to take a quick look. You could use short sections to support different areas of the curriculum and to build background on various women who have had a great impact on US history. It is important for you to read the note from the author as you use this book since there are many more than the hundred featured women who have had a tremendous impact on our history.

River Boy: The Story of Mark Twain

Written by William Anderson
Illustrated by Dan Andreasen
HarperCollins 2003, ISBN 0–06–028400–5

> Be prepared for an inspiring view when you open this treasure to the endpapers that feature a steamboat chugging down the mighty Mississippi River. Life along the river revolved around the sighting of the steamboats especially for young boys. This wonderful book invites you into the life of the young Samuel Clemens who later wrote under the pen name of Mark Twain. Read and enjoy as you learn that young Sam was prone to pulling pranks as he dreamed of being a steamboat captain. His wanderlust led him to earn his pilot's license and his life of adventure on the river became the basis for his writing. His most famous book, *The Adventures of Tom Sawyer,* is about his life in Hannibal, Missouri.

Thomas Jefferson

Written and Illustrated by Cheryl Harness
National Geographic 2004, ISBN 0–7922–6496–7

> Once when President John Kennedy was honoring the Nobel Prize winners at the White House, he made this statement: *I think this is the most*

extraordinary collection of talent, of human knowledge, that has ever been gath-ered together in the White House, with the possible exception of when Thomas Jefferson dined alone. With these words on the front flap, Harness offers us an inside view of an extremely talented author of the Declaration of Indepen-dence who also became the third President of the United States. The book provides readers with an incomparable glimpse into the life of this great American. The pictures sprinkled throughout the text help history come alive right in your classroom.

When Mr. Jefferson Came to Philadelphia: What I Learned of Freedom, 1776

Written by Ann Turner
Illustrated by Mark Hess
HarperCollins 2004, ISBN 0–06–027580–4

We hold these truths to be self-evident, that all men are created equal . . . With these stirring words our Declaration of Independence came into reality from the pen of Thomas Jefferson. This astonishingly beautiful book blends the story of Jefferson during the days men were debating separation from En-gland with the story of a young boy whose parents owned the boarding house where Jefferson was staying. The text is short but powerful, which will appeal to children as this important event in history is revealed to them from a different point of view. Don't miss this one.

Will Rogers: An American Legend

Written by Frank Keating
Illustrated by Mike Wimmer
Silver Whistle/Harcourt 2002, ISBN 0–15–202405–0

With words like *he saw oceans of wheat and dreamed of touching distant skies,* Keating, a former governor and first-time author, gives us a rich glimpse into the life of the famous Will Rogers. The text on each page is short, yet it clearly provides the complete story of this outstanding American. Along with Wimmer's almost photographic art, this one belongs on your social studies shelf and will help children breathe life into history.

A Woman for President: The Story of Virginia Woodhull

Written by Kathleen Krull
Illustrated by Jane Dyer
Walker Books 2004, ISBN 0–8027–8908–0

The Author's Note at the back of the book offers little-known history about the plight of Virginia Woodhull. For example, did you know that Virginia ran for president against Ulysses S. Grant but spent Election Day in jail? Did you know she became the first woman to own a newspaper? Did you know she was the first woman to speak to Congress and the first woman to sit on the Wall Street stock exchange? When we notice the name of Jane Dyer as the illustrator, we expect a gorgeous book and this one is nothing less. It is beautifully done and will stretch your insights about this period of history as well. This is an upper-grade picture book that will be of great interest, especially during an election year or when zooming in on the role of women in shaping the history of our nation.

America Bookshelf Three: Historic Landmarks and Symbols

Across America: I Love You
Written by Christine Loomis
Illustrated by Kate Kiesler
Hyperion 2000, ISBN 0–7868–0366–5

From the ragged shoreline of the Pacific through the rugged rise of the Rocky Mountains to the carefully tilled fields of the heartland of America, Loomis takes us on a cross-country journey that invites everyone to look at our beautiful country with new eyes. She takes us to every region with her well-crafted language while Kiesler provides a visual portrait of all parts of the country we visit in this delightful book. This one will stir up your patriotism and will make you stand taller the next time you hear the National Anthem and "America the Beautiful."

Beautiful for Spacious Skies
Written by Katharine Lee Bates
Illustrated by Wayne Thiebaud
Edited by Sara Jane Boyers
Chronicle Books 1994, ISBN 0–8118–0832–7

Bates wrote the poem that later became one of the all-time favorite American patriotic songs. Hopefully, by using this book with its lovely art supporting the phrases of the poem, children will unpack the true meaning behind the lyrics. The font is enlarged with only phrases on each full spread making it appealing to young and old alike.

Bebop Express

Written by H. I. Panahi
Illustrated by Steve Johnson and Lou Fancher
Geringer Books/HarperCollins 2005, ISBN 0–06–057190–X

The sounds of jazz are uniquely American. Listen and you'll hear sounds you won't find in any other genre of music. Through her words Panahi has succeeded in capturing that essence and gives students the flavor and mood of jazz without leaving the classroom. From the bebopping, doo-wapping of the jazz heard in the clubs of New York, you ride the train across America to meet jazz sounds unique to other areas. The trip ends in our beloved New Orleans, the jazz enriched city of the South where street musicians fill the air with *blee bah blee bah, dool doot bah!* The book is filled with alliteration and a rhythm that would be a music teacher's dream. Make this one even more meaningful and play a little jazz recording just as you reach the last words. Oh yeah . . . !

By the Dawn's Early Light: The Story of the Star-Spangled Banner

Written by Steven Kroll
Illustrated by Dan Andreasen
Scholastic 1994, 2000, ISBN 0–590–45055–7

If you are fascinated by the history of our country, you will simply have to have this indispensable book to read to children. Not only is it well-written in a dramatic style that keeps you hanging on to find out what happened, but the art is simply gorgeous. Invite children to hear what inspired Francis Scott Key, a Washington lawyer, to write the words that would later be ones we sing with great reverence at most US events. This is a wonderful supplement for the teaching of American history.

Capital!: Washington D.C. from A to Z

Written by Laura Krauss Melmed
Illustrated by Frané Lessac
HarperCollins 2003, ISBN 0–688–17561–9

This is a book you will want to use over time. Take it slowly and in small installments so that you can linger with the information and images. It simply has so much material that you would never want to rush through the book by reading it aloud page by page in one sitting. The material is interesting and will take students into our nation's capital city. It can also lead to another research project using the same structure. Once again, the art is in a cartoon style that will likely engage children and draw them in to learn more about the rich history of our diverse nation.

The Flag Maker: A Story of the Star-Spangled Banner

Written by Susan Campbell Bartoletti
Illustrated by Colaire A. Nivola
Houghton Mifflin 2004, ISBN 0–618–26757–3

If you want students to understand how the flag became a symbol during a crucial time in the history of our country, this one is a must-read. Young Caroline and her mother were seamstresses who made flags of all kinds for the soldiers who were fighting against the British in an attempt to win freedom for the American Colonies. When the soldiers came and requested a very large flag that the British could see from a long distance, they began sewing. The flag soon outgrew their sewing room and had to be moved to a larger warehouse. On the night of the battle at Fort McHenry that star-spangled banner was still waving over the land of the free and home of the brave. The Author's Note at the back provides additional information about this important time in our country's history.

The Flag We Love

Written by Pam Muñoz Ryan
Illustrated by Ralph Masiello
Charlesbridge 1996, ISBN 0–88106–844–6

If you've had trouble explaining to children the history behind one of our most important symbols, the American flag, this is the book for you. Ryan and Masiello take readers on a historical tour that is inspiring and informative. The enlarged font is child-friendly and doesn't overwhelm readers because the art finishes the meaning. This one will become an essential book for you every year as you teach children about our country and the significance of this important symbol.

Ghosts of the White House

Written and Illustrated by Cheryl Harness
Simon & Schuster 1998, ISBN 0–689–80872–0

As James Buchanan was leaving the White House and Abraham Lincoln was moving in following his election in 1861, Buchanan told him: *If you are as happy, my dear sir, on entering this house as I am in leaving it and returning home, you are the happiest man in the country.* This is only one of the unique quotes concerning the White House that are in this book. The volume is filled with gossip about all the presidents and first ladies who have occupied the White House. Much of it is written as a comic book with sidebars containing a concise history of the president being featured on the pages. Both you and your children will enjoy this one.

I Pledge Allegiance

Written by Bill Martin Jr. and Michael Sampson
Illustrated by Chris Raschka
Candlewick 2002, 2004, ISBN 0–7636–2527–2

Have you ever listened in as young children repeat the Pledge of Allegiance to the Flag every morning? Do children really understand what the words mean and why we say the pledge anyway? How do you explain to children all the words of the Pledge of Allegiance? Well, Martin and Sampson give you this indispensable resource in which they have divided the pledge into phrases and feature only one phrase per page. Along with the phrase running across the bottom of the page is an explanation of what the phrase or words mean. This one is very simple, but very powerful.

If the Walls Could Talk: Family Life at the White House

Written by Jane O'Connor
Illustrated by Gary Hovland
Wiseman/Simon & Schuster 2004, ISBN 0–689–86863–4

It is difficult for children to understand that presidents have a somewhat normal life with pets and accidents and the daily occurrences just like their own. This book offers delicious tidbits that will intrigue students as they get a peek into what life is like for a president and a president's family. The book opens with facts that many children may not know about the White House. Every page is full of details about the featured presidents beginning with George Washington and moving chronologically to George W. Bush. The last page is worth the price of the book; it shows all the modern-day presidents and their wives with a short blurb about each. This title can help you demonstrate how research doesn't always tell everything in minute detail. The cartoonlike drawings will capture students' interest in learning more about the history of our presidents. Here, again, is another nice alternative and/or supplement to the history/social studies textbook.

Liberty!

Written and Illustrated by Allan Drummond
Frances Foster/Farrar, Straus and Giroux 2002, ISBN 0–374–34385–3

The note from the author at the front of the book gives a history of the Statue of Liberty. The text itself is very short, told in an entertaining style, and supported by cartoonlike art. The font is enlarged, which makes this a great read-aloud for younger children. This one would be great to pair with *The Story of the Statue of Liberty* (Mulberry 1986; see page 185).

Liberty's Journey

Written by Kelly DiPucchio
Illustrated by Richard Egielski
Hyperion 2004, ISBN 0–7868–1876–X

Upon a salt-licked island shore
stands a lady folks adore.
A mighty beacon by the sea,
she greets the tired, the poor, the free.

These lyrical lines open the story of how Lady Liberty leaves her island home to travel across the United States from shore to shore to see the sights. When she reaches the Golden Gate Bridge, a young boy tells her how much she is missed by the people in New York. Suddenly her wanderlust is satisfied and she longs to return home.

O, Say Can You See?: America's Symbols, Landmarks, and Inspiring Words

Written by Sheila Keenan
Illustrated by Ann Boyajian
Scholastic 2004, ISBN 0–439–42450–X

Keenan has provided us with a picture book that is simply full of interesting information about the symbols of our nation. Providing this book for children will help them understand the importance of symbols and how they help us as a nation (community) to feel pride in ourselves and to establish an identity. Therefore, this book will help children be more conscious about what it means to be an American. Here are just a few morsels of information to whet your appetite: Do you know why the Liberty Bell has a crack in it? Which president never got to live in the White House? How many steps are in the Statute of Liberty? Kids will simply "eat this up," so be prepared to let them hover with it for many days. It's much too long for one sitting, but too good to miss. So search through and select a few morsels to draw them in, then leave the feast within their reach and watch the feeding frenzy.

The Story of the Statue of Liberty

Written and Illustrated by Betsy and Giulio Maestro
HarperTrophy 1986, 1989, ISBN 0–688–08746–9

Isn't it amazing that the monument standing in the New York Harbor to welcome visitors to America, serving as a symbol of the freedom in the New World, should be a gift from an artist in France? Since this book comes in paperback, you will want several copies because once children become fascinated by the designing and building and history of this statue, it will become a favorite. (That is even true for adults who love the Statue of Liberty.) This little book is full of insights that will fascinate and inform students.

The Train of States

Written and Illustrated by Peter Sis
Greenwillow 2004, ISBN 0–06–057838–6

What a wonderful resource this book will be to any classroom launching a study of the fifty states. Sis uses antique circus train cars as the backdrop to feature each state presented in chronological order by the date each obtained statehood. Every page contains many facts about the featured state including its motto, bird, flower, tree, and so on. Study every car carefully and examine all the borders closely to find even more information. This book offers a delightful alternative to an overwhelming textbook and serves as an excellent starting point for further inquiry.

Twenty-One Elephants

Written by Phil Bildner
Illustrated by LeUyen Pham
Simon & Schuster 2004, ISBN 0–689–87011–6

From her window in Brooklyn, Hannah watches the building of the Eighth Wonder of the World that connects Brooklyn to Manhattan—the Brooklyn Bridge. At first, many of the residents of Brooklyn won't travel across the suspension bridge because they feel it is unsafe. Hannah's family, the people at her school, and the people at the market by her church all feel it's unsafe and refuse to let Hannah cross it. A year passes and it hasn't fallen even though people cross it every day, yet Hannah's dad still refuses to let her go across. When the circus comes to town, Hannah has an idea of how she can prove to her parents that the bridge is safe. She talks Mr. Barnum into leading his twenty-one elephants across the bridge to show everyone how safe it is. Thereafter, she and her dad walk across the bridge many days. *Twenty-One Elephants* is a bit of history told in a fictional story that will truly engage and delight children.

Wackiest White House Pets

Written by Gibbs Davis
Illustrated by David A. Johnson
Scholastic 2004, ISBN 0–439–44373–3

Take a look at this book for the inside story on the most unusual pets of some of our former presidents; when we say *unusual,* we aren't talking about cats or dogs. Each spread features one president and reveals the family's unusual pet of choice. Here's a little sample: Did you know that some of our famous leaders favored horses, grizzly cubs, parrots, elephants, and even an alligator rather than the typical pets we've grown use to seeing with presidents as they return to the White House from trips? Some of these rather unusual pets actually lived at the White House but were later donated to zoos. You'll just have to read to believe and find out the story behind some unusual inhabitants of the White House. A rather serious listing is also provided to inform readers about all those other presidents who had rather ordinary pets.

We the Kids: The Preamble to the Constitution of the United States

Written by Our Founding Fathers
Foreword and Illustrated by David Catrow
Dial 2002, 2005, ISBN 0–8037–2553–1

Catrow's foreword is worth the price of the book because he explains in simple terms what the Constitution is and why we have it. Then he provides a listing of the "big words" found in it and what they mean. With full-page art in the now very recognizable Catrow style, he gifts us with the actual words of the Constitution presented in an enlarged font. This is a must-have if you are teaching about the Constitution.

America Bookshelf Four: The US Presidency and Voting in the United States

Hail to the Chief: The American Presidency

Written by Don Robb
Illustrated by Alan Witschonke
Charlesbridge 2000, ISBN 0–88106–392–4

This title is an excellent choice to use with your classroom as a minitextbook on the US presidency. Every spread, supported by the artwork of Witschonke, brings into focus a different element of the job. As a bonus, you will find a listing of websites and additional readings at the back of the book.

My Teacher for President

Written by Kay Winters
Illustrated by Denise Brunkus
Dutton 2004, ISBN 0–525–47186–3

Oh, Winters was so clever with this adorable book. Hats off to whoever selected Brukus as the illustrator because her art tells "the other half" of the story in a glorious way. The book begins with a boy writing to a TV station asking how he can help his teacher become president. After all, she is used to living in white houses, being followed around everywhere, having people pay attention when she enters the room, attends meetings—and the list goes on and on. The structure of this very short story has only one sentence per page. The print is always placed on the left page. The sentence defines what she is doing in her *teacher role*. On the opposite page, you see the teacher doing the same things in a *presidential role*. This one is a must-read and a must-have for a classroom library.

So You Want to Be President?

Written by Judith St. George
Illustrated by David Small
Philomel 2000, ISBN 0–399–23407–1

This is a rather long story for a picture book, but considering the number of presidents it portrays, it is simply delightful. While many facts are presented, there are also some *"spit-fire" comments and comical anecdotes* about several of the presidents that may surprise you but will surely thrill the kids. With Small's characteristic illustration style, which won him the cherished Caldecott, this book will be enjoyed while it informs children.

Vote!

Written and Illustrated by Eileen Christelow
Clarion 2003, ISBN 0–618–24754–8

Have you found it difficult to explain to children how voting works? If so, this could be the book you have been searching for. Christelow provides a complete description of the process in terms children can understand. Readers will find information that provides historical background about voting in a democratic society. The art is presented in a cartoon style that is likely to engage children without overwhelming them as they study the process of elections and unpack the complex concepts. To extend a study, the book contains a glossary, Internet resources, and a timeline of voting rights that will be helpful.

Woodrow for President: A Tail of Voting, Campaigns and Elections

Written and Illustrated by Peter W. Barnes and Cheryl Shaw Barnes
Vacation Spot Pubications 1999, ISBN 1–893–62201–0

Using Woodrow, a mouse, as the main character and a delightful play on words, the authors will assist you in explaining the process of voting. Woodrow is a good citizen who befriends others. When it is time for someone to run for city council, everyone in town thought of Woodrow and he is elected. Later he runs for the state senate and after that for governor; he wins both of the subsequent elections. Throughout the story, terms are explained so that children get a general idea about the process of running for an office. Of course, Woodrow goes all the way and runs for president. At the back of the book, there is a contract between America's children and adults promising to exercise the right to vote. This would be a nice book to use when our country is in the midst of a major election.

You're on Your Way, Teddy Roosevelt

Written by Judith St. George
Illustrated by Matt Faulkner
Philomel 2004, ISBN 0–399–23888–3

All of us, especially children, have a difficult time imagining the famous people we read about in history ever having been children. This book lets us into the life of a young Teddy Roosevelt who battled asthma throughout childhood to become a great leader. He experienced many failures and could never seem to live up to the expectations of his parents who were supportive and worked to help little Teddy overcome his illnesses. The book is written in short chapters with delightful pictures that extend the story.

America Bookshelf Five: "Let's Play Ball"— Baseball, America's Game

OK, we admit it; we couldn't decide where to place this shelf. But, we couldn't leave it out. There are so many books about baseball, and we know that kids (of all ages) love the game; we just couldn't leave them out of this book.

Casey at the Bat

Written by Ernest Lawrence Thayer
Illustrated by LeRoy Neiman
Introduction by Joe Torre
Ecco 2000, 2002, ISBN 0–06–009068–5

Ernest Lawrence Thayer wrote the original poem in 1888 as a salute to the nation's pastime. Neiman has revived the poem and illustrated it with his striking charcoal drawings to bring pleasure to a new generation of baseball lovers. There are only a few words on each page, and they are in a very large font. Neiman's sketches do much of the work of telling the story of the game.

Casey at the Bat: A Ballad of the Republic Sung in the Year 1888

Written by Ernest Lawrence Thayer
Illustrated by Christopher Bing
Handprint 2000, ISBN 1–929766–00–9

If you have children in your classroom who are resistant to reading, this could be a book to change their minds. Once you show and explain how the newspaper clippings work to tell the story of Casey, you won't have any argument when it's time for independent reading—well, not as long as this book survives the many, many page turnings that are sure to occur. The entire book has the look of a scrapbook with clippings and pictures from period newspapers. The story, however, is in its original form as when Thayer first wrote of the mighty *Casey at the Bat*.

Coming Home: A Story of Josh Gibson, Baseball's Greatest Home Run Hitter

Written by Nanette Mellage
Illustrated by Cornelius Van Wright and Ying-Hwa Hu
BridgeWater/Troll 2001, ISBN 0–8167–7010–7

> Josh Gibson was only eighteen when he joined the all-negro baseball team in Pennsylvania. In those days of segregation, black ballplayers weren't allowed to play on the same teams as white players. The story was written as a tribute to the talent of this young man who had such strength that it sounded like thunder when he hit the ball. His fans began calling him "Thunder," and it became a chant on the day his team met in Yankee Stadium to play another undefeated team in the Negro League. On that day in 1930, Gibson hit the longest home run in history. The watercolor hues are gorgeous and offer another dimension to an already appealing story.

Dad, Jackie, and Me

Written by Myron Uhlberg
Illustrated by Colin Bootman
Peachtree 2005, ISBN 1–56145–329–3

> This is a moving memoir-like story of growing up in Brooklyn during the days Jackie Robinson became the first African American to be drafted to play in the majors for the Brooklyn Dodgers. The narrator's father, who was deaf, felt a soul-to-soul connection with Jackie as they both battled to overcome prejudice. The Author's Note makes this book an even more powerful memory of the groundbreaking event in US history. Uhlberg tells that his dad, who was also deaf, read the papers every day and clipped every article he could find about Jackie. He placed those articles in a scrapbook. The endpapers include period newspaper clippings that readers will want to linger with to learn even more about the famous Jackie Robinson.

Dirt on Their Skirts: The Story of the Young Women Who Won the World Champsionship

Written by Doreen Rappaport and Lyndall Callan
Illustrated by E. B. Lewis
Dial 2000, ISBN 0–8037–2042–4

> We recommend that you and your students spend some time examining the period team photographs on the front and back endpapers before reading this retelling of the 1942 All-American Girls Professional Baseball League

championship game. The children are sure to be fascinated by the uniforms. As you begin reading aloud, let the art of E. B. Lewis and the language of this story carry you into that championship game through the eyes of a young girl whose father had just returned home from fighting overseas in World War II. Now, instead of mailing him the score cards, he can go to the games with her to cheer her team on. The book provides a play-by-play of the game that went into extra innings before Margaret's team won. An Author's Note at the back gives you the history of why the all-girls team was formed. Read this one along with *Girl Wonder: A Baseball Story in Nine Innings* by Deborah Hopkinson.

Hank Aaron: Brave in Every Way

Written by Peter Golenbock
Illustrated by Paul Lee
Gulliver/Harcourt 2001, ISBN 0–15–202093–4

Growing up in the South, Hank Aaron was a hero for many youngsters regardless of race or gender. The flap of this book jacket sums up this book so nicely: *On April 8, 1974, American watched as Hank Aaron stepped up to the plate. The pitch was low and down the middle. Hank swung—and hit home run number 715! With that hit, Hank Aaron surpassed Babe Ruth's legendary record and realized a lifelong dream.* Hank Aaron is born three years before Marian Anderson is allowed to sing on the steps of the Lincoln Memorial. And maybe his parents have not heard about this important happening in the life of another African American, but they dream that their boy will have the opportunity to make a difference in the world. They are in the middle of the Great Depression but the family surrounds little Hank with love and time to play ball. His mama's advice is always, *Set goals for yourself and always work to be your best!* Read this incredible story of a young man who did just that and became a hero to many. Lee's full-page illustrations extend the story and will serve to hold the attention of all those who take the time to peek inside.

Home Run: The Story of Babe Ruth

Written by Robert Burleigh
Illustrated by Mike Wimmer
Silver Whistle/Harcourt 1998, 2003, ISBN 0–15–200970–1

The book begins with *He is the Babe* and across from that one sentence standing alone on the page is a glorious picture of none other then George

Herman Ruth. Then, you are off and reading one exceptionally well-written book on the impact the Babe had on the game of baseball. Ruth began playing major league baseball when he was only nineteen years old, which is why the other players began calling him "the Babe." Burleigh does a magnificent job of making you feel as though you are standing on home plate watching and waiting for that perfect ball. He knows just when to speed the story up and the perfect moment to slow the pace. Add to that Mike Wimmer's exquisite artwork, so finely detailed that you have to look twice to be sure it isn't a photograph, and you have a winner.

Just Like Josh Gibson

Written by Angela Johnson
Illustrated by Beth Peck
Simon & Schuster 2004, ISBN 0–689–82628–1

Growing up in the 1940s wasn't easy, especially if you were a girl who liked to play baseball. She heard it all the time, . . . *too bad she's a girl* because she could sure play baseball. Her idol was Josh Gibson, the *Babe Ruth of the Negro League.* When her dad pitches to her, she pretends to be playing in the big league. When she gets to practice with the boys, she pretends. One day when one of the baseball players gets hurt and the team is one short, they come calling. It is said that as she hit, caught, and pitched that day, she was just like her idol . . . Josh Gibson.

Luke Goes to Bat

Written and Illustrated by Rachel Isadora
G. P. Putnam's Sons 2005, ISBN 0–399–23604–X

Here's another book that gives us a look at the Brooklyn Dodgers during that famous year of 1951 when Jackie Robinson became the first black major league baseball player. This one features a little boy named Luke who wants more than anything to be allowed to play stickball with the older boys in the street. But each time he asks, they refuse. After every game he observes, he'd leaves and goes to practice so that he'll be ready when his day comes. At night, he climbs up on his roof and watches the Dodgers game at Ebbets Field. When the cheers go up, Luke just knows his favorite player, Jackie Robinson, has hit a home run. One day his grandmother got tickets for the game and his prayers are answered when Jackie hits a home run. That night when he goes to the roof just to look at the lights of Ebbets Field, there is Jackie Robinson's home run ball. What more could be said?

Mama Played Baseball

Written by David A. Adler
Illustrated by Chris O'Leary
Gulliver/Harcourt 2003, ISBN 0–15–202196–5

During World War II, many things changed in America while the men were in Europe. One of those things was the role of women. Women began doing things that only men had done prior to the war. In this nostalgic story, Amy's mom needs a job while her husband is at war. She decides on the new All-American Girls Professional Baseball League. With help from Amy, she practices until she is good enough to make the team. That league was one way for Americans at home to take their minds off the war and missing family members. When dad comes home, everyone celebrates his arrival as well as the efforts of Amy's mom to make the team.

Mighty Jackie: The Strike-Out Queen

Written by Marissa Moss
Illustrated by C. F. Payne
Wiseman/Simon & Schuster 2004, ISBN 0–689–86329–2

Babe Ruth was thought to be the best player in the major leagues during the late 1920s and early 1930s. In those years before the season began, the major league teams traveled around the country to play local teams. This story is about one of those games. No one could believe the pitcher for the Chattanooga Lookouts was a girl and only seventeen years old. She was a joke to the mighty Yankees and their outstanding player Babe Ruth. They jeered her when she went out on the mound. But what they didn't count on was the heart of the girl with the ball in her hand. The pacing of the language is superb. This one deserves to be read; even those who aren't baseball fans will appreciate the storytelling in this finely crafted book.

Players in Pigtails

Written by Shana Corey
Illustrated by Rebecca Gibbon
Scholastic 2003, ISBN 0–439–18305–7

Katie Casey wasn't good at being a girl . . . at least not the kind of girl everyone thought she should be. . . . But there was one thing Katie was good at, BASE-BALL. None of this pleased her parents, but when Katie has the opportunity to travel to Chicago and try out for the All-American Girls Professional

Baseball League, she is on her way. It is difficult for people to accept that girls want to play baseball, not to mention be any good at it. But when *PLAY BALL* is shouted in the stadium and the girls prove they can hit, run, catch, and throw as well as men, the cheers go up for the team.

Roberto Clemente: Pride of the Pittsburgh Pirates

Written by Jonah Winter
Illustrated by Raul Colon
Atheneum 2005, ISBN 0–689–85643–1

This is a story of the determination to follow a dream despite poverty and lack of support. Clemente was born in Puerto Rico and wanted nothing more than to play major league baseball. His family could not afford to buy him a bat, a ball, or a glove. Yet, with a coffee sack wrapped around his hand for a glove, he practiced. He practiced and practiced until he was the best in his country at the game. One league led into the next until he made it to the majors. People in America had never heard about this boy from Puerto Rico who could do such unbelievable things with the baseball and a bat. Before his death, he had 3,000 hits—the scoreboard depicted on that page tells more of the history of that day. When the 1972 season was over, he was flying to Central America to help in the aftermath of an earthquake when the engine in his plane failed and Clemente dropped to his death.

The Shot Heard 'Round the World

Written by Phil Bildner
Illustrated by C. F. Payne
Simon & Schuster 2005, ISBN 0–689–86273–3

Here is one more telling of the famous 1951 Brooklyn Dodgers when Jackie Robinson became the first black player in the National League. This book is told through the eyes of a young boy whose life revolves around those Dodger games and his spirits ride with them through a perfect season. And now they must face the Giants, another New York team. The entire city is caught up in the furor of both of their successful seasons because everyone was either a Dodgers' fan or a Giants' fan. Game day finds everyone hustling to the game or huddled around the radio listening. With bated breath, game day arrives and the pennant will go home with one of the teams. The Dodgers, having led throughout the game, face the bottom of the ninth with a three-run lead. Two players hit singles before the third batter hits a home run that makes a sound the boys felt could be heard around the world. As the Giants win the pennant, the fans of the Brooklyn Dodgers are crushed, but with *hearts that ran blue,* all they could do was wait another year. The art is amazing and puts the reader right there with those boys listening to the sounds of the game pour out of the radio.

■ *Building Background for a Study of Living Through Conflict, Working Toward Peace*

This collection of books includes shelves for only a few of the major conflicts in which our nation has been involved. While reading for these shelves, we looked for those titles that seemed to be the most attuned to the fact that children would be the audience. We weren't trying to shelter them from the reality of wars and other conflicts; rather, we looked for titles that would keep the focus on the human stories connected to efforts to resolve conflicts. We have tried to create shelves of books that will enable read-alouds to reach listeners heart to heart and head to head and soul to soul. That is, the goal is to try to help children know that these events in history are about more than keeping score of how many battles were won and lost.

You will notice too that we have included books that address the Oklahoma City bombing and the tragic events of September 11, 2001. We chose them for similar reasons; too many of our children see reports of these events on the news and never know the human stories behind them. We hope you recognize that this collection was selected with care because the topics are sensitive, and we know that children will be the listeners.

Living Through Conflict, Working Toward Peace Bookshelf One: Revolutionary War

The Scarlet Stockings Spy

Written by Trinka Hakes Noble
Illustrated by Robert Papp
Sleepy Bear Press 2004, ISBN 1–58536–230–1

> Begin your reading with the Author's Note because it will make the book come alive for students with added knowledge about the author. The story is set in Philadelphia in 1777 in the time of Revolutionary War. *Uncertainty*

settled over the city like soot. Suspicions skulked through the cobblestone streets like hungry alley cats. Rumors multiplied like horseflies. Spies were everywhere. Maddy Rose becomes one of those spies; because of her young age, she can move about the street without being noticed. Her father was killed a year earlier and her brother Jonathan joined Washington's army so there is only Maddy Rose and her mother. She learns how to signal Jonathan by hanging certain garments on her clothesline. She learns how to notice everything and to hear everything around her to be useful to her brother. When her brother gets killed (the art on this page is particularly outstanding), Maddy Rose takes Jonathan's blue coat, her scarlet stockings, and her white petticoat and makes a flag to hang when the war is over and the Colonists have prevailed. Don't miss this one if you're studying American history. The art is colorful and crisp and, above all, simply memorable.

Living Through Conflict, Working Toward Peace Bookshelf Two: Civil War

The Blue and the Gray

Written by Eve Bunting
Illustrated by Ned Bittinger
Scholastic 1996, ISBN 0–590–60200–4

Bunting begins the story with two young boys who are going to live in a new subdivision built in the middle of what once was fields and forest. As the boys look out over the field, their dad reminds them that once this very land was a battlefield where many people fought against each other: . . . *North against South, the blue against the gray. White against black. White against white. Us against us.* As the boys walk with dad, he continues telling them the history of the war. The story goes back and forth between the current day where a black and a white boy can be friends to the days when the air was filled with the echoes of the horrors of battle and death. The art-filled pages are moving.

Cassie's Sweet Berry Pie: A Civil War Story

Written and Illustrated by Karen B. Winnick
Boyds Mills 2005, ISBN 1–56397–984–5

This fictional story, set during the Civil War, tells of a young girl caring for her brother and sister. Their daily routines reveal a way of life typical for many families at that time. Food was limited to what their family could grow and that often meant very scarce resources. So when Cassie finds some berries one day, she hopes to bake a pie because the family has not had one for many months. Just as she begins to mix all the ingredients her Mama has carefully saved for the pie, she hears the pounding of hooves outside their cabin. She knows that means the Yankees are approaching and that means danger. To save her siblings and their food from the Yankees, this clever girl uses the berries to paint measles on the faces of the young children. The sight of those spotted faces sends the Yankees on their way, leaving the family and their food safe for another day.

Diary of a Drummer Boy

Written by Marlene Targ Brill
Illustrated by Michael Garland
Millbrook Press 1998, 2000, ISBN 0–7613–1388–5

When the Civil War began, young males who could not even vote became drummer boys whose job was to lead soldiers into battle with their drums. The story is told as the diary of Orion Howe who is only twelve years old. The diary format enables Brill to share with readers all the events surrounding a family in 1860. Young Howe spends three years in the war before finally arriving at home again and every entry into his diary provides further description of the war's events. Garland's art is so crisp and realistic you will want to frame many of them. Each painting supports the text and extends understanding and insights.

Drummer Boy: Marching to the Civil War

Written by Ann Turner
Illustrated by Mark Hess
HarperCollins 1998, ISBN 0–06–027696–7

This thirteen-year-old boy feels compelled to help keep his country together, but he is too young to join the army. So, he lies about his age to enlist and soon becomes a valuable solider who learns to beat the drum to signal the men or to raise their spirits. The words from the front flap sum up the story quite well: *Beautiful, haunting text and stunning paintings bring to life what it must have been like to be a very young soldier in the Civil War. It is an unforgettable homage to the bravery and resourcefulness of children in uncommon situations.*

Pink and Say

Written and Illustrated by Patricia Polacco
Philomel 1994, ISBN 0–399–22671–0

This book is a Civil War story about two young Union boys—Sheldon Russell Curtis (Say), a white boy, and Pinkus, a slave boy with *skin the color of polished mahogany.* Pinkus comes upon the wounded Say and, with difficulty, carries him many miles to his home deep within Confederate territory in Georgia. During the time that Pink's mother, Moe Moe Bay, nurses Say, a friendship is born between the boys. This tender story has lots of Civil War and slavery history woven through it, but above all the book is a story of a friendship that transcends many obstacles.

Red Legs: A Drummer Boy of the Civil War

Written and Illustrated by Ted Lewin
HarperCollins 2001, ISBN 0–688–16024–7

Lewin weaves an intriguing tale that takes the reader into battle with a young drummer boy leading the charge. As you read aloud, students will fall silent and hold their breaths when the young one is shot and drops to the ground. Let this event hang in the air for a moment like the resounding echo of the shot fired just seconds before. Don't turn the page just yet, let students linger with Lewin's captivating images. Then, when you turn that last page, let your voice drop to a softer tone and announce that this is the story of a Civil War reenactment. Read the Author's Note to be able to explain what that means and how Ted Lewin came to create this remarkable tale. Lewin's art is equally as significant as his story because it makes an unfamiliar part of history come alive for kids. This has become one of our all-time favorite books to use in the curriculum connection section. We are certain it will soon become one of yours as well.

The Silent Witness: A True Story of the Civil War

Written by Robin Friedman
Illustrated by Claire A. Nivola
Houghton Mifflin 2005, ISBN 0–618–44230–8

In July 1861, the first battle of the Civil War was waged in Manassas, Virginia, on the front lawn of Wilmer McLean's home. Suddenly the peaceful country became harsh and dangerous with all the troops camped around their home.

Soon after the war began, Wilmer decided to move his young family to a village called the Appomattox Court House. Then on April 9, 1865, four long years after the war began, General Lee and General Grant met in that same Court House to end the war. Left in the room was little Lulu's rag doll. The soldiers dubbed the doll *The Silent Witness*. Once the surrender papers were signed, one of the Union soldiers stuffed the little doll into his pocket as a souvenir. Lulu never saw her doll again. Embedded within the story, you will find many facts about the events between 1861 and 1865. The book will strengthen any study you do concerning the Civil War.

Living Through Conflict, Working Toward Peace Bookshelf Three: World War II

Faithful Elephants: A True Story of Animals, People and War

Written by Yukio Tsuchiya
Translated by Tomoko Tsuchiya Dykes
Illustrated by Ted Lewin
Houghton Mifflin 1951, 1988, ISBN 0–395–46555–9

During World War II after bombs were dropped on Japan, the government officials became afraid that bombs would break open the cages at the zoo and the captive animals would be freed. To ensure the safety of the people, an order was given to put all the animals to death. The animals were poisoned with injections, but the needles just broke in the thick skin of elephants. The zookeepers tried feeding them poisoned potatoes but the elephants wouldn't eat them. The decision was then made to starve the three elephants. Slowly one by one the three elephants succumbed to painful deaths. The zookeepers were heartbroken and railed against the war that had caused them to do such a horrible thing. The beloved elephants were buried in honor with a marble marker to commemorate their lives.

The Greatest Skating Race: A World War II Story from the Netherlands

Written by Louise Borden
Illustrated by Niki Daly
McElderry/Simon & Schuster 2004, ISBN 0–689–84502–2

This read-aloud will keep your students leaning in, urging you to turn the pages, eager to hear the conclusion as three young children escape the

Germans by skating the canals connecting the towns in the Netherlands and Belgium. Let your voice build suspense as the father of the youngest two is arrested and the mother must send her children away to keep them safe from the Germans. When the mother asks her friends for help, they decide the only way to escape is for the children to skate the long way to their aunt's house in Belgium. Many of the words may be difficult to pronounce, even with the guide at the bottom, so this is one you will have to practice. It will be well worth the time you invest. This is truly a remarkable story that can help students understand the struggles of World War II.

Mercedes and the Chocolate Pilot: A True Story of the Berlin Airlift and the Candy That Dropped from the Sky

Written by Margot Theis Raven
Illustrated by Gijsbert van Frankenhuyzen
Sleeping Bear Press 2002, ISBN 1–58536–069–4

During World War II life was grim in America, but for families in Europe, life was often quite unbearable. When West Berlin was cut off from the rest of the world, pilots began flying in needed supplies across enemy territory to help civilians there. One of those pilots knew that the children living there had not had candy for a long time and began making little parachutes attached to candy to drop to them. One of those children was seven-year-old Mercedes and the story unfolds for readers through her excited eyes. This story features the power of human kindness in the midst of untold horror and pain. The art, by van Frankenhuyzen, will help children understand some of the devastation caused by war.

 *Living Through Conflict, Working Toward Peace Bookshelf Four: Japanese Internment*

Baseball Saved Us

Written by Ken Mochizuki
Illustrated by Dom Lee
Lee & Low 1993, 1995, ISBN 1–880000–19–9

During World War II after the bombing of Pearl Harbor, the US government moved all the Japanese people living in the United States to internment camps. This story takes place in one of the camps, which were hot during the day and very cold at night. Since they were built in the middle of the desert, dust storms were plentiful. One of the men living in the camp decides to help his people think of something other than the endless misery by building a baseball field and establishing teams. The art begins in muddy browns and gradually changes to an array of color as the story moves from misery to a new focus when the entire camp is pulling and cheering together, leaving their loneliness behind for many hours during each game. It should be noted that the US government admitted in 1988 that it had been a mistake to isolate the Japanese Americans during that time.

The Bracelet

Written by Yoshiko Uchida
Illustrated by Joanna Yardley
PaperStar/Putnam 1976 (Philomel), 1993, ISBN 0–698–11390–X

In 1942 during World War II, all Japanese Americans were sent to internment camps. Young Emi's family is separated when her father gets sent to a different camp. On the last day before they have to leave their home, Emi's friend Laurie brings her a bracelet to help her remember their friendship. Somehow, during the difficult days of settling into the camp, she loses the bracelet and no matter how much they look for it, the precious bracelet cannot be found. During the hours that follow, Emi grows to realize that people do not need objects to help them remember the people they love. They have all they need right inside of them.

Home of the Brave

Written and Illustrated by Allen Say
Houghton Mifflin 2002, ISBN 0–618–21223–X

While *Home of the Brave* provides another look at the Japanese internment camps, it is written in the form of a man's dreamlike, confused state as he wanders into the desert camp where he discovers only lost children. The illustrations are muted, adding to the haunting message of the text. Our suggestion would be to use this book only after building a solid background of understanding about the camps during that period of time.

I Am an American: A True Story of Japanese Internment

Written by Jerry Stanley
Illustrated with actual photographs
Scholastic 1994, 1998, ISBN 0–590–68444–2

The world changed for all Americans on December 7, 1941. But the change was especially significant for Japanese Americans. Great distrust of anyone with Japanese heritage spread throughout the United States following the bombing of Pearl Harbor by Japan. This story documents those tense times in our history and reminds us all of the impact of war. To understand this period of history requires that we help students develop adequate background knowledge. Toward that goal, we have recommended two picture books: *Baseball Saved Us* and *So Far from the Sea*. Now, we add this ninety-page book with photographs from the era that will provide an even more in-depth understanding of this painful time in our history.

Music for Alice

Written and Illustrated by Allen Say
Houghton Mifflin 2004, ISBN 0–618–31118–1

The human spirit can overcome great obstacles if there is courage and determination to do so. Alice and her husband Mark, both Japanese Americans, were living in Oregon when the government rounded up all people of Japanese decent and moved them to camps out in the desert. Once there amidst the dust, they become committed to bringing beauty to the land and begin planting flowers—acres and acres of flowers. Alice, a former dancer, works the fields right alongside her husband. Together they become very successful. Eventually (after the war ends), they decide to sell their flower farm in the desert and move to a different climate. Years later Mark dies and Alice decides to move back to Oregon. There she finally finds the peace to dance once more.

So Far from the Sea

Written by Eve Bunting
Illustrated by Chris K. Soentpiet
Clarion 1998, ISBN 0–395–72095–8

The front and back covers of this book tell a powerful story even before you read the words on the pages. But take the time to move inside, read about a period of time in our history when some cultures were treated differently and unfairly because of their ethnicity. Following the bombing of Pearl Harbor in 1941, all Japanese American families were sent to internment camps. This story features one family and chronicles their time in the Manzanar War Relocation Center in California. It is told through the eyes of the little boy who spent many months there with his family. Now that he is grown with a family of his own, he brings them back for one last visit to the camp where his father died *so far from the sea* that he so longed to see before his death. Chris Soentpiet does an amazing presentation with his art by alternating the colored spreads with the black-and-white sketches to ensure that readers develop an even greater degree of understanding of the time.

Living Through Conflict, Working Toward Peace Bookshelf Five: Division of North Korea from South Korea

My Freedom Trip: A Child's Escape from North Korea

Written by Frances Park and Ginger Park
Illustrated by Debra Reid Jenkins
Boyds Mills 1998, ISBN 1–56397–468–1

To set the stage for the events that happen in this book, the following message is provided as a prelude to the story: *Many years ago . . . soldiers drew a big line that divided Korea into two countries. . . . In North Korea we could no longer speak our minds, or come and go as we pleased. We lost our freedom. Many of us secretly escaped to South Korea, the freedom land. This is my story . . .* The story will remind you of many of the stories of The Underground Railroad. It is filled with suspense and the pages reveal admirable courage. The difference between this story and those of The Underground Railroad is that in Korea each person goes along with one leader who knows the journey. Little Soo's father goes first and shortly after his successful escape, Little Soo follows. Unfortunately, Little Soo's mother is never able to escape and that journey separates the father and daughter from their wife and mother forever.

Living Through Conflict, Working Toward Peace Bookshelf Six: The Vietnam War

America's White Table

Written by Margot Theis Raven
Illustrated by Mike Benny
Sleeping Bear Press 2005, ISBN 1–58536–216–6

Although we had never heard of this tradition, there have been families across America who have participated in this touching ceremony since the years of the Vietnam war. The quiet ceremony honors those who served and those who didn't come home. The tradition is to set a richly appointed table where no one sits. The table looms large during each of the ceremonies. Raven tells this remarkable story through the eyes of Katie, a little girl who has been asked by her mother to set the white table. As Katie prepares the table, her mom tells the story of Uncle John who lost many of his friends during the war. Mom's words are in italics and the illustrations are in black and white. And gracefully scrolling along the bottom are words of *My Country 'Tis of Thee.*

The Wall

Written by Eve Bunting
Illustrated by Ronald Himler
Clarion 1990, 1992, ISBN 0–395–62977–2

The narrator is a young boy who has come with his dad to find his grandfather's name on the Vietnam Wall in Washington, DC. *This is the wall, my grandfather's wall. On it are the names of those killed in a war long ago.* Bunting uses simple and direct language to reach deep into the dad's wounded heart as he encounters his father's name engraved on the wall. The reader is there to see and hear as people bring things to honor the dead soldiers and leave them at the base of the monument. Even the boy's dad pulls out his wallet and leaves a picture of the boy among all the other items.

Living Through Conflict, Working Toward Peace
Bookshelf Seven: Contemporary Events

Gleam and Glow

Written by Eve Bunting
Illustrated by Peter Sylvada
Harcourt 2001, 2005, ISBN 0–15–202596–0

Not until you read the Author's Note do you know which country or war the story is about. Even so, this is a stunning story that will leave you hanging at the end of every page as a young family in a war-torn country escapes their homeland soon after the father goes to be a part of the underground. The mother and her two young children are very frightened as they listen to the tales of visitors who are stopping off to rest with them. One of the visitors leaves his two fish because he is too weary to carry them any farther. The children name the two fish *Gleam and Glow* and find comfort in caring for them. Shortly after this visit, the young family must also leave. Against the children's pleas to carry the new pets with them, they must leave the fish in a pond behind their house knowing that their lives will be short when their food runs out. After months and months away and having been reunited with their father, the family returns to their home only to find a skeleton of their old house. But there in the pond where they left them, they find *Gleam and Glow* along with dozens and dozens of their children.

The Librarian of Basra: A True Story from Iraq

Written and Illustrated by Jeanette Winters
Harcourt 2005, ISBN 0–15–205445–6

Included at the back of the book is an Author's Note that lets readers know that this astonishing story of courage and determination is a true one. Alia, the librarian in the town of Basra, sets out on a mission to save the books from destruction as war approaches in early 2003. Alia transports stacks of books from the library to her home by night to avoid suspicion. But before she can complete her plan, war breaks out and she is forced to move the remaining books to a restaurant across the wall from the library. Without thought for her own safety, Alia hides as many of her treasured books as possible before the library is finally burned to the ground. Now, Alia dreams of peace for her country and a new library to house her beloved books. The text is short but important because this significant book puts a human face to the many good citizens in every land, even in a time of war.

The Little Chapel That Stood

Written by A. B. Curtis
Illustrated by Mirto Golino
OldCastle/Hyperion 2003, ISBN 0–932529–77–1

Ground Zero smoldered, dark and grim. Our hearts stood still, then we pitched in. Helpers brought shovels, and pails, or pans. If they had nothing else, they dug with their hands to clear the mountain of crumpled steel from a nightmare that was all too real. Directly across from where the World Trade Center stood is the little chapel of St. Paul's. It is dwarfed amidst 150-year-old syca-mores and towering buildings that once surrounded it. But on September 11, 2001, it withstood the blast as the Twin Towers crumbled and hot coals, barbs of steel, equipment, furniture, and tons of paper and litter rained down on its roof. The walls of this chapel soon served as a haven for all the men and women working to rescue the living or to recover bodies. Today that little chapel (the very one where George Washington worshiped when he lived in New York City) still stands with many mementos of those sad and terrifying days following the fall of the towers. This tender book recalls those days of heroes, of fear, and of patriotism.

One April Morning: Children Remember the Oklahoma City Bombing

Written by Nancy Lamb and Children of Oklahoma City
Illustrated by Floyd Cooper
HarperCollins 1996, ISBN 0–688–14666–X

This story of the day of the Oklahoma City bombing will leave you breathless with its examples of beauty in the face of such tragedy and loss. Nancy tells you how she went back to her hometown to talk to the children who experienced the day the earth shook and windows in their schools and homes were shattered. She uses quotes from the children, extending the text she has written to describe the horror of that eventful day in US history. However, the beauty of human compassion and kindness is expressed when she explains how Americans joined hands from across the nation to assist fellow citizens in their efforts to regroup, repair, and learn to cope with their losses. The story is one of great sorrow surrounded by great pride and unfailing human love.

September Roses

Written and Illustrated by Jeanette Winter
Farrar, Straus and Giroux 2004, ISBN 0–374–36736–1

When a flower show is canceled on September 11, 2001, in New York City, two sisters who flew in from South Africa to enter their roses in the show must decide what to do with all of them. When a kind man from a nearby church offers to let them sleep at his house because all the hotels are full, they ask him what to do with the more than 2,000 roses. He takes them to Union Square where mourners have gathered to remember and pray for all the people affected by the tragedy. There the sisters use their roses to build a replica of the Twin Towers.

September 12th: We Knew Everything Would Be All Right

Written and Illustrated by first-grade students of H. Byron Masterson Elementary in Kennett, Missouri
Scholastic 2002, ISBN 0–439–44246–X

> Even if this book had not been in response to the terrifying events of September 11, 2001, it would be a fine one to use with young children who need reassurance in the face of unnamed fears. This one does just that in such a powerful way.

There's a Big, Beautiful World Out There!

Written and Illustrated by Nancy Carlson
Viking 2002, ISBN 0–670–03580–7

> *There's a lot to be scared of, that's for sure!* This is the opening line of this wonderful story for young children about all the things in our world that can cause fear and worry. The second half of the story highlights the opposite of those fears and reassures children of the wonderful things that are in their world to be experienced. It was written by Nancy Carlson as a book of comfort for children following the horrors of September 11, 2001.

Understanding September 11th: Answering Questions About the Attacks on America

Written by Mitch Frank
Photographs and maps from various sources
Viking/Penguin 2002, ISBN 0–670–03587–4

> This book was not written to be used as a read-aloud; rather, it is intended as a resource to assist adults who are trying to explain the events of September 11 to children. Frank provides the reader with a timeline running across the bottom of every page that places the details of this tragic time in sequence. We've included it because this title will lend support for several of the other books on this sensitive topic that are recommended for read-alouds.

A Closing Word

T**HE BRIDGE METAPHOR** was selected for this book because we see picture books as the most versatile of resources for teaching and learning. They have the very real potential for bringing together ideas, images, content, vocabulary, language, and art in the minds of any learner. Picture books often do become a bridge to span the curriculum, connecting each subject and each topic into one interconnected entity. This makes it possible for both teaching and learning to travel freely in the territory of ideas and information.

Clearly, we were not able to include every book that has the potential to build those bridges. There are just too many books and no one volume could have that much space. We therefore are keenly aware of the fact that there are titles that could and should have been included. It is like the slogan, *So Many Books—So Little Time.* For us, it is *So Many Books—So Little Space.* Alas, this is the situation—there are no more blank pages, yet shelves and shelves of books remain that we would love to tell you about.

Several months ago when we turned in the completed manuscript of our companion book, *Learning Under the Influence of Language and Literature: Making the Most of Read-Alouds Across the Day* (2006), our editor, Lois Bridges, pointed out that we had *significantly* exceeded the word limit. We decided that cutting books from the fifth opportunity to read aloud would keep that book intact and maintain the focus on reading aloud across the day. As we began the painful and agonizing process of cutting away book after book, a vision emerged for a second book—a vision focused completely on building bridges across the curriculum with picture books. This book began in just that way.

Here, we encourage you, once again, to view a carefully chosen read-aloud not as "one more thing to do" in an already full day but as a thoughtful, planful, and reflective instructional act. As you have read through each of the four curriculum chapters, we hope that this book has become a resource—one you can trust and bring into planning sessions. This book is meant to save you enormous amounts of planning time and to serve as a bridge to viewing your personal library with renewed enthusiasm.

Reading Aloud Across the Curriculum and our companion title, *Learning Under the Influence of Language and Literature,* have been labors of love. We have sought to select and recommend only the best books from our collections for your classroom. Now, we hope that these selections will be joined by annotations of your own and that the new resources you develop will support many months of instruction to enrich the academic lives of children.

Our hope in writing this is that our passion for the role of picture books as art, literature, and valuable instructional resources will validate your practice, extend your vision for teaching, deepen your knowledge of books, and rekindle your commitment to bringing beautiful books and precious children together. We are honored that you have taken the time to read this book and that you have allowed us to share in the rewarding journey of providing a more thoughtful curriculum for children.

Works Cited

Harvey, Stephanie, and Anne Goodvis. 2005. *The Comprehension Toolkit: Language and Lessons for Active Literacy.* Portsmouth, NH: Heinemann.

Laminack, Lester, L., and Reba M. Wadsworth. 2006. *Learning Under the Influence of Language and Literature: Making the Most of Read-Alouds Across the Day.* Portsmouth, NH: Heinemann.

National Council of Teachers of English. 1996. *Standards for the English Language Arts.* Urbana, IL: NCTE.

Van de Walle, John A. 2001. *Elementary and Middle School Mathematics: Teaching Developmentally* (4th edition). New York: Longman.

Whitin, David J., and Sandra Wilde. 1995. *It's the Story That Counts.* Portsmouth, NH: Heinemann.

Index

WITHDRAWN

MAY 0 7 2024

DAVID O. McKAY LIBRARY
BYU-IDAHO